CISCO SECURITY
ARCHITECTURES

McGRAW-HILL CISCO TECHNICAL EXPERT TITLES

Fischer *Configuring Cisco Routers for ISDN*   0-07-02273-5
Gai *Internetworking IPv6 with Cisco Routers*   0-07-022836-1
Lewis *Cisco TCP/IP Professional Reference*   0-07-041140-1
Parkhurst *Cisco Router OSPF Design and Implementation*   0-07-048626-3
Parkhurst *Cisco Multicast Routing and Switching*   0-07-134647-3
Rossi *Cisco and IP Addressing*   0-07-134925-1
Rossi *Cisco Catalyst LAN Switching*   0-07-134982-0
Sackett *Cisco Router Handbook*   0-07-058097-9
Slattery/Burton *Advanced IP Routing in Cisco Networks*   0-07-058144-4
Van Meter *Cisco and Fore ATM Internetworking*   0-07-134842-5

To order or receive additional information on these or any other McGraw-Hill titles, in the United States please call 1-800-722-4726, or visit us at www.computing.mcgraw-hill.com. In other countries, contact your McGraw-Hill representative.

Cisco
Security
Architectures

Gilbert Held
Kent Hundley

McGraw-Hill

New York • San Francisco • Washington, D.C. • Auckland • Bogotá
Caracas • Lisbon • London • Madrid • Mexico City • Milan • Montreal
New Delhi • San Juan • Singapore • Sydney • Tokyo • Toronto

Library of Congress Cataloging-in-Publication Data

Held, Gilbert, 1943—
    Cisco security architectures / Gilbert Held, Kent Hundley.
       p.   cm.
    (Includes index.)
    ISBN 0-07-134708-9
    1. Computer networks—Security measures. 2. Computer network
architectures. I. Hundley, Kent. II. Title.
TK5105.59.H45 1999
005.8—dc21   99-22659
                                                     CIP

McGraw-Hill

*A Division of The **McGraw·Hill** Companies*

1 2 3 4 5 6 7 8 9 0 AGM/AGM 9 0 4 3 2 1 0 9

ISBN: 0–07–134708–9

The sponsoring editor for this book was Steven Elliot, and the production supervisor was Clare Stanley. It was set by D&G Limited, LLC.

Printed and bound by Quebecor/Martinsburg

CONTENTS AT A GLANCE

CONTENTS

Contents

Chapter 8   Advanced Cisco Router Security Features   173

PREFACE

In the past, the strength of countries and organizations were measured in terms of production, with tons of steel, barrels of oil, and similar metrics used to gauge their place among contemporaries. Today, the strength of countries and organizations is more dependent upon their capacity to transfer information. That information can range in scope from satellite images of terrorists' base camps in a village in Afghanistan, which are used to wage retaliatory strikes by countries, to the flow of financial information between organizations and the use of ATM machines by consumers. If this information flow is disrupted or altered, the effect on countries, organizations, and individuals can be severe or even disastrous. Just imagine if a person could intercept the flow of financial information and reroute the flow of funds into an account in Switzerland or in the Bahamas. Depending on whose account was diverted, countries, businesses, or individuals might become candidates for national or Chapter 11 bankruptcy.

The key to securing networks is obtained through the use of appropriate equipment and policies that govern the use of such equipment. When we talk about securing computer networks to include Internet access, most people rightfully think of Cisco Systems, because that company provides approximately 80 percent of the routers used to connect organizational networks to the Internet. Thus, the focus of this book reflects its title and deals with Cisco Systems equipment, covering in detail the operation and utilization of that company's routers and firewalls.

While the only network that is completely secure is the one that is truly isolated and is contained in a locked laboratory or closet, information presented in this book was written to provide you with a solid foundation concerning tools and techniques you can use to secure your Cisco Systems-based network. By obtaining a detailed understanding of how to correctly configure access lists, as well as enabling different firewall functions, you can avoid many common mistakes that result in network vulnerability. When appropriate, we will include real-life examples obtained from several decades of collective consulting experience. To avoid embarrassing previous and current clients, we will use pseudonyms to hide the guilty. Because security is a learning process, you should note errors and omissions—as well as techniques—that can result in potential security problems, to ensure that such errors and omissions are avoided. Thus, by focusing on how to correctly configure equipment, we will provide you with the information necessary to minimize the vulnerability of your organization's network. While nobody can guarantee a perfectly secure network, the information contained in this book should assist you in your goal of obtaining the foundation needed to minimize potential network vulnerabilities.

As professional authors, we highly value reader feedback. If you wish to share your thoughts concerning the scope and depth of topics covered in this book, or if there are areas you would like to see covered in a future edition, you can contact us either through our publisher or directly via e-mail.

Gilbert Held
Macon, GA
235–8068@mcimail.com

Kent Hundley
Stanford, KY
kent_hundley@ins.com

ACKNOWLEDGMENTS

Although you might not realize it, a book is similar to many sports representing a team effort. Without the effort of an acquisitions editor with the knowledge and foresight to back a proposal, it would be difficult, if not impossible, to have a manuscript published. It is always a pleasure to work with a knowledgeable acquisitions editor, and Steve Elliot is no exception. Thus, we would be remiss if we did not thank Steve for backing this writing project.

As an old-fashioned author who spends a significant amount of time traveling to various international locations, Gil Held long ago recognized that the variety of electrical receptacles made pen and paper far more reliable than the use of a notebook, which was difficult to recharge. Converting his writings and drawings into a professional manuscript is a difficult assignment, especially when balancing the effort with family obligations. Once again, Gil is indebted to Mrs. Linda Hayes for her fine effort in preparing the manuscript that resulted in the book you are reading.

Writing is a time-consuming effort, requiring many weekends and evenings that would normally be spent with family. Thus, last but not least, we truly appreciate the support and understanding of our families and friends as we wrote this book, checked galley pages, and verified the techniques presented in this book. Kent would like to extend a special thanks to his wife, Lori, for her support during the months of effort that have culminated in this work.

1

Introduction

In the preface to this book, we noted that the strength of countries, organizations, and individuals in a modern society depends to a great extent upon the flow of information. That information flow must be transported from source to destination in a reliable manner, such that the receiver can be assured of the identity of the originator —as well as the fact that the received data was not altered. In addition, some types of information should be excluded from recognition by other parties. Thus, at a minimum, there are several security-related issues associated with the transmission of information to include authentication and encryption.

When constructing data networks, authentication and encryption might only represent a portion of security features and techniques you might wish to consider. To obtain an appreciation for the variety of security features and techniques you might wish to consider, let's first examine the need for security—along with some of the potential threats that result in the requirements to obtain security-related equipment to protect the modern organizational network.

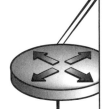

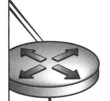

The Need for Security

Figure 1–1 illustrates an example of a corporate network that is connected to the Internet. Although many people might be tempted to consider security equipment as a necessity to protect the computers on the private network from people who can access the Internet, that might not be the only networking boundary that requires a degree of protection. The private network, regardless of its structure, might also require one or more security devices, techniques, and policies to protect equipment on that network from inadvertent or intentional employee actions. Thus, in this section, we will examine the need for security from both external and internal threats.

Public Network Threats

In this section, we will consider public network threats to represent potential or actual threats originating on a public network. These threats are directed at an organization's private network but are also connected to the public network. Because the Internet literally represents a network of interconnected networks without a boundary, the organizational network becomes accessible to the tens of millions of people who now access the Internet. Without a method to control access to the segments shown behind the organizational router, each workstation and server operated by the organization becomes vulnerable to intentional, malicious actions that could emanate from anywhere on the globe. Such malicious actions could include an attempted break-in into a server or the transmission of e-mail to a workstation user with an executable virus either embedded in the e-mail as a macro or added as a file attachment.

A second area of concern with respect to the network configuration illustrated in Figure 1–1 involves two items: the transmission line that connects the organizational router to the *Internet Service Provider* (ISP) router, and the ISP's connection to the Internet. Once data traffic leaves the premises of the organization, ensuring that the transmission is not read nor modified becomes more difficult. This occurs because physical security employed via building passes and employee recognition can prevent a person from gaining access to a wire closet and using a protocol analyzer to record traffic. Once data flows beyond the physical span of control of the organization, however, that organization must then rely upon authentication and encryption to verify the originator of the message—and the fact that its contents are not disclosed.

Figure 1–1
Public network
threats

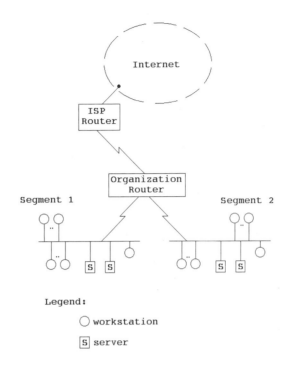

Another problem area that deserves attention when connecting to a public network—such as the Internet—involves a series of activities that are commonly referred to collectively as denial-of-service attacks. In its simplest fashion, one or more malicious individuals can write a program that randomly selects source addresses for use in packet requests transmitted to one or more of your organizational servers. By transmitting a continuous stream of service requests, your servers do what they are programmed to do: respond. Because the response is transmitted to a non-existent address, the servers keep a session connection open a bit longer than normal until a timer expires. The volume of service requests and the prolonged session connection time, however, cumulatively results in the use of all of the server's resources—in effect, denying service to legitimate users.

Without having to write specialized software, the possibility exists for people to easily overload an organization's public network connection. For example, assume your organization has one or more FTP servers and supports anonymous FTP access. A person, either inadvertently or intentionally, could access the FTP server and enter the command MGET *.*, causing all the files in the directory to be transferred. If your FTP server has a few gigabytes of files and a 56Kbps connection to the Internet, one MGET command will saturate your Internet connection—perhaps interfering with customers attempting to obtain pricing or place orders on your organizational Web servers. Thus, there are a number of factors you must consider when connecting a private network to the Internet. Now that we have an appreciation for some of the threats to a private network via a public network, let's turn our attention to private network threats.

Private Network Threats

In this section, we will examine some actual and potential threats to a private network emanating from a private network. In doing so, we will again reference the network structure shown in Figure 1–1, focusing our attention on the two segments behind the organizational router.

If we assume the private network was segmented to enable accounting and personnel operations to be separated from other organizational functions, then one or more servers on one segment more than likely are limited to supporting users only on that segment. This situation means that a curious or malicious employee could conceivably attempt to access the accounting or personnel server to perhaps increase a payment to a friend, change the pay grade of an employee, or perform another most questionable activity. Because the router is the first line of defense that bars user access from one segment to the other, without implementing any access lists, data can flow freely between segments. Even with an access list in place, the possibility exists for a disgruntled employee to use another station, whose address is enabled in the access list, for access to the other segment. Or, with a degree of technical knowledge, the employee could attempt to gain access to the router's command port and alter the access list. Assuming a disgruntled employee can access the other segment, the task is relatively simple to use the contents of an electronic dictionary in an attempt to gain access to an account on a server. In fact, as we will note later in this book, routers do not examine the contents of the information field packets. This fact means that once access is obtainable to a server, either from the public network or from the private network, the router cannot distinguish a series of client-server request-responses from a series of repeated logon attempts.

Thus, by itself, a router provides a limited degree of security that many organizations will usually supplement through the use of a firewall, authentication server, and virus scanning software. Concerning the latter, monitoring the use of the telephone and the corporate Internet location to prevent employees from inadvertently downloading a file containing a virus is difficult, if not impossible. In addition, many malicious people develop virus-based macros and executable programs that they either embed in an e-mail or attach to their electronic message—which results in another potential security hazard that network managers, LAN administrators, and network users must consider. Now that we have an appreciation for a few of the major security threats to a network, let's focus our attention on the role of routers in defending a network.

The Role of Routers

From an operational perspective, the major function of a router is to transfer packets from one network to another. Routers operate at the network layer that represents the third layer of the OSI Reference Model. By examining the network address of packets, routers are programmed to make decisions concerning the flow of packets. Another function that goes hand-in-hand with routing packets between networks is the creation and maintenance of routing tables. Such protocols as the *Routing Information Protocol* (RIP), *Open Shortest Path First* (OSPF), and the *Border Gateway Protocol* (BGP), represent only three of more than 50 routing protocols that have been developed over the past 20 years. With respect to security, the router represents the first line of protection for a network. That protection is in the form of access lists, which are created to enable or deny the flow of information through one or more router interfaces.

Cisco System routers support two types of access lists: basic and extended. A *basic* access list controls the flow of information based on network addresses. An *extended* access list enables the flow of information to be controlled by both network address and the type of data being transferred within a packet. Although access lists can be considered to represent the first line of protection for a network, as currently implemented they usually do not examine the actual contents of the information fields of packets—nor do they maintain information about the "state" of a connection. In other words, each packet is examined individually without the router attempting to determine whether the packet is part of a legitimate conversation stream.

Two notable exceptions to this rule are *context-based access control* (CBAC) and *Reflexive access control lists* (Reflexive ACLs). CBAC is the heart of the Cisco firewall feature set, which is a specific code revision available for the Cisco 1600- and 2500-series routers. Beginning with IOS 12.0T, CBAC is available on the 3600-series router and might be available on other platforms when newer versions of Cisco's IOS are introduced. This feature is capable of maintaining information about the state of an existing connection and examining application layer information for a limited number of TCP and UDP protocols. It provides a significantly greater level of security than traditional access lists. Reflexive ACLs are a new feature introduced in the 11.3

revision of the Cisco IOS. Reflexive ACLs maintain a degree of "pseudo-state" information by creating dynamic entries in traditional ACLs, once a legitimate conversation is started. Future packets are evaluated against the dynamic entries in the Reflexive ACL to determine whether they are part of an existing connection. Once the conversation is ended, the dynamic entries are deleted from the ACL. Reflexive ACLs, however, do not understand higher-layer protocols and are not suitable for use with some multi-channel protocols such as FTP. CBAC and Reflexive ACLs will be covered in detail later in this book.

Despite these features, all ACLs are still incapable of authenticating the originator of data, which verifies that the contents of a packet were not altered, and encrypting the information field of packets to hide their contents from observation. Recognizing the limitations of access lists, both Cisco systems and other hardware and software vendors developed a series of other security devices that we will briefly review in this introductory chapter.

Other Security Devices

Limitations associated with router ACLs resulted in the development of several additional security devices. Those devices include firewalls, proxy servers, encryption servers, authentication servers, and virus scanning servers. Because some firewalls can be configured to support one or more of the functions of stand-alone servers limited to supporting a single security function, we will focus our attention in this section on the firewall and its general capabilities.

Firewall Features

Many firewalls include a large number of security-related features. Those features range in scope from packet filtering, which in some ways is similar to the operation of router access lists, to network address translation, authentication services, selective encryption of the contents of packets based on their destination address, alarm generation, and proxy services. Because one or more of these features might not be fully recognizable to some readers, let's briefly review the general function associated with each security feature. Later in this book when we discuss Cisco security products in detail, we will also discuss each of these firewall features in considerably more detail.

Packet Filtering

Although most firewalls perform packet filtering in a manner similar to router access lists, they might also include an additional capability far beyond basic and extended lists. That additional capability is usually in the form of a policy creation capability, which enables the firewall administrator to associate certain types of filtering to specific groups of users. That association can also include time-of-day and day-of-week control, which represents two additional features included with the packet filtering capability of many firewalls.

Network Address Translation

The purpose of network address translation is to translate the Layer 3 source and/or destination addresses inside IP packets. This function enables an organization to hide the addresses of devices behind a firewall from observation by other computer users located in front of the firewall. This function also protects devices behind the network from a direct attack, because all responses are directed directly to the firewall that must then perform a reverse translation.

Authentication Services

The purpose of authentication is to verify the identity of the originator of a data flow. The most common form of authentication, and the one most familiar to the vast majority of readers, is the user ID-password association. Unfortunately, many popular applications such as FTP servers use clear-text passwords that can be intercepted and easily read and understood. In addition, an appropriate password does not indicate that the holder of the password is entitled to have the password.

One of the more popular types of authentication is a credit card-size smart card with a pseudo-random number generator and six-digit display. This card generates a new six-digit random number every minute. A firewall that supports this method of authentication has the same pseudo-random number generator that is associated with each user via a *personal identification number* (PIN). The remote user who requires authentication is prompted to enter his or her PIN number, followed by their security card six-digit pseudo-random number, which—when verified by the firewall—authenticates the remote user.

Encryption

To effectively encrypt packets, a firewall must include a facility to identify those packets. This task is normally accomplished by associating one or more destination addresses, or groups of addresses, to one or more encryption methods. The reason that encryption must be selectively performed results from the fact that most times users access different destinations. Some destinations might represent non-organizational locations for which encryption is not required, while other destinations might represent locations accessed via a public packet network that expects to receive encrypted data. The situation in which data flows between two organizational locations via a public packet network results in the creation of a *Virtual Private Network* (VPN). The process of encrypting the flow of data creates a secure tunnel through the VPN.

Alarm Generation

Many firewalls include the capacity to set thresholds governing certain conditions. Once those thresholds are reached, the firewall can be configured to generate an audible alarm, send an e-mail to one or more individuals, execute a predefined program, or even send a message that causes the *local area network* (LAN) administrator's beeper to activate at 3 A.M.

Proxy Services

A *proxy* represents an intermediary. When applied to a network, proxy services result in a firewall receiving application requests, examining those requests, and if configured to do so, acting on those requests prior to passing the request to the device actually performing the service. Examples of proxy services include an FTP proxy and a Telnet proxy. Now that we have an appreciation for many of the key features of a firewall, we will conclude this chapter by previewing the succeeding chapters in this book.

Book Preview

In this section, we will obtain an overview of the focus of succeeding chapters in this book. You can use the information in this section either by itself or in conjunction with the index, as a mechanism to directly locate specific areas of interest.

The TCP/IP Protocol Suite

Chapters 2 through 4, which discuss different protocols, are included in this book as tutorial information covering two of the most popular protocol suites used throughout the world. Information in these chapters is included because an understanding of Layer 2 frames and Layer 3 and Layer 4 packets is necessary to obtain an appreciation for how routers and firewalls operate.

In Chapter 2, we will focus our attention on the TCP/IP protocol suite. In doing so, we will briefly review the *International Standards Organization* (ISO) *Open System Interconnection* (OSI) Reference Model. Once this task is accomplished, we will turn our attention to the TCP/IP protocol suite and the relationship of that suite to the ISO's OSI Reference Model.

The Internet Protocol

In Chapter 3, we begin our detailed examination of the Internet protocol. In this chapter, we will examine the composition of the IP header, as well as review IP addressing. Concerning the latter, we will examine several types of addressing—as well as the purpose of subnet masking and the manner by which subnets are created and identified.

TCP and UDP

Moving up the TCP/IP protocol stack, Chapter 4 is focused on the *Transmission Control Protocol* (TCP) and the *User Datagram Protocol* (UDP). Because most network security methods involve the use of TCP and UDP port numbers, after we review the header format for each protocol, a comprehensive list of 'well-known' ports will be presented and will serve as a reference for performing security-related tasks described in the remainder of this book.

NetWare

Because NetWare protocols transport more than 50 percent of the information flow on private networks, this protocol cannot be overlooked when developing security methods to protect an organization's computational facilities. In Chapter 5, we will examine the IPX and SPX headers—as well as the manner by which Novell networks implement network and host station addressing.

Router Hardware and Software

A Cisco Systems router can be considered to represent a fine painting with a variety of components, which fit together to provide functionality in a manner similar to brush strokes which are used to create that painting. To obtain an appreciation for configuring access lists, as well as other security-related router features, you should obtain a basic understanding of the hardware and software components of a Cisco router, which is the purpose of Chapter 6.

In Chapter 6, we will first review the basic Cisco router hardware and software components. Once this task is accomplished, we will obtain an understanding of the use of different router operational modes and conclude this chapter by focusing our attention on router EXEC commands.

Working with Access Lists

Using the information presented in the preceding chapters as a foundation, Chapter 7 examines Cisco Systems router access lists in detail. After examining the syntax and format of access lists we will turn our attention to the construction of access lists, using several networking examples to illustrate how an access list can become your first line of network defense. In Chapter 8, we examine how you can construct a Cisco firewall using such enhanced IOS security features as Context Based Access Control, Reflexive ACLs, and network address translation. Chapter 9 explores IPX and layer 2 access lists.

The PIX Firewall

In Chapter 10, to conclude the book, we investigate the Cisco PIX in detail, first examining its features and functions. Once this task is accomplished, we will examine how the PIX is configured, turning our attention to its configuration commands. This description will provide us with the capacity to illustrate several examples of its configuration as a mechanism to enhance network security.

2

The TCP/IP Protocol Suite

The purpose of this chapter is to provide readers with an overview of the TCP/IP protocol suite, paving the way for detailed information concerning different layers of the protocol suite that will be presented in two succeeding chapters. Because the TCP/IP protocol suite represents a layered architecture, we will commence this chapter with a brief overview of the *International Standards Organization*'s (ISO) *Open Systems Interconnection* (OSI) Reference Model. After examining the role and functions associated with each of the seven layers in the ISO Reference Model, we will turn our attention to the TCP/IP protocol suite. In doing so, we will discuss the design of the TCP/IP protocol suite, which, although a layered suite, predates the development of the ISO Reference Model. By comparing and contrasting the TCP/IP protocol suite to the ISO Reference Model, we will obtain an appreciation for the manner in which the TCP/IP protocol stack operates with respect to an international standard.

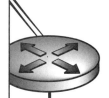

The ISO Open Systems Interconnection Reference Model

The ISO *Open Systems Interconnection* (OSI) Reference Model was developed as a mechanism to facilitate communications interoperability as well as to simplify communications in general. The *International Standards Organization* (ISO) is a standards-making body that consists of over 100 members of the United Nations. The ISO is a non-government entity that has consultative status within the United Nation's Economic and Social Council. Its development of the seven-layer *Open Systems Interconnection* (OSI) Reference Model is one of the most notable achievements in the field of communications.

The ISO's Reference Model defines the communications process as a set of seven layers, with specific communications-related functions isolated and associated with each layer. By subdividing a complex process into seven defined layers, it becomes easier to develop an overall process through a logical subdivision of effort. In addition, by defining the functions associated with each layer and how one layer interoperates with another, it becomes possible for different companies to develop products that operate at the same or different layers of the Reference Model and to interoperate with products developed by other vendors.

Figure 2–1 illustrates the seven layers of the ISO's OSI Reference Model. Each layer except the physical layer covers lower-layer processes, in effect isolating them from higher-layer functions. In this way, each layer performs a distinct set of functions that provides a set of services to the higher layer. Through layer isolation, the characteristics of one layer can change without impacting the remainder of the model, assuming that supporting services remain the same. Thus, users can mix and match OSI-conforming communications products to satisfy a particular networking requirement.

Layers of the OSI Reference Model

With the exception of layers 1 and 7, each layer in the ISO's OSI Reference Model is bounded by the layers above and below it. Layer 1, the physical layer, can be considered to be bound below by the transmission medium over which data flows. Layer 7, which has no upper boundary, represents the application that in effect represents an upper boundary. Within each of the server layers, a group of functions provides a defined set of services at that layer as well as to any higher layers. To obtain an appreciation for

Figure 2–1
The ISO's Open System Interconnection Reference Model

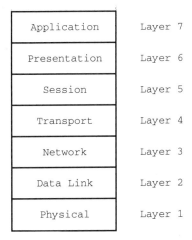

Application	Layer 7
Presentation	Layer 6
Session	Layer 5
Transport	Layer 4
Network	Layer 3
Data Link	Layer 2
Physical	Layer 1

the manner by which the ISO's Reference Model operates, let's examine each of the layers in the model.

Layer 1—The Physical Layer

The lowest layer in the Reference Model is the physical layer. This layer defines the rules necessary for communications to occur on different media used to interconnect two or more devices. Thus, layer 1 is concerned with the electrical and physical connection between devices required to support the transfer of information.

One example of the physical layer many readers commonly use without actually thinking about the ISO's Reference Model is the cable between a PC and modem. The cable interface that includes the assignment of pins and the manner in which the connector on each end of the cable mates with the PC and modem is defined by the RS–232 standard, which represents a physical layer standard.

Layer 2—The Data Link Layer

The layer above the physical layer is referred to as the data link layer. This layer defines the method by which a device gains access to the medium specified by the physical layer.

Another key function of the data link layer is to define the manner in which information is transported. This definition includes the addressing scheme used to ensure data correctly flows from originator to receiver and the format of fields used to convey addressing, data, and error detection information. By defining data formats to include procedures to correct transmission errors, this layer becomes responsible for the reliable delivery of information. As we will note later in this chapter, Ethernet, Token Ring, and the TCP/IP *Point-to-Point Protocol* (PPP) represent examples of data link layer protocols.

Layer 3—The Network Layer

The third layer in the ISO's OSI Reference Model is the network layer. As its name suggests, this layer is responsible for arranging a logical connection through a network to enable a route to be established to connect source to destination. A key function incorporated into the network layer is network addressing, which enables data to be routed between networks.

The routing process itself supports the transfer of information between networks as well as packet sequencing and flow control. The sequencing of packets ensures they are rearranged in their correct order if they flow over different paths between source and destination and arrive out of order, while flow control ensures the orderly flow of information between nodes and networks. Several common network layer protocols include the *International Telecommunications Union* (ITU) X.25 packet switching protocol, Novell NetWare's *Internetwork Packet Exchange* (IPX), and the *Internet Protocol* (IP).

Layer 4—The Transport Layer

The fourth layer in the ISO's OSI Reference Model is the transport layer. This layer is responsible for guaranteeing that the transfer of information occurs correctly after a layer 3 protocol establishes a route through a network. The transport layer is responsible for controlling the flow of information when a session is established as well as tearing down the connection after a session is completed. It's also responsible for controlling the communications session. In doing so, the transport layer performs error control, sequence checking, and other end-to-end communications functions that can affect the reliability of the data transfer.

Although most transport layer protocols include a mechanism that provides end-to-end reliability, it's an optional feature associated with the transport layer. Similarly, although most transport layer protocols are connection-oriented, requiring the destination to acknowledge its capability to receive data prior to a transmission session being established, this is also an optional feature. Instead of operating as a connection-oriented protocol, a transport layer protocol can operate on a best-effort basis. This means that the protocol will initiate transmission without knowing if the destination is ready to receive or if it is even operational. Although this method of operation may appear awkward, the originator sets a timer that decrements in value. If no response is received to the initial packet flow by the time the timer expires, the originator assumes the destination is not reachable and terminates the session. This second method of operation avoids the relatively long handshaking sequence associated with some transport layer protocols. Examples of transport layer protocols include Novell's NetWare, the *Transmission Control Protocol* (TCP), and the *User Datagram Protocol* (UDP).

Layer 5—The Session Layer

The session layer provides a set of rules for establishing and terminating the operation of an activity transported by the lower layers in the Reference Model. Functions performed by the session layer can include establishing and terminating node connections, dialogue control, and end-to-end data control.

Layer 6—The Presentation Layer

The sixth layer in the ISO's OSI Reference Model is the presentation layer. This layer is primarily responsible for formatting, data transformation, and syntax-related operations. One of the primary functions of this layer that is probably overlooked is to convert transmitted data at the receiver into a display format for a receiving device. Concerning receiving devices, different presentation layers reside on different computers, so data that is displayed on one PC would more than likely differ from the manner data is displayed on another terminal. Other functions that can be performed by the presentation layer include encryption/decryption and compression/decompression.

Layer 7—The Application Layer

At the top of the ISO's OSI Reference Model is the application layer. This layer can be seen as a window through which the application gains access to all the services provided by the seven-layer model. Functions that can be performed at the application layer include email transmission, file transfers, and client-server query/response.

The first four layers in the Reference Model are fairly well defined; however, the functions associated with the upper three layers can vary considerably based upon the application, the type of data transported, and how a device's display is used for the presentation of information. As we will note when we turn our attention to the TCP/IP protocol suite later in this chapter, the functions of the individual upper layers of the Reference Model can be grouped together into one layer.

Data Flow

Because one of the driving forces behind layering is the capability to sub-divide communications processes into distinct entities, a mechanism is required to identify the process performed at each layer, as data flows from the application layer downward for delivery via a transmission medium. This identification mechanism consists of a series of headers that are appended to data as it flows in distinct packets down the application suite. At the receiver, the headers are removed in the reverse order from which they were added, resulting in the original data without a header being received at the application layer of the destination. Figure 2–2 illustrates the theoretical data flow within an ISO Reference Model network.

Figure 2–2

Data flow within an ISO Reference Model network

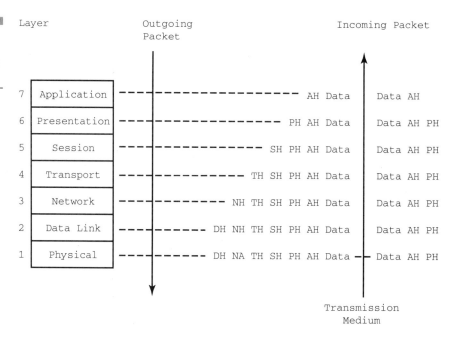

```
Layer                      Outgoing                          Incoming Packet
                           Packet

7   Application   ----------------------------- AH Data      Data AH

6   Presentation  ------------------------- PH AH Data       Data AH PH

5    Session      --------------------- SH PH AH Data        Data AH PH

4   Transport     ----------------- TH SH PH AH Data         Data AH PH

3    Network      ------------- NH TH SH PH AH Data          Data AH PH

2   Data Link     --------- DH NH TH SH PH AH Data           Data AH PH

1    Physical     ----- DH NA TH SH PH AH Data -- Data AH PH

                                                            Transmission
                                                            Medium
```

```
Legend:

   AH   Application Header
   PH   Presentation Header
   SH   Session Header
   TH   Transport Header
   NH   Network Header
   DH   Data Link Header
```

In examining Figure 2–2, note that as data flows down the ISO Reference Model, headers are added at each layer other than the physical layer. At the physical layer, data is encoded into a suitable format for transmission and then placed onto the transmission media as a serial data stream. At the receiver, the serial data stream is decoded and formed into packets that in effect move up the Reference Model. As the packet flows up the model, succeeding layers remove applicable headers, resulting in the data being passed from the application layer to the application without any headers.

Layer Subdivision

Prior to turning our attention to the TCP/IP protocol suite, a brief discussion is in order covering layer subdivision resulting from the efforts of the *Institute of Electrical and Electronic Engineers* (IEEE).

The IEEE is responsible for developing *Local Area Network* (LAN) standards, and its efforts are commonly incorporated by the *American National Standards Institute* (ANSI). When the IEEE began developing LAN standards, it realized that it was desirable to subdivide the data link layer into *logical link control* (LLC) and *media access control* (MAC) sublayers. The MAC sublayer defines how a station gains access to a LAN and obviously differs for different types of LANs, such as Ethernet and Token Ring. The LLC sublayer can then be used for controlling the establishment, maintenance, and termination of a logical connection between workstations. This subdivision enables an LLC standard to be applicable to different types of LANs.

The address associated with IEEE workstations normally represents the six-byte address burnt into *read-only memory* (ROM) on each network adapter card. The first three bytes of the address are assigned by the IEEE to an adapter card manufacturer and represent the manufacturer ID portion of the address. The following three bytes are used by the adapter card manufacturer to uniquely identify each adapter card they produce. If the manufacturer is successful at selling adapter cards, they will typically request another manufacturer ID from the IEEE when all three bytes of unique addresses for their previously assigned manufacturer ID are used.

Figure 2–3 illustrates the general format of an IEEE adapter card address. Because this address is used at the MAC layer when Ethernet or Token Ring frames are transported on a LAN to identify the destination and source of each frame, these addresses are also referred to as MAC addresses.

Figure 2–3
The MAC address

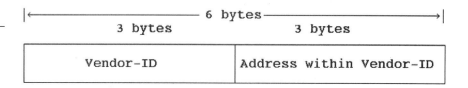

Two types of addresses can be associated with each Ethernet or Token Ring workstation. When a burnt-in ROM address is used, it is referred to as a *universal administered address,* because it is universally assigned by the IEEE. The second type of MAC address is assigned by the network manager or LAN administrator. This type of MAC address results in a batch file statement being used to set a locally generated address that overrides the built-in ROM address. This type of MAC address is referred to as a *locally administered address.* Regardless of the type of MAC address, it represents a layer 2 address that is 48 bits in length. As we will shortly note, a translation process is required to associate a layer 3 address to a layer 2 address when TCP/IP is used.

The TCP/IP Protocol Suite

TCP/IP represents one of the earliest developed layered protocol suites, preceding the ISO's OSI Reference Model by approximately 20 years. The development of the TCP/IP protocol suite has its roots in the establishment of the *Advanced Research Agency Network* (ARPANET), which was funded by the U.S. Department of Defense. The research performed by ARPANET resulted in a collection of network protocols that provide services at the network and transport layers of the ISO's OSI Reference Model as well as over 80 applications that roughly correspond to layers 5 through 7 of the Reference Model.

Comparison to the ISO Reference Model

If we begin our comparison from the bottom of the protocol stack, we should note that the dashed lines surrounding Ethernet, Token Ring, and FDDI indicate that those protocols are not part of the TCP/IP protocol suite. Instead, the *Address Resolution Protocol* (ARP), which can be considered as a facility of the *Internet Protocol* (IP), provides a mechanism that enables IP-addressed packets to be correctly delivered to workstations that use MAC addressing, such as workstations on an Ethernet, Token Ring, or FDDI network. Thus, although layer 2 protocols are not part of the TCP/IP protocol suite, it includes a facility that enables layer 3 packets to be delivered via layer 2 frames. When we turn our attention to IP and its addressing in Chapter 3, "The Internet Protocol," we will also examine ARP. Figure 2–4 provides a general comparison of the TCP/IP protocol suite to the several layers of the ISO Reference Model.

Internet Protocol (IP)

Moving up the protocol layer, IP represents a network layer protocol. IP has a header in which 32-bit addresses are currently used to reference source and destination. The 32-bit address is normally subdivided in a network address portion and an interface address portion, with the former representing a specific network and the latter representing a specific interface on the network.

Although not technically accurate, the interface portion of the address is commonly referred to as a *host address.* The reason this is not technically correct is due to the fact that a host can have multiple interfaces, with each interface having a distinct address. In Chapter 3, we will examine the IP header and IP addressing in detail.

ISO Layers   The TCP/IP Protocol Suite

Figure 2–4
Comparing the
TCP/IP Protocol Suite
to the ISO Reference
Model

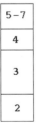

ISO Layers	The TCP/IP Protocol Suite						
5–7	FTP	Telnet	SMTP	HTTP	SNMP	NFS	BOOTP
4	TCP				UDP		
3	IP (ICMP, ARP)						
2	Ethernet		Token-Ring		FDDI		. . .

Legend:
ARP   Address Resolution Protocol
BOOTP   Bootstrap Protocol
FTP   File Transfer Protocol
HTTP   HyperText Transmission Protocol
ICMP   Internet Control Message Protocol

Internet Control Message Protocol (ICMP)

The *Internet Control Message Protocol* (ICMP) represents an error-reporting mechanism that enables routers that encounter an error to report the error to the originator of the packet. Although ICMP is shown in Figure 2–4 as a layer 3 protocol, from a technical perspective an IP message is transported within an IP datagram in exactly the same manner as datagrams transporting information. ICMP is transported by IP and you can configure extended access lists to filter based upon the type of ICMP message. We will examine ICMP in detail in Chapter 3 when we turn our attention to IP.

TCP and User Datagram Protcol (UDP)

TCP represents one of two layer 4 protocols supported by the TCP/IP protocol suite. TCP is a reliable connection-oriented protocol used to transport certain applications. Returning to Figure 2–4, we note that FTP, Telnet, SMTP, and HTTP are transported by TCP. UDP represents a connectionless protocol that operates on a best effort basis. Examples of applications transported by UDP include SNMP, NFS, and BOOTP.

Both the use of UDP and TCP result in the prefix of an appropriate header to application data. When TCP is used as the transport layer, the TCP header and application data are referred to as a TCP segment. When UDP is used as the transport layer, the UDP header and application data are referred to as a UDP datagram.

To enable TCP and UDP to transport multiple types of applications between the same addresses or to a similar destination address, each header includes a "port" number. By assigning port numbers to each application, an interface can receive a series of packets, with each packet containing a different type of application data. This explains how a Web server can also support Telnet and FTP and allow users to access different applications via a common IP address. In Chapter 4, we will examine the composition of the TCP and UDP headers as well as the use of different port numbers.

Data Delivery

In concluding this section, let's turn our attention to the delivery of application data from a host on one network to a host on another network. Figure 2–5 illustrates the formation of a LAN frame containing TCP/IP application data. Assuming a router is connected to the LAN, it strips off the LAN header and trailer and uses a *wide area network* (WAN) protocol to transport the IP datagram. At the destination network, another router receives the inbound packet, removes the WAN header and trailer, and encapsulates the IP datagram into a LAN frame for delivery to the appropriate IP address.

Figure 2–5
LAN frame formation

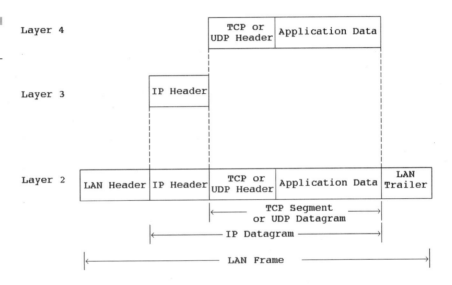

CHAPTER **3**

The Internet Protocol

In Chapter 2, we obtained an introduction to the TCP/IP protocol suite, leaving it for later chapters to investigate layer 3 and layer 4 protocols in detail. We will now begin our in-depth investigation of TCP/IP, focusing our attention upon the *Internet Protocol* (IP). In this chapter, we will examine the fields within the IP header, IP addressing, and, because ICMP messages are transported via IP, we will conclude our examination of layer 3 operations by discussing the *Internet Control Message Protocol* (ICMP). As we will note later in this book, the filtering of IP packets can occur based upon IP addresses as well as ICMP message types and control field values. Thus, this chapter provides a foundation for understanding the operation of filtering functions based upon IP addresses, ICMP message types, and Control field values.

The IP Header

Figure 3–1 illustrates the fields contained in the IP header. In examining the figure, note that the header contains a minimum of 20 bytes of data, and the width of each field is shown with respect to a 32-bit word. To obtain an appreciation for the functions performed by the IP header, let's examine the functions of the fields in the header.

Vers Field

The Vers field consists of four bits that identify the version of the IP protocol used to create the datagram. The current version of the IP protocol is four and the next generation IP protocol is assigned version number six.

Hlen and Total Length Fields

The Hlen field is four bits in length. This field, which follows the Vers field, indicates the length of the header in 32-bit words. In comparison, the Total Length field indicates the total length of the datagram to include its header and higher layer information. Since 16 bits are used for this field, an IP datagram can be up to 2^{16}, or 65,535, octets in length.

Service Type Field

The purpose of the Service Type field is to indicate how the datagram is processed. Three of the eight bits in this field are used to denote the precedence or level of importance assigned by the sender. Thus, this field proves a priority mechanism for the routing of IP datagrams.

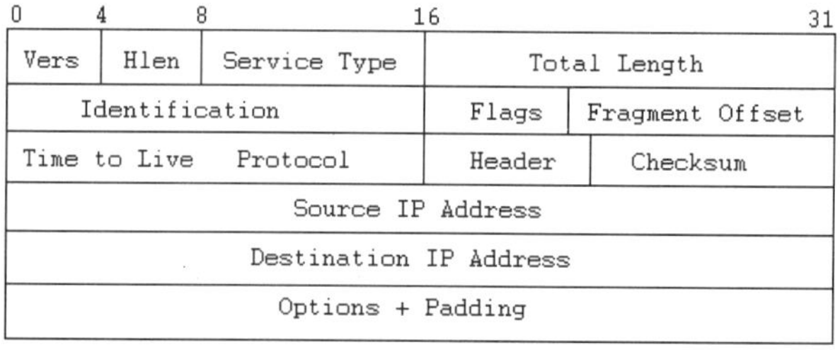

Figure 3–1
The IP header

0 4 8		16			31
Vers	Hlen	Service Type	Total Length		
Identification			Flags	Fragment Offset	
Time to Live	Protocol		Header	Checksum	
Source IP Address					
Destination IP Address					
Options + Padding					

Identification and Fragment Offset Fields

The Identification field enables each datagram or fragmented datagram to be identified. If a datagram is fragmented into two or more pieces, the Fragment Offset field specifies the offset in the original datagram of the data being transported. Thus, this field indicates where a fragment belongs in the complete message. The actual value in this field is an integer that corresponds to a unit of eight octets, providing an offset in 64-bit units.

It is important that security devices be able to recognize all fragments as members of the same datagram. Some recent attacks exploit holes in firewall and router code that block the initial fragment of a data packet but allow the remaining fragments to pass through. This attack takes advantage of the fact that the layer 4 header information is contained only in the first datagram fragment. Once this fragment is blocked, if the blocking device does not keep a record of the discarded initial packet, it may mistakenly allow subsequent unauthorized fragments through. Although an actual application connection cannot be established without the layer 4 header information in the initial fragment, an attacker might be able to create a denial of service attack by sending many fragmented datagrams to a particular host. The host must hold the fragments in memory while it waits for all fragments to arrive, consuming valuable resources. The specifics of this attack and its prevention will be covered in greater detail in later chapters.

Time to Live Field

The *Time to Live* (TTL) field specifies the maximum time that a datagram can exist. This field prevents a misaddressed datagram from endlessly wandering the Internet or a private IP network. Because an exact time is difficult to measure, it is commonly used as a hop count field. In other words, routers decrement the value of this field by one as a datagram flows between networks. If the value of the field reaches zero, the datagram is discarded.

Flags Field

The Flags field contains two bits that are used to denote how fragmentation occurs, with a third bit in the field presently unassigned. The setting of one of the two fragmentation bits can be used as a direct fragment control mechanism because a value of 0 indicates the datagram can be fragmented, while a value of 1 indicates that it should not. The second bit is set to 0 to indicate that a fragment in a datagram is the last fragment, while a value of 1 indicates more fragments follow.

Protocol Field

The purpose of the Protocol field is to identify the higher level protocol used to create the message carried in the datagram. For example, a value of decimal 6 would indicate TCP, while a value of decimal 17 would indicate UDP.

The 8-bit Protocol field enables protocols to be uniquely defined under IP version 4. Table 3–1 lists the current assignment of Internet protocol numbers. Note that although TCP and UDP by far represent the vast majority of Internet traffic, other protocols can also be transported and a large block of protocol numbers are currently unassigned. Under the evolving IP version 6, the Protocol field is named the Next Header field.

Table 3–1

Assigned Internet
Protocol
Numbers

Decimal	Keyword	Protocol
0	HOPOPT	IPv6 Hop-by-Hop Option
1	ICMP	Internet Control Message
2	IGMP	Internet Group Management
3	GGP	Gateway-to-Gateway
4	IP	IP in IP (encapsulation)
5	ST	Stream
6	TCP	Transmission Control Protocol
7	CBT	CBT
8	EGP	Exterior Gateway Protocol
9	IGP	any private interior gateway (used by Cisco for their IGRP)
10	BBN-RCC-MON	BBN RCC Monitoring
11	NVP-II	Network Voice Protocol Version 2
12	PUP	PUP

Decimal	Keyword	Protocol
13	ARGUS	ARGUS
14	EMCON	EMCON
15	XNET	Cross Net Debugger
16	CHAOS	Chaos
17	UDP	User Datagram
18	MUX	Multiplexing
19	DCN-MEAS	DCN Measurement Subsystems
20	HMP	Host Monitoring
21	PRM	Packet Radio Measurement
22	XNS-IDP	XEROX NS IDP
23	TRUNK−1	Trunk−1
24	TRUNK−2	Trunk−2
25	LEAF−1	Leaf−1
26	LEAF−2	Leaf−2
27	RDP	Reliable Data Protocol
28	IRTP	Internet Reliable Transaction
29	ISO-TP4	ISO Transport Protocol Class 4
30	NETBLT	Bulk Data Transfer Protocol
31	MFE-NSP	MFE Network Services Protocol
32	MERIT-INP	MERIT Internodal Protocol
33	SEP	Sequential Exchange Protocol
34	3PC	Third-Party Connect Protocol
35	IDPR	Inter-Domain Policy Routing Protocol
36	XTP	XTP
37	DDP	Datagram Delivery Protocol
38	IDPR-CMTP	IDPR Control Message Transport Protocol
39	TP++	TP++ Transport Protocol
40	IL	IL Transport Protocol

continues

Table 3–1

Decimal	Keyword	Protocol
41	IPv6	IPv6
42	SDRP	Source Demand Routing Protocol
43	IPv6-Route	Routing Header for IPv6
44	IPv6-Frag	Fragment Header for IPv6
45	IDRP	Inter-Domain Routing Protocol
46	RSVP	Reservation Protocol
47	GRE	General Routing Encapsulation
48	MHRP	Mobile Host Routing Protocol
49	BNA	BNA
50	ESP	Encap Security Payload for IPv6
51	AH	Authentication Header for IPv6
52	I-NLSP	Integrated Net Layer Security
53	SWIPE	IP with Encryption
54	NARP	NBMA Address Resolution Protocol
55	MOBILE	IP Mobility
56	TLSP	Transport Layer Security Protocol (using Kryptonet key management)
57	SKIP	SKIP
58	IPv6-ICMP	ICMP for IPv6
59	IPv6-NoNxt	No Next Header for IPv6
60	IPv6-Opts	Destination Options for IPv6
61		any host internal protocol
62	CFTP	CFTP
63		any local network
64	SAT-EXPAK	SATNET and Backroom EXPAK
65	KRYPTOLAN	Kryptolan
66	RVD	MIT Remote Virtual Disk Protocol
67	IPPC	Internet Pluribus Packet Core
68		any distributed file system

Decimal	Keyword	Protocol
69	SAT-MON	SATNET Monitoring
70	VISA	VISA Protocol
71	IPCV	Internet Packet Core Utility
72	CPNX	Computer Protocol Network Executive
73	CPHB	computer Protocol Heart Beat
74	WSN	Wang Span Network
75	PVP	Packet Video Protocol
76	BR-SAT-MON	Backroom SATNET Monitoring
77	SUN-ND	SUN ND PROTOCOL-Temporary
78	WB-MON	WIDEBAND Monitoring
79	WB-EXPAK	WIDEBAND EXPAK
80	ISO-IP	ISO Internet Protocol
81	VMTP	VMTP
82	SECURE-VMTP	SECURE-VMPT
83	VINES	VINES
84	TTP	TTP
85	NSFNET-IGP	NSFNET-IGP
86	DGP	Dissimilar Gateway Protocol
87	TCF	TCF
88	EIGRP	EIGRP
89	OSPFIGP	OSPFIGP
90	Sprite-RPC	Sprite RPC Protocol
91	LARP	Locus Address Resolution Protocol
92	MTP	Multicast Transport Protocol
93	AX.25	AX.25 Frames
94	IPIP	IP-within-IP Encapsulation Protocol
95	MICP	Mobile Internetworking Control Protocol
96	SCC-SP	Semaphore Communications Sec. Protocol

continues

Table 3–1

Continued

Decimal	Keyword	Protocol
97	ETHERIP	Ethernet-within-IP Encapsulation
98	ENCAP	Encapsulation Header
99		any private encryption scheme
100	GMTP	GMTP
101	IFMP	Ipsilon Flow Management Protocol
102	PNNI	PNNI over IP
103	PIM	Protocol Independent Multicast
104	ARIS	ARIS
105	SCPS	SCPS
106	QNX	QNX
107	A/N	Active Networks
108	IPPCP	IP Payload Compression Protocol
109	SNP	Sitara Networks Protocol
110	Compaq-Peer	Compaq Peer Protocol
111	IPX-in-IP	IPX in IP
112	VRRP	Virtual Router Redundancy Protocol
113	PGM	PGM Reliable Transport protocol
114		any 0-hop protocol
115	L2TP	Layer Two Tunneling Protocol
116	DDX	D-II Data Exchange (DDX)
117–254		Unassigned
255		Reserved

Source and Destination Address Fields

The source and destination address fields are both 32 bits in length. Each address represents both a network and a host computer on the network. Because it is extremely important to understand the composition and formation of IP addresses to correctly configure devices connected to an IP network, we will next turn our attention to this topic. Once we obtain an understanding of IP addressing, we will then examine the address resolution process required to enable layer 3 packets that use IP addresses to be correctly delivered via layer 2 addressing.

In this section, we turn our attention to the mechanism that enables TCP and UDP packets to be transmitted to unique or predefined groups of hosts. That mechanism is the addressing method used by the IP, commonly referred to as IP addressing. The current version of the IP is version 4. The next generation IP, which is currently being operated on an experimental portion of the Internet, is referred to as version 6 and noted by the mnemonic IPv6. Because of significant differences in the method of addressing used by each version of the IP, we will cover both versions in this section. First, we will focus our attention on the addressing used by IPv4. Once we obtain an appreciation for how IPv4 addresses are formed and used, we will turn our attention to IPv6. By first covering the addressing used by IPv4, we will also obtain the ability to discuss address compatibility methods that will allow IPv6 addresses to be used to access devices configured to respond to IPv4 addresses.

Overview

IP addresses are used by the IP to identify distinct device interfaces such as interfaces that connect hosts, routers, and gateways to networks as well as to route data to those devices. Each device interface in an IP network must be assigned to a unique IP address so that it can receive communications addressed to it. This means that a multiport router will have one IP address for each of its network connections.

IPv4 uses 32-bit binary numbers to identify the source and destination addresses in each packet. This address space provides 2,294,967,296 distinct addressable devices, which exceeded the world's population when the Internet was initially developed. However, the proliferation of personal computers, the projected growth in the use of cable modems that require individual IP addresses, and the fact that every interface on a gateway or router must have a distinct IP address has contributed to a rapid depletion of available IP addresses. Recognizing that hundreds of millions of people who currently do not have access may eventually be connected to the Internet, and also recognizing the potential for cell phones and even pacemakers to communicate via the Internet, the *Internet Activities Board* (IAB) commenced work on a replacement for the current version of IP during 1992.

Although the addressing limitations of IPv4 was of primary concern, the efforts of the IAB resulted in a new protocol with a number of significant improvements over IPv4 to include the use of 128-bit addresses for source and destination devices. This new version of IP, IPv6, was finalized during 1995 and is currently being evaluated on an experimental portion of the Internet. Because this section is concerned with IP addressing, we will cover the addressing schemes, address notation, host address restrictions, and special addresses associated with both IPv4 and IPv6.

IPv4

The IP was officially standardized in September of 1981. Included in the standard was a requirement that each host connected to an IP-based network must be assigned a unique 32-bit address value for each network connection. This requirement resulted in some networking devices, such as routers and gateways, that have interfaces to more than one network as well as host computers with multiple connections to the same or different network being assigned a unique IP address for each network interface. Figure 3–2 illustrates two bus-based Ethernet LANs connected by the use of a pair of routers. Note that each router has two interfaces, one rep-

Figure 3–2
IP addressing

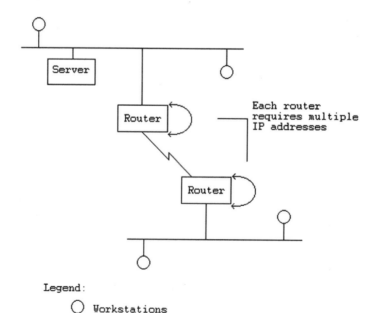

resented by a connection to a LAN and the second represented by a connection to a serial interface. That interface provides router-to-router connectivity via a *wide area network* (WAN). Thus, each router has two IP addresses, one assigned to its LAN interface and the other assigned to its serial interface. By assigning addresses to each specific device interface, this method of addressing enables packets to be correctly routed when a device has two or more network connections.

The Basic Addressing Scheme

When the IP was developed, it was recognized that hosts would be connected to different networks and that those networks would be interconnected to form an Internet. Thus, in developing the IP addressing scheme, it was also recognized that a mechanism would be required to identify a network as well as a host connected to a network. This recognition resulted in the development of a two-level addressing hierarchy that is illustrated in Figure 3–3.

Under the two-level IP addressing scheme, all hosts on the same network must be assigned the same network prefix but must have a unique host address to differentiate one host from another. Similarly, two hosts on different networks must be assigned different network prefixes; however, the hosts can have the same host address. This concept is similar to your telephone number. No one in your area code can have exactly the same phone number as your own, but it's likely that somewhere the same phone number exists in a different area code.

Address Classes

When IP was standardized, it was recognized that a single method of subdividing the 32-bit address into network and host portions would be wasteful with respect to the assignment of addresses. For example, if all addresses were split evenly, resulting in 16 bits for a network number and 16 bits for a host number, the result would allow a maximum of 65,534

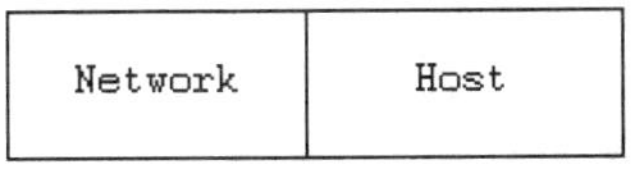

Figure 3–3
The two-level IP
addressing hierarchy

Network	Host

(2^16—2) networks with up to 65,534 hosts per network. Then the assignment of a network number to an organization that only had 100 computers would result in a waste of 65,434 host addresses that could not be assigned to another organization. Recognizing this problem, the designers of IP decided to subdivide the 32-bit address space into different address classes, resulting in five address classes being defined. Those classes are referred to as Class A through Class E.

Class A addresses are for very large networks, while Class B and Class C addresses are for medium-sized and small networks, respectively. Class A, B, and C addresses incorporate the two-level IP addressing structure previously illustrated in Figure 3–3. Class D addresses are used for IP multicasting, in which a single message is distributed to a group of hosts dispersed across a network, and Class E addresses are reserved for experimental use. Both Class D and Class E addresses do not incorporate the two-level IP addressing structure used by Class A through Class C addresses.

Figure 3–4 illustrates the five IP address formats to show the bit allocation of each 32-bit address class. In examining the figure, note that the address class can easily be determined through examining one or more of the first four bits' values in the 32-bit address. Once an address class is identified, the remainder of the address' subdivision into the network and host address portions is automatically noted.

To obtain an appreciation of each address class, let's examine the composition of the network and host portion of each address when applicable, because doing so provides some basic information that can be used to indicate how such addresses are used. Concerning the allocation of IP addresses, it should be noted that specific class addresses are assigned by the InterNIC.

Class A

A Class A IP address is defined by a 0-bit value in the high-order bit position of the address. This class of addresses uses seven bits for the network portion and 24 bits for the host portion of the address. As a result of this subdivision, 128 networks can be defined with approximately 16.78 million hosts capable of being addressed on each network. Due to the relatively small number of Class A networks that can be defined and the large number of hosts that can be supported per network, Class A addresses are primarily assigned to large organizations and countries that have national networks.

Class B

A Class B network is defined by the setting of the IP address' two high-order bits to 10. The network portion of a Class B address is 14 bits in

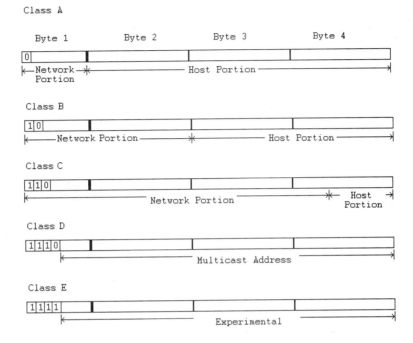

Figure 3–4
IP address formats

width, while the host portion is 16 bits wide. This results in Class B addresses having the capability of being assigned to 16,384 networks, with each network able to support up to 65,534 hosts. Due to the manner by which Class B addresses are subdivided into network and host portions, such addresses are normally assigned to relatively large organizations with tens of thousands of employees.

Class C

A Class C address is identified by the first three bits of its IP address having the value 110. This results in the network portion of the address having 21 bits, while the host portion of the address is limited to eight-bit positions.

The use of 21 bits for a network address enables approximately two million distinct networks to be supported by the Class C address class. Because eight bits are used for the host portion of a Class C address, this means that each Class C address can theoretically support up to 256 hosts. However, an address of all zeros and an address of all ones cannot be used, reducing the number of host addresses to 2^8-2 or 254.

Due to the subdivision of network and host portions of Class C addresses, they are primarily assigned for use by relatively small networks, such as an organizational LAN. Because it is quite common for many organizations to have multiple LANs, it is also quite common for multiple Class C addresses to be assigned to organizations that require more than 254 host addresses but are not large enough to justify a Class B address. Although Class A through C addresses are commonly assigned by the InterNIC to Internet service providers for distribution to their customers, Class D and E addresses represent special types of IP addresses.

Class D

A Class D IP address is defined by the value 1110 in the first four bits in the address. The remaining bits are used to form what is referred to as a multicast address. Thus, the 28 bits used for that address enable approximately 268 million possible multicast addresses.

Multicast is an addressing technique that allows a source to send a single copy of a packet to a specific group through the use of a multicast address. Through a membership registration process, hosts can dynamically enroll in multicast groups. Thus, the use of a Class D address enables up to 268 million multicast sessions to simultaneously occur throughout the world. Until recently, the use of multicast addresses was relatively limited, yet its use is considerably increasing as it provides a mechanism to conserve bandwidth, which is becoming a precious commodity.

To understand how Class D addressing conserves bandwidth, consider a video presentation routed from the Internet onto a private network that users working at 10 hosts on the network wish to receive. Without a multicast transmission capability, 10 separate video streams would be transmitted onto the private network, with each stream consisting of packets with 10 distinct host destination addresses. In comparison, through the use of a multicast address, one data stream would be routed to the private network.

Because a video stream can require a relatively large amount of bandwidth in comparison to interactive query-response client-server communications, the capability to eliminate multiple data streams via multicast transmission can prevent networks from being saturated. This capability can also result in the avoidance of session time-outs when client-server sessions are delayed due to high LAN utilization levels, providing another reason for the use of multicast transmission.

Class E

The fifth address class defined by the IP address specification is a reserved address class known as Class E. A Class E address' first four bits contain the value of 1111. This results in the remaining 28 bits being capable of supporting approximately 268.4 million addresses. Class E addresses are restricted for experimentation.

Dotted-Decimal Notation

Recognizing that the direct use of 32-bit binary addresses is both cumbersome and unwieldy to deal with, a technique more acceptable for human use was developed. That technique is referred to as *dotted-decimal notation* in recognition of the fact that the technique developed to express IP addresses occurs via the use of four decimal numbers separated from one another by decimal points.

Dotted-decimal notation divides the 32-bit IP address into four eight-bit (one byte) fields, with the value of each field specified as a decimal number, which can range from 0 to 255 in bytes 2, 3, and 4. In the first byte of an IP address, the setting of the first four bits in the byte that is used to denote the address class limits the range of decimal values that can be assigned to that byte. For example, from Figure 3–4, a Class A address is defined by the first bit position in the first byte being set to 0. Thus, the maximum value of the first byte in a Class A address is 127. Table 3–2 summarizes the numeric ranges for Class A through Class C IP addresses.

To illustrate the formation of a dotted-decimal number, let's first focus our attention on the decimal relationship of the bit positions in a byte. Figure 3–5 indicates the decimal values of the bit positions within an eight-bit byte. Note that the decimal value of each bit position corresponds to 2^n, where n is the bit position in the byte. Using the decimal values of the bit positions shown in Figure 3–5, let's assume the first byte

Table 3–2

Class A Through C Address Characteristics

Class	Length of Network Address (Bits)	First Number Range (Decimal)
A	8	0–127
B	16	128–191
C	24	192–223

Figure 3–5

Decimal values of bit positions in a byte

128	64	32	16	8	4	2	1

in an IP address has its bit positions set to 01100000. Then the value of that byte expressed as a decimal number becomes 64 + 32, or 96. Now let's assume that the second byte in the IP address has the bit values 01101000. The decimal value of that binary byte is 64 + 32 + 8 or 104. Let's further assume that the last two bytes in the IP address have the bit values 00111110 and 10000011. Then the third byte would have the decimal value 32 + 16 + 8 + 4 + 2 or 62, while the last byte would have the decimal value 128 + 2 + 1, or 131.

Based on the preceding information, the dotted decimal number 96.104.62.131 is equivalent to the binary number 01100000011010000011111010000011. Obviously, it is easier to work with as well as remember four numbers separated by periods, rather than a string of 32 digits.

Reserved Addresses

Three blocks of IP addresses were originally reserved for networks that would not be connected to the Internet. Those address blocks were defined in RFC 1918, Address Allocation for Private Internets, and are summarized in Table 3–3.

Both security considerations and the difficulties in obtaining large blocks of IP addresses resulted in many organizations using the addresses listed in Table 3–3 for connecting their network to the Internet. Because the use of any private Internet address by two or more organizations would result in addressing conflicts and the unreliable delivery of information, those addresses are not directly used. Instead, organizations commonly install a proxy firewall that provides address translation between a large number of private Internet addresses used on the internal network and a smaller number of assigned IP addresses. Not only does this technique allow organizations to connect large internal networks to the Internet without being able to obtain relatively scarce Class A or B addresses, the proxy firewall hides internal addresses from the Internet community.

Table 3–3	**Address Blocks**
Reserved IP Addresses for Private Internet Use	10.0.0.0 — 10.255.255.255
	172.16.0.0 — 172.31.255.255
	192.168.0.0 — 192.168.255.255

Any hacker that attempts to attack a host on your network actually has to attack your organization's proxy firewall.

As an alternate to the use of a proxy firewall, you can use a router with a *network address translation capability* (NAT). NAT also hides your organization's internal IP addresses from the Internet community amd provides a mechanism to economize valuable IP addresses. Later in this book the use of proxy services on firewalls as well as network address translation will be covered.

Networking Basics

As previously noted, each IP network has a distinct network prefix and each host on an IP network has a distinct host address. When two IP networks are interconnected by the use of a router, each router port that represents an interface is assigned an IP address that reflects the network it is connected to. Figure 3–6 illustrates the connection of two networks via a router, indicating possible address assignments.

Note that the first decimal number (192) of the four-byte dotted-decimal numbers on the left of Figure 3–6 denotes a Class C address. This is because 192 decimal is equivalent to 11000000 binary. Because the first two bits are set to the bit value 11, this indicates a Class C address. Also note that the first three bytes of a Class C address indicate the network, while the fourth

Figure 3–6
Router connections to networks require an IP address for each connection.

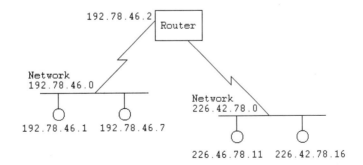

byte indicates the host address. Thus, the network shown in the left portion of Figure 3–6 is denoted as 192.78.46.0, with device addresses that can range from 192.78.46.1 through 192.78.46.254.

In the lower right portion of Figure 3–6, two hosts are shown connected to another network. Note that the first byte for the four-byte dotted-decimal number assigned to each host and the router port is decimal 226, which is equivalent to binary 11100010. Because the first two bits in the first byte are again set to 11, the second network also represents the use of a Class C address. Thus, the network address is 226.42.78.0, with device addresses on the network ranging from 226.42.78.01 to 226.42.78.254.

Although it would appear that 256 devices could be supported on a Class C network (0 through 255 used for the host address), in actuality the host portion field of an IP address has two restrictions. First, the host portion field cannot be set to all zero bits. This is because an all-zeros host number is used to identify a base network or subnetwork number. Concerning the latter, we will shortly discuss subnetworking. Secondly, an all-ones host number represents the broadcast address for a network or subnetwork. Due to these restrictions, a maximum of 254 devices can be defined for use on a Class C network. Similarly, other network classes have the previously discussed addressing restrictions, which reduce the number of distinct addressable devices that can be connected to each type of IP network by two. Because, as previously explained, an all-zeros host number identifies a base network, the two networks shown in Figure 3–6 are shown numbered as 192.78.46.0 and 226.42.78.0.

Subnetting

One of the problems associated with the use of IP addresses is the necessity to assign a distinct network address to each network. This can result in the waste of many addresses as well as require a considerable expansion in the use of router tables. To appreciate these problems, let's return to Figure 3–6, which illustrates the connection of two Class C networks via a router.

Assume each Class C network supports 29 workstations and servers. Adding an address for the router port, each Class C network would use 30 out of 254 available addresses. Thus, the assignment of two Class C addresses to an organization with a requirement to support two networks with a total of 60 devices would result in 448 (254 $\cdot$ 2—60) available IP addresses being wasted. In addition, routers would have to recognize two network addresses instead of one. When this situation is multiplied by numerous organizations requiring multiple networks, the effect on routing tables becomes more pronounced, resulting in extended search times as routers sort through their routing tables to determine an appropriate route to a network. Recognizing the preceding problems, RFC 950 became a standard in 1985. This standard defines a procedure to subnet or divide a single Class A, B, or C network into subnetworks.

Through the process of subnetting, the two-level hierarchy of Class A, B, and C networks shown in Figure 3–4 is turned into a three-level hierarchy. In doing so, the host portion of an IP address is divided into a subnet-portion and a host-portion. Figure 3–7 provides a comparison between the two-level hierarchy initially defined for Class A, B, and C networks and the three-level subnet hierarchy.

Through the process of subnetting, a Class A, B, or C network address can be divided into different subnet numbers, with each subnet used to identify a different network internal to an organization. Because the network portion of the address remains the same, the route from the Internet to any subnet of a given IP network address is the same. This means that routers within the organization must be able to differentiate between different subnets, but routers outside the organization consider all subnets as one network.

To illustrate the subnet process as well as obtain an appreciation of how it facilitates the use of IP addresses in a less wasteful manner and reduces routing table entries, let's examine the process. In doing so, we will discuss the concept of masking and the use of the subnet mask, both of which are essential to the extension of the network portion of an IP address beyond its network portion of the address.

To illustrate the concept of subnetting, let's return to the two networks previously illustrated in Figure 3–6, 192.78.46.0 and 226.42.78.0. Let's assume that instead of two networks geographically separated from one another at two distinct locations, we require the establishment of five networks at one

Figure 3–7

Comparing the three-level subnet hierarchy to the two-level network class hierarchy

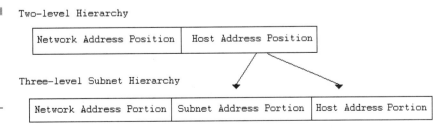

location. Let's further assume that each of the five networks can support a maximum of 15 stations. Although your organization could apply for four additional Class C addresses, doing so would waste precious IP address space because each Class C address supports a maximum of 254 devices. In addition, if your internal network is connected to the Internet, entries for four additional networks would be required in a number of routers in the Internet in addition to your organization's internal routers.

Instead of requesting four additional Class C addresses, let's use subnetting, dividing the host portion of the IP address into a subnet number and a host-number. Because we need to support five networks at one location, we must use a minimum of three bits from the host-portion of the IP address as the subnet number. Note that the number of subnets you can obtain is 2^n-1, where n is the number of bits. When n equals 2, this yields three subnets, which is too few. When n equals 3, we get 7, which gives enough subnets for our example. Because a Class C address uses one eight-bit byte for the host identification, this means that a maximum of five bit positions can be used (8–3) for the host number. Assuming we intend to use the 192.78.46.0 network address for our subnetting effort, we would construct an extended network prefix based on combining the network-portion of the IP address with its subnet number.

Figure 3–8 illustrates the creation of five subnets from the 192.78.46.0 network address. The top entry in Figure 3–8, which is labeled "Base Network," represents the Class C network address with a host address byte field set to all zeros. We previously decided to use three bits from the host portion of the Class C IP address to develop an extended network prefix. Thus, the five entries in the code below indicate the use of three bits from the host position in the address to create extended prefixes that identify five distinct subnets created from one IP Class C address.

Figure 3–8
The Internet versus
the internal network
view of subnets

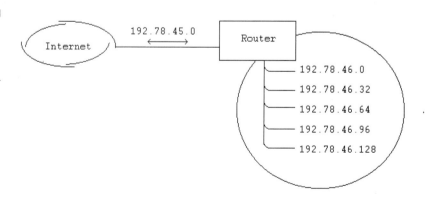

```
Base Network:  11000000.01010000.00101110.00000000 = 192.78.46.0
Subnet #0:     11000000.01010000.00101110.00000000 = 192.78.46.0
Subnet #1:     11000000.01010000.00101110.00100000 = 192.78.46.32
Subnet #2:     11000000.01010000.00101110.01000000 = 192.78.46.64
Subnet #3:     11000000.01010000.00101110.01100000 = 192.78.46.96
Subnet #4:     11000000.01010000.00101110.10000000 = 192.78.46.128
```

For each subnet, there are two addressing restrictions that reduce the number of hosts or more correctly, the interfaces, that can be supported. The addressing restrictions are the same as in a regular IP network; you cannot use a base subnet address of all zeros, nor all ones. Thus, for subnet 0 in Figure 3–8, valid addresses would range from 1 to 30. Similarly, for subnet 1, valid addresses would range from 33 to 62.

One point of interest worth noting is that the zero subnet was at one point considered anathema by the Internet community and its use was highly discouraged. Although this viewpoint has fallen from favor, some devices still do not support the use of subnet zero and do not allow their interface address to be configured with an address on the zero subnet. Cisco routers support the use of subnet zero, but this support must be explicitly enabled in the router configuration. By default, the router will give you a "inconsistent network mask" error when attempting to configure an interface on subnet zero. It is highly encouraged that you test each device class in your network for support of subnet zero before designing an IP address scheme using this subnet, or just avoid its use.

To the Internet, all five networks appear as the network address 192.78.46.0, with the router responsible for directing traffic to the appropriate subnet. It is important to note that externally, or to the Internet, there is nothing to indicate that the dotted decimal numbers in the right column represent distinct subnets. This is because the Internet views the first byte of each dotted decimal number and notes that the first two bits are set. Doing so tells routers on the Internet that the address is a Class C address, that the first three bytes represent the network portion of the IP address, and that the fourth byte represents the host address. Thus, to the outside world, address 192.78.46.32 would not be recognized as subnet 1. Instead, a router would interpret the address as network 192.78.46.0 with host address 32. Similarly, subnet four would appear as network address 192.78.46.0 with host address 128. Internally within an organization, however, each of the addresses listed in the right column in Figure 3–8 would be recognized as a subnet. To visualize this dual interpretation of network addresses, Figure 3–8 illustrates the Internet versus the private network view of subnets.

As we might logically assume from our prior discussion of Class C addresses, any address with the network prefix 192.78.46.0 is routed to the corporate router. Although we noted how subnet addresses are formed, we have yet to discuss how we assign host addresses to devices connected to different subnets or how the router can break down a subnet address so it can correctly route traffic to an appropriate subnet. Thus, a discussion of host addressing on subnets to include the role of the subnet mask is in order.

Host Addresses on Subnets

We previously subdivided the host portion of a Class C address into a three-bit subnet field and a five-bit host field. Because the host field of an IP address cannot contain all zero bits nor all one bits, the use of five bits in the host portion of each subnet address means that each subnet can support a maximum of 2^5-2, or 30 addresses. Thus, we could use host addresses 1 through 30 on subnet 0, 33 through 62 on subnet 1, and so on. Figure 3–9 illustrates the assignment of host addresses for subnet 3 whose creation was previously indicated in the block of five code entries earlier.

```
Subnet #3:  11000000.01010000.00101110.01100000 = 192.78.45.96
Host #1:    11000000.01010000.00101110.01100001 = 192.78.46.97
Host #2:    11000000.01010000.00101110.01100010 = 192.78.46.98
Host #3:    11000000.01010000.00101110.01100011 = 192.78.46.99

Host #30:   11000000.01010000.00101110.01111110 = 192.78.46.126
```

In examining these host addresses, note that we start with the subnet address 192.78.46.96, which indicates the subnet in its first three bits. The remaining five bits define the host address on each subnet. Thus, the address 192.78.46.96 represents the third subnet, while addresses 192.78.46.97 through 192.78.46.126 represent hosts 1 through 30 that can reside on subnet 3.

Although we now have an appreciation for creating subnets and host addresses on subnets, an unanswered question is how do devices on a pri-

---

Figure 3–9
The relationship between the IP address and the subnet mask is shown.

```
IP Address:   192.78.46.97     11000000.01010000.00101110.01100001
Subnet Mask:  255.255.255.244  11111111.11111111.11111111.11100000
```

Extended Network Address

vate network recognize subnet addressing? If a packet arrives at an organizational router with the destination address 192.78.46.97, for example, how does the router know to route that packet onto subnet 3? The answer to this question involves what is known as the subnet mask.

The Subnet Mask

The subnet mask represents a mechanism that enables devices on a network to determine the separation of an IP address into its network, subnet, and host portions. To accomplish this, the subnet mask consists of a sequence of one-bits that denotes the length of the network and subnet portions of the IP network address. For example, let's assume our network address is 192.78.46.96 and we want to develop a subnet mask that can be used to identify the extended network. Because we previously used three bits from the host portion of the IP address, the subnet mask would become

```
11111111.11111111.11111111.11100000
```

Similar to the way IP addresses can be expressed using dotted-decimal notation, we can also express subnet masks using that same notation. By doing so, we can express the subnet mask as

```
255.255.255.224
```

The subnet mask tells the device examining an IP address which bits in the address should be treated as the extended network address, consisting of network and subnet addresses. The remaining bits that are not set in the mask indicate the host on the extended network address. However, how does a device determine the subnet of the destination address? Because the subnet mask indicates the length of the extended network to include the network and subnet fields, knowing the length of the network portion of the address provides a device with the capability to determine the number of bits in the subnet field. Once this is accomplished, the device can determine the value of the bits that indicate the subnet.

To illustrate this concept, let's use the IP address 192.78.46.97 and the subnet mask 255.255.255.224, with the latter used to define a 27-bit extended network. The relationship between the IP address and the subnet mask is shown in Figure 3–9.

Because the first two bits in the IP address are set, this indicates a Class C address. Since a Class C address consists of three bytes used for the network address and one byte for the host address, this means the subnet must be three bits in length (27–24). Thus, bits 25 through 27, which are set to 011 in the IP address, identify the subnet as subnet 3. Because the last five bits in the subnet mask are set to zero, this means that those bit positions in the IP address identify the host on subnet 3. Because those last five bits have the value 00001, the IP address references host 1 on subnet 3 on network 192.78.46.0.

To facilitate working with subnets, Table 3–4 provides information on the number of subnets that can be created for Class B and Class C networks, their subnet masks, the number of hosts per network, and the total number of hosts supported by a particular subnet mask. Note that the total number of hosts can vary considerably based on the use of different subnet masks and should be carefully considered prior to your subdivision of a network.

Table 3–4

Subnet Mask
Reference

Number of Subnet bits	Subnet Mask	Number of Subnetworks	Hosts/ Subnet	Total Number of Hosts
		Class B		
1	-	-	-	-
2	255.255.192.0	2	16382	32764
3	255.255.224.0	6	8190	49140
4	255.255.240.0	14	4094	57316
5	255.255.248.0	30	2046	61380
6	255.255.252.0	62	1022	63364
7	255.255.254.0	126	510	64260
8	255.255.255.0	254	254	64516
9	255.255.255.128	510	126	64260
10	255.255.255.192	1022	62	63364
11	255.255.255.224	2046	30	61380
12	255.255.255.240	4094	14	57316
13	255.255.255.248	8190	6	49140

Number of Subnet bits	Subnet Mask	Number of Subnetworks	Hosts/ Subnet	Total Number of Hosts
14	255.255.255.252	16382	2	32764
15	-	-	-	-
16	-	-	-	-
		Class C		
1	-	-	-	-
2	255.255.255.192	2	62	124
3	255.255.255.224	6	30	180
4	255.255.255.240	14	14	196
5	255.255.255.248	30	6	170
6	255.255.255.252	62	2	124
7	-	-	-	-
8	-	-	-	-

Configuration Examples

When configuring a workstation or server to operate on a TCP/IP network, most network operating systems require you to enter a minimum of three IP addresses and an optional subnet mask or mask bit setting. The first address is the IP address assigned to the workstation or server. The two additional addresses consist of the IP address of the gateway or router that is responsible for relaying packets with a destination not on the local network to a different network, and a name resolver, which is also referred to as the *Domain Name Server* (DNS). The name resolver is a computer responsible for translating mnemonic names assigned to computers into IP addresses.

Figure 3–10 illustrates the first configuration screen in a series of screens displayed by the Windows 95 TCP/IP Properties dialog box. The IP address screen illustrated in the figure provides you with the ability to enter an IP address that is assigned to the workstation or server running Microsoft's TCP/IP protocol stack. The configuration screen also provides you with the ability to enter the number of subnet mask bits in the form

Figure 3–10

The Windows 95
TCP/IP Properties
screen enables you
to set the IP address
of the host running
the program's TCP/IP
protocol stack.

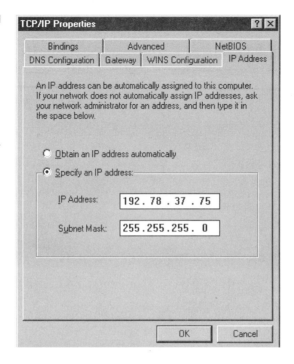

of a dotted-decimal number. Table 3–5 compares the number of subnet bits to host bits and indicates the resulting decimal mask.

In examining the screen displayed in Figure 3–10, note that simply clicking on different tabs results in the display of new configuration screens. For example, Figure 3–11 illustrates the DNS Configuration screen that provides a name resolution process. Here you would enter the address of one or more *Domain Name Servers* (DNS) as well as the name assigned to your host and its DNS domain name. In this example, the host name is shown entered as "gil," while the DNS domain name is "feds.gov." This informs the domain server at the indicated address that requests to access the host with the mnemonic gil.feds.gov should be routed to the IP address previously entered into the IP Configuration screen. Thus, this display screen provides network users with the ability to have their computer identified by a name rather than a more cumbersome IP address. The specification of at least one domain server's IP address also enables the use of mnemonic names to access other computers. This is because the computer now knows to send the name-to-IP address resolution requests to the indicated domain server IP address.

Table 3–5

Subnet Masks

Subnet Bits	Host Bits	Decimal Mask
0	8	0
1	7	28
2	6	192
3	5	224
4	4	240
5	3	248
6	2	252
7	1	254
8	0	255

Figure 3–11
The Windows 95 DNS Configuration tab in the TCP/IP Properties dialog box enables a host to be configured so it can be identified by its mnemonic name. The specification of the IP address of a domain server also enables the use of mnemonic names to access other computers.

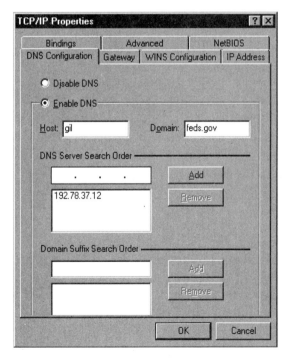

Classless Networking

As previously noted, the use of individual Class A, B, and C addresses can result in a significant amount of unused address space, making their use very inefficient. Recognizing this inefficiency, another method has been developed to assign IP addresses to organizations. This method results in a more efficient assignment of IP addresses, as it better ties the number of distinct IP addresses to the requirements of an organization. Because the technique does away with network classes, it is commonly referred to as *classless networking*.

Under classless networking, an organization is assigned a number of bits to use as the local part of its address that best corresponds to the number of addresses it needs. If an organization requires 4,000 IP addresses, for example, it would be given 12 bits (4,096 distinct addresses) to use as the local part of its address. The remaining 20 bits in the 32-bit address space are then used as a prefix to denote what is referred to as a supernetwork. To denote the network part of a classless network, the forward slash (/) is used, followed by the number of bits in the prefix. Thus, the previously mentioned classless network would be denoted as /20.

Currently, address allocations used for classless networking are taken from available Class C addresses. Thus, obtaining a 20-bit prefix is equivalent to obtaining 16 continuous Class C addresses. Table 3–6 lists the classless address blocks that can be assigned from available Class C address space.

Table 3–6

Classless Network Address Assignments

Network Part	Local Bits	Equivalent Number of Class C Addresses	Distinct Addresses
124	8	1	256
123	9	2	512
122	10	4	1024
121	11	8	2048
120	12	16	4096
119	13	32	8192
118	14	64	16284
117	15	128	32768

In addition to providing a better method for allocating IP addresses, classless addressing enables a router to forward traffic to an organization using a single routing entry. Due to the tremendous growth of the Internet, classless addressing provides a more efficient mechanism for locating entries in router tables. This is because one classless entry can replace up to 129 Class C addresses, enabling a router to locate entries faster as it searches its routing tables. Thus, you can expect the use of classless addressing to increase as a mechanism to both extend the availability of IP addresses as well as enable routers to operate more efficiently as we wait for IPv6 to be deployed.

IPv6

IPv6 was developed as a mechanism to simplify the operation of the IP, provide a mechanism for adding new operations as they are developed through a header daisy chain capability, add built-in security and authentication, and extend source and destination addresses to an address space that could conceivably meet every possible addressing requirement for generations. This latter task is accomplished through an expansion of source and destination addresses to 128 bits and is the focus of this section.

Address Architecture

IPv6 is based on the same architecture used in IPv4, resulting in each network interface requiring a distinct IP address. The key differences between IPv6 and IPv4 with respect to addresses are the manner by which an interface is identified and the size and composition of the address. Under IPv6, an interface can be identified by several addresses to facilitate routing and management. In comparison, under IPv4, an interface can be assigned only one address. Concerning address size, IPv6 uses 128 bits, or 96 more bits than an IPv4 address.

Address Types

IPv6 addresses also include unicast and multicast, which were included in IPv4. In addition, IPv6 adds a new address category known as *anycast*. Although an anycast address identifies a group of stations similar to a multicast address, a packet with an anycast address is delivered to only one station, the nearest member of the group. The use of anycast addressing can facilitate network restructuring while minimizing the amount of configuration changes required to support a new network structure. This is because an anycast address can be used to reference a group of routers, and the alteration of a network when stations use anycast addressing would enable them to continue to access the nearest router without a user having to change the address configuration of their workstation.

Address Notation

Because IPv6 addresses consist of 128 bits, a mechanism is required to facilitate their entry as configuration data. The mechanism replaces those bits with eight 16-bit integers separated by colons, with each integer represented by four hexadecimal digits. For example:

```
6ACD:00001:00FC:B10C:0001:0000:0000:001A
```

To facilitate the entry of IPv6 addresses, you can skip leading zeros in each hexadecimal component. That is, you can write 1 instead of 0001 and 0 instead of 0000. Thus, this capability to suppress zeroes in each hexadecimal component would reduce the previous network address to

```
6ACD:1:FC:B10C:1:0:0:1A
```

Under IPv6, a second method of address simplification was introduced, the double-colon convention (:). Inside an address, a set of consecutive null 16-bit numbers can be replaced by two colons. Thus, the previously reduced IP address could be further reduced as

```
6ACD:1:FC:B10C:1::1A
```

It is important to note that the double-colon convention can only be used once inside an address. The reason for this is because the reconstruction of the address requires the number of integer fields in the address to be subtracted from eight to determine the number of consecutive zero value fields the double-colon represents. Otherwise, the use of two or more double-colons would create an ambiguity that would not allow the address to be correctly reconstructed.

Address Allocation

The use of a 128-bit address space provides a high degree of address assignment flexibility beyond that available under IPv4. IPv6 addressing enables

Internet service providers to be identified and includes the capability to identify local and global multicast addresses, private site addresses for use within an organization, hierarchical geographical global unicast addresses, and other types of addresses. Table 3–7 lists the initial allocation of address space under IPv6.

Table 3–7

IPv6 Address
Space Allocation

Fraction of Allocation	Prefix (Binary)	Address Space
Reserved	0000 0000	1/256
Unassigned	0000 0001	1/256
Reserved for NSAP Allocation	0000 001	1/128
Reserved for IPX Allocation	0000 010	1/128
Unassigned	0000 011	1/128
Unassigned	0000 1	1/32
Unassigned	0001	1/16
Unassigned	001	1/8
Provider-based Unicast Address	010	1/8
Unassigned	011	1/8
Reserved for Geographic-based Unicast Address	100	1/8
Unassigned	101	1/8
Unassigned	110	1/8
Unassigned	1110	1/16
Unassigned	1111 0	1/32
Unassigned	1111 10	1/64
Unassigned	1111 110	1/128
Unassigned	1111 1110 0	1/512
Link-Local Use Addresses	1111 1110 10	1/1024
Site-Local Use Addresses	1111 1110 11	1/1024
Multicast Addresses	1111 1111	1/256

The *Internet Assigned Numbers Authority* (IANA) has been assigned the task of distributing portions of IPv6 address space to regional registries around the world, such as the InterNIC in North America, RIPE in Europe, and APNIC in Asia. To illustrate the planned use of IPv6 addresses, let's turn our attention to what will probably be the most common type of IPv6 address, the provider-based address.

Provider-Based Addresses

The first official distribution of IPv6 addresses is accomplished by using provider-based addresses. Based on the initial allocation of IPv6 addresses, as shown in Table 3–7, each provider-based address has the three-bit prefix 010. That prefix is followed by fields that identify the registry that allocated the address, service provider, and subscriber. The subscriber field actually consists of three subfields, a subscriber ID that can represent an organization, and variable network and interface identification fields used in a manner similar to IPv4 network and host fields. Figure 3–12 illustrates the initial structure for a provider-based address.

Special Addresses

Under IPv6 are five special types of unicast addresses that were defined, one of which deserves special attention. That address is the Version 4 address, which was developed to provide a migration capability from IPv4 to IPv6.

In a mixed IPv4 and IPv6 environment, devices that do not support IPv6 are mapped to version 6 addresses using the following form:

```
0:0:0:0:0:FFFF:w.x.y.z
```

Figure 3–12
Provider-based
address structure

Prefix	Registry ID	Provider ID	Subscriber ID	Subnet ID	Station ID

```
Legend:
        Prefix          three bits set to 010
        Registry        5 bits identifies organization that
                        allocated the address
        Provider        24 bits with 16 used to identify ISP and 8
                        used for future extensions
        Subscriber      32 bits with 24 used to identify the
                        subscriber and 8 for extension
        Subnet          16 bits to identify the subnetwork
        Station         48 bits to identify the station
```

Here w.x.y.z represents the original IPv4 address. Thus, IPv4 addresses are transported as IPv6 addresses through the use of the IPv6 version 4 address format. This means that an organization with a large number of workstations and servers connected to the Internet only has to upgrade their router to support IPv6 addressing when IPv6 is deployed. Then they can gradually upgrade their network on a device-by-device basis to obtain an orderly migration to IPv6. Now that we have an appreciation for IPv4 and IPv6 addressing, let's turn our attention to the address resolution process and ICMP prior to exploring TCP and UDP in Chapter 4, "TCP and UDP."

Address Resolution

The physical address associated with a *local area network* (LAN) workstation is often referred to as its hardware or *Media Access Control* (MAC) address. In actuality, that address can be formed via software to override the burnt-in address on the network adapter card, a technique referred to as *locally administrated addressing.* When the built-in hardware address is used, this addressing technique is referred to as *universally administrated addressing,* as it represents a universally unique address whose creation we will shortly discuss. For both techniques, frames that flow at the data link layer use six byte source and destination addresses formed either via software or obtained from the network adapter.

Figure 3–13 illustrates the formats for both Ethernet and Token Ring frames. Both networks have been standardized by the *Institute of Electrical and Electronic Engineers* (IEEE) and use six byte source and destination addresses. The IEEE assigns blocks of addresses six hex characters in length to vendors that represent the first 24 bits of the 48-bit field used to uniquely identify a network adapter card. The vendor then encodes the remaining 24 bits or six hex character positions to identify the adapter manufactured by the vendor. Thus, each Ethernet and Token Ring adapter has a unique hardware of burnt-in identifiers that denote the manufacturer and the adapter number product by the manufacturer. If an organization decides to override the hardware address, they can do so via software; however, a 48-bit address must still be specified for each station address.

When an Ethernet or Token Ring station has data to transmit, it encodes the destination address and source address fields with 48-bit numbers that identify the layer 2 locations on the network to receive the frame and the layer 2 device that is transmitting the frame. In comparison, at the network layer, IP uses a 32-bit address that has no relation to the MAC or layer 2 address. Thus, a common problem associated with the routing of an IP datagram to a particular workstation on a LAN involves the delivery of the datagram to its correct destination. This delivery process requires an IP device that must

Figure 3-13
Ethernet and Token
Ring frame formats

Ethernet Frame Format

Preamble (1)	Start of Frame Delimiter (7)	Destination Address (6)	Source Address (6)	Type/ Length (2)	Information (46 to 1500)	FCS (4)

Token Ring Frame Format

Starting Delimiter (1)	Access Control (1)	Frame Control (1)	Destination Address (1)	Source Address (6)	Routing Information (Optional)

Variable Information	FCS (4)	Ending Delimiter (1)	Frame Status (1)

Legend: FCS   Frame Check Sequence
         (n)   n bytes represents field length

transmit a packet via a layer 2 delivery service to obtain the correct MAC or layer 2 address so it can take a packet and convert it into a frame for delivery.

In the opposite direction, a workstation must be able to convert a MAC address into an IP address. Both of these address translation problems are handled by protocols developed to provide an address resolution capability. One protocol, known as the *Address Resolution Protocol* (ARP), translates an IP address into a hardware address. The *Reverse Address Resolution Protocol* (RARP), as its name implies, performs a reverse translation or mapping, converting a hardware layer 2 address into an IP address.

Operation

Figure 3–14 illustrates the format of an ARP packet. Note that the numbers in some fields indicate the number of bytes when a field spans a four-byte boundary.

The 16-bit Hardware Type field indicates the type of network adapter. A value of one, for example, indicates a 10 Mbps Ethernet, six indicates an IEEE 802 network, and 16 indicates *Asynchronous Transmission Mode* (ATM). Similarly, the 16-bit Protocol Type field indicates the protocol for which an address resolution process is being performed. For IP, the Protocol Type field has a value of hex 0800. The Hardware Length field denotes the number of bytes in the hardware address. The value of this field is six for both

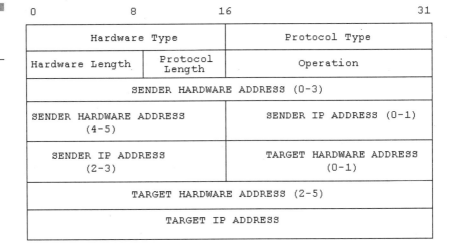

Figure 3–14
The ARP packet
format

Ethernet and Token Ring. The Protocol Length field is similar to the Hardware length field, indicating the length of the address for the protocol to be resolved. For IPv4, the value of this field is four. The Operation field has a value of one for an ARP Request and when a target station responds, the value of this field is changed to two to denote an ARP replay.

The Sender Hardware Address field is six bytes in length and indicates the hardware address of the station generating the ARP Request or ARP Reply. That address is followed by a four-byte Sender IP Address field. This field, as its name implies, indicates the IP address of the originator of the packet. The next to last field, Target Hardware Address, is originally set to zero in an ARP Request. The last field, Target IP Address, is set to the IP address for which the originator needs a hardware address.

To obtain a general appreciation for the operation of ARP, let's say a user located on an Ethernet network wants to transmit a datagram to another computer on the same network. The first computer would transmit an ARP packet that would be carried as an Ethernet broadcast frame to all stations on the network. Thus, the packet would be transported to all devices on the Ethernet LAN. The packet would contain the destination IP address that is known, because the computer is transmitting the IP address to a known location. The field in the ARP packet used for the target hardware address, however, is set to all zeros because the transmitting station does not know the destination hardware address. Each device on the Ethernet LAN will read the ARP packet as it is transmitted as a broadcast frame, but only the station that recognizes that it has the destination field's IP address will copy the frame off the network and respond to the ARP request. When it does, it transmits an ARP reply in which its physical address is inserted in the ARP target hardware address field that was previously set to zero.

To alleviate the necessity to constantly transmit ARP packets as well as to lower the utilization level of the LAN, the originator records received information in a table known as an ARP cache. The use of the ARP cache allows subsequent datagrams with previously learned correspondences between IP addresses and MAC addresses to be quickly transmitted to the appropriate hardware address on the network.

The standard also calls for devices on the network to update their own ARP table with the MAC and IP address pair of the originator of the ARP request. Additionally, when a device initializes its network connection during the boot process, it issues a "gratuitous ARP," which is an ARP request for its own IP address. This is how a station determines if another device on the network is using its assigned IP address and becomes aware if there is a conflict.

Finally, there is a feature in the standard called proxy ARP. Proxy ARP is a mechanism that allows a device to answer an ARP request on behalf of another device. This feature is necessary when the actual intended recipient of the ARP request does not reside on the same physical subnet as the originator of the request. Because the ARP request is a layer 2 broadcast, it is blocked at the router interface.

If, for example, the originating device has a standard Class C subnet mask, the device would assume that any address within that class resides on its own physical network and would expect it to respond to an ARP request. If the network has actually been subnetted into two parts, however, some of the hosts would reside on the other side of a router and the ARP request would not be seen on the second subnet. The reason the originating host might not have the correct subnet mask could be because of limitations of the operating system or a misconfiguration.

In this scenario, the router is aware of both subnets and can answer the ARP request on behalf of other devices on the second subnet by supplying its own MAC address. The originating device enters the routers MAC address in its ARP cache and correctly sends packets destined for the end host to the router. This feature is enabled by default on Cisco routers.

An additional use of this feature is that with most operating systems if you enter your own IP address as your default gateway address on your host, the host issues an ARP request for every destination, even those it knows to be on remote networks. The benefit of this is that if multiple routers are on the subnet or the router IP address is unknown, your ARP request is automatically answered via the proxy ARP feature without having to configure a single, static default gateway. As we can see, ARP provides a well-thought out methodology for equating physical hardware addresses to IP logical addresses and allows IP addressing at layer 3 to occur independently from LAN addressing at layer 2.

Now that we have an appreciation for ARP, we will conclude our examination of the IP by turning our attention to ICMP.

ICMP

As briefly noted in Chapter 2, "The TCP/IP Protocol Suite," the *Internet Control Message Protocol* (ICMP) represents an error-reporting mechanism that is transported via IP datagrams. The format of an ICMP message and its relationship to an IP datagram is illustrated in Figure 3–15. Note that although each ICMP message has its own format, they all begin with the same three fields: an eight-bit Type field, an eight-bit Code field, and a 16-bit Checksum field.

The ICMP Type field defines the meaning of the message as well as its format. Perhaps the two most familiar ICMP messages are type 0 and type 8. A Type field value of eight represents an echo request, while a Type 0 ICMP message denotes a reply. Although their official names are Echo Reply and Echo Request, most persons are more familiar with the term ping, which is used to reference both the request and reply. Table 3–8 lists the values of ICMP Type fields that currently identify specific types of ICMP messages.

The second field common to each ICMP header is the Code field. This field provides additional information about the message and may not be meaningful for certain messages. For example, both Type field values of

Figure 3–15
ICMP messages are transported via encapsulation within an IP datagram.

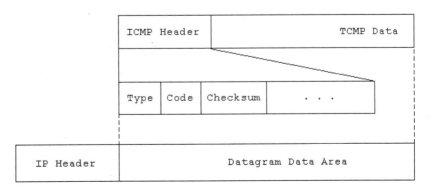

Table 3–8

ICMP Type
Field Values

Type	Name
0	Echo Reply
1	Unassigned
2	Unassigned
3	Destination Unreachable
4	Source Quench
5	Redirect
6	Alternate Host Address
7	Unassigned
8	Echo Request
9	Router Advertisement
10	Router Selection
11	Time Exceeded
12	Parameter Problem
13	Timestamp
14	Timestamp Reply
15	Information Request
16	Information Reply
17	Address Mask Request
18	Address Mask Reply
19	Reserved (for Security)
20–29	Reserved (for Robustness Experiment)
30	Traceroute
31	Datagram Conversion Error
32	Mobile Host Redirect
33	IPv6 Where-Are-You
34	IPv6 I-Am-Here
35	Mobile Registration Request
36	Mobile Registration Reply

Type	Name
37	Domain Name Request
38	Domain Name Reply
39	Skip
40	Photuris
41–255	Reserved

zero and eight always have a Code field value of zero. In comparison, a Type field value of three (Destination Unreachable) can have one of 16 possible Code field values, which further defines the problem. Table 3–9 lists the Code field values presently assigned to ICMP messages based on their Type field values. As we will note when we examine ICMP filtering, Cisco uses similar but different names for many ICMP message types and Control field values, yet the effect of their use is for a router to examine the contents of IP datagrams transporting ICMP messages and to perform filtering based on the values of ICMP Type and Code fields.

Table 3–9

ICMP Code Field Values Based on Message Type

Message Type	Code Field Values
3	Destination Unreachable
Codes	
0	Net Unreachable
1	Host Unreachable
2	Protocol Unreachable
3	Port Unreachable
4	Fragmentation Needed and Don't Fragment was Set
5	Source Route Failed
6	Destination Network Unknown
7	Destination Host Unknown
8	Source Host Isolated

Table 3–9

ICMP Code Field
Values Based on
Message Type

	Codes	
	9	Communication with Destination Network is Administratively Prohibited
	10	Communication with Destination Host is Administratively Prohibited
	11	Destination Network Unreachable for Type of Service
	12	Destination Host Unreachable for Type of Service
	13	Destination Host Unreachable for Type of Service
	14	Communication Administratively Prohibited
	15	Precedence cutoff in effect

Message Type	Code Field Values	
5	Redirect	
	Codes	
	0	Redirect Datagram for the Network (or subnet)
	1	Redirect Datagram for the Host
	2	Redirect Datagram for the Type of Service and Network
	3	Redirect Datagram for the Type of Service and Host
6	Alternate Host Address	
	Codes	
	0	Alternate Address for Host
11	Time Exceeded	
	Codes	
	0	Time to Live exceeded in Transit
	1	Fragment Reassembly Time Exceeded
12	Parameter Problem	
	Codes	
	0	Point Indicates the Error.
	1	Missing a Required Option
	2	Bad Length

Message Type	Code Field Values	
40	Photuris	
	Codes	
	0	Reserved
	1	Unknown security parameters index
	2	Valid security parameters, but authentication failed
	3	Valid security parameters, but decryption failed

ICMP is a very simple but powerful protocol. One of its more powerful features allows messages to be sent to devices that redirect them to different, next-hop IP addresses for certain destinations. If a message is sent to a router, an attacker could conceivably redirect packets to flow over a different path; ICMP prevents this. Additionally, because ICMP echo and echo-reply packets (ping) are almost universal troubleshooting tools and are allowed through most firewalls, programs have been written to exploit the use of these messages to create denials of service attacks through the use of directed broadcast pings (a directed broadcast ping is a ping to all hosts on a network or subnet). These types of attacks and the defense against them will be covered in more detail in later chapters.

TCP and UDP

Both TCP and UDP represent Layer 4 transport protocols. As previously discussed in Chapter 2, "The TCP/IP Protocol Suite," and in Chapter 3, "The Internet Protocol," there are significant differences between the functionality of each transport protocol. TCP is a connection-oriented, reliable transport protocol that creates a virtual circuit for the transfer of information. In comparison, UDP is a connectionless, unreliable transport protocol that results in routers forwarding datagrams without requiring a session between originator and recipient to be created. This method of transmission can be considered to represent a best-effort forwarding method and does not require the handshaking process used by TCP to establish and maintain a communications session. This contrast also means that you can consider a comparison of TCP and UDP as a trade-off between reliability and performance. Now that we have reviewed the general differences between TCP and UDP, let's turn our attention to the format of their headers to include their port number fields, which are used by routers and firewalls in conjunction with IP address fields as a mechanism to filter packets.

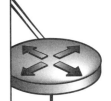

The TCP Header

At the transport layer, TCP accepts application data in chunks up to 64K bytes in length. Those chunks are fragmented into a series of smaller pieces that are transmitted as separate IP datagrams, typically 512 or 1,024 bytes in length. The actual selection of the length of a datagram depends upon the length supported by source and destination networks and any intermediate networks. In other words, TCPs at each end denote the maximum datagram length they support, and TCPs select the smallest mutually supported size.

Because IP provides no guarantee mechanism to ensure that datagrams will be correctly received, both for content and sequence, the TCP header has the responsibility to provide the mechanism for reliable and orderly delivery of data. To do so, the TCP header includes a field that is used for the sequencing of datagrams and a Checksum field for reliability. Because traffic from different applications, such as FTP and HTTP, can flow from or to a common host, a mechanism is required to differentiate the type of data carried by each datagram. This data differentiation is accomplished by the use of a destination port field, which contains a number that identifies the process or application in the datagram. In actuality, the TCP header plus data is referred to as a segment, so the port number identifies the type of data in the segment. The IP header is added to the TCP header to form the datagram that will contain the source and destination IP address. Now that we have a general appreciation for the TCP header and its relationship to the application process and IP header, let's turn our attention to the fields in the TCP header, whose structure is illustrated in Figure 4–1.

Figure 4–1
The TCP Header

2	Source Port
2	Destination Port
4	Sequence Number
4	Acknowledgement Number
2	Data Offset/Control Flags
2	Window
2	Checksum
2	Urgent Pointer
2	Data

Source and Destination Port Fields

The source and destination port fields are each 16 bits in length. Each field identifies a user process or application, with the first 1,024 (zero to 1023) of 65,536 available port numbers standardized with respect to the type of traffic transported via the use of a specific numeric value. The source port field is optional, and when this field is not used, it is set to a value of zero. In actuality, the use of TCP and UDP source and destination port numbers depends upon the user program using the transport layer protocol. In other words, if the user program is quiescent and is waiting for requests, the program is designed to look for a specific port number, such as 21 for a destination port, when FTP is used. For user programs that originate traffic, such programs commonly use random port numbers for the source port. For example, when you first open FTP to transfer a file port number 1234 might be used as the source port number—while later in the day, when you open an FTP application to transmit another file source port number 2048 might be used. For all FTP usage, however, the destination port would be fixed at 21, which is the standardized port number for an FTP server. When the server responds, the server will place the source port number in the destination port field—which enables the file originator to correctly identify the response to its datagram. As we will note later in this section, each datagram has a sequence number which enables the opposite end of the transmission to ensure that datagrams are received in their correct order—and that none are lost. The term *Well-Known Port*, which is commonly used to denote an application layer protocol or process, actually references a port address at or below 1023. Both TCP and UDP headers contain fields for identifying source and destination ports. Telnet, for example, which is transported by TCP, uses the Well-Known Port number 23, while SNMP, which is transported by UDP, uses the Well-Known Port number 161.

Port Numbers

Port numbers transported by TCP and UDP can vary from a value of zero through 65535. This "universe" of port numbers is divided into three ranges referred to as *Well-Known Ports, Registered Ports,* and *Dynamic* or *Private Ports.* Well-Known Ports are those ranges whose values are between zero and 1023. Registered Ports are those ranges whose values are between 1024 and 49151, while Dynamic or Private Ports are those ranges whose values are between 49152 and 65535.

Well-Known Ports are assigned by the *Internet Assigned Numbers Authority* (IANA) and are used to indicate the transportation of standardized processes. Where possible, the same Well-Known Port number assignments are used with TCP and UDP. Ports used with TCP are normally used to provide connections that transport long-term conversations.

NOTE: In some literature, Well-Known Port numbers are specified as being in the range of values from zero through 255. While that range was correct several years ago, the range for assigned ports managed by the IANA were recently expanded to include the range of values from zero through 1023.

Although the vast majority of TCP/IP applications use Well-Known Port values, not all applications do so. Many new applications that remain to be standardized, such as Internet telephony applications, use proprietary port assignments. Most of those port numbers are in the range from 49152 through 65535 and represent Dynamic or Private Ports. This author, however, has also encountered products that use registered port values in the range of 1024 through 49151. Table 4–1 provides a summary of some of the more popular Well-Known Ports to include the service supported by a particular port and the type of port, TCP, or UDP for which the port number is primarily used.

Table 4–1

Well-known TCP and UDP services and port use

Keyword	Port Service	Port Type	Number
TCPMUX	TCP Port Service Multiplexer	TCP	1
RJE	Remote Job Entry	TCP	5
ECHO	Echo	TCP and UDP	7
DAYTIME	Daytime	TCP and UDP	13
QOTD	Quote of the Day	TCP	17
CHARGEN	Character Generator	TCP	19
FTD-DATA	File Transfer (Default Data)	TCP	20
FTP	File Transfer (Control)	TCP	21
TELNET	Telnet	TCP	23
SMTP	Simple Mail Transfer Protocol	TCP	25

Keyword	Port Service	Port Type	Number
MSG-AUTH	Message Authentication	TCP	31
TIME	Time	TCP	37
NAMESERVER	Host Name Server	TCP and UDP	42
NICNAME	WhoIs	TCP	43
DOMAIN	Domain Name Server	TCP and UDP	53
BOOTPS	Bootstrap Protocol Server	TCP	67
BOOTPC	Bootstrap Protocol Client	TCP	68
TFTP	Trivial File Transfer Protocol	UDP	69
FINGER	Finger	TCP	79
HTTP	World Wide Web	TCP	80
KERBEROS	Kerberos	TCP	88
RTELNET	Remote Telnet Service	TCP	107
POP2	Post Office Protocol Version 2	TCP	109
POP3	Post Office Protocol Version 3	TCP	110
NNTP	Network News Transfer Protocol	TCP	119
NTP	Network Time Protocol	TCP and UDP	123
NETBIOS-NS	NetBIOS Name Server	UDP	137
NETBIOS-DGM	NetBIOS Datagram Service	UDP	138
NETBIOS-SSN	NetBIOS Session Service	UDP	139
NEWS	News	TCP	144
SNMP	Simple Network Management Protocol	UDP	161
SNMTTRAP	Simple Network Management Protocol Traps	UDP	162
BGP	Border Gateway Protocol	TCP	179
HTTPS	Secure HTTP	TDP	413
RLOGIN	Remote Login	TCP	513
TALK	Talk	TCP and UDP	517

Sequence and Acknowledgment Number Fields

The *Sequence* number field is 32 bits in length and provides the mechanism for assuring the sequentiality of the data stream. The *Acknowledgment* number field, which is also 32 bits in length, is used to verify the receipt of data.

The Acknowledgment number field informs the recipient that the datagram the sender transmitted arrived at its destination. Because it would be inefficient to acknowledge each datagram, a variable window is supported by the protocol. In other words, returning an acknowledgment field value of seven would indicate the receipt of all data up to the seventh datagram. To ensure that lost datagrams or lost acknowledgments do not place this transport protocol in an infinite waiting period, the originator will retransmit data if the originator does not receive a response within a predefined period of time. The previously described use of the acknowledgment field is referred to as *Positive Acknowledgment or Retransmission* (PAR). PAR requires that each unit of data must be explicitly acknowledged. If a unit of data is not acknowledged by the time the originator's timeout period is reached, the previous transmission is retransmitted. When the acknowledgment field is in use, a flag bit referred to as the *ACK* flag in the code field will be set. We will shortly discuss the six bits in that field.

The Sequence number field is of particular interest when discussing network security. Many operating systems implement their TCP/IP stack in a manner that causes the sequence numbers to be predictable. In other words, if a client connects to a server three times in rapid succession and watches the sequence numbers sent by the server, the numbers will follow a pattern—which can be used to guess what the next sequence number will be. This function is important, because an attacker can then carry out the TCP three-way handshake without actually seeing the responses from the server. This type of an attack is called *session hijacking* and is described later in this chapter.

The attacker would initially use his or her real IP address to discern how the sequence numbers are incremented. Then, the attacker would spoof his or her source IP address so that packets sent from his or her machine would appear to originate from a machine the server trusted. The attacking machine would never receive the replies, because the return packets would be routed to the real client. If the attacker can guess the sequence numbers, however, the attacker does not need to see the replies to establish a connection.

Once the three-way handshake is complete, the attacker can fairly easily issue application commands without seeing the response. Most simple applications, such as Telnet, have predictable responses, so it is not too difficult to carry on a conversation without seeing the responses from the server. Note that to make this attack work, the attacker would have to "anesthetize" the real client by performing a DoS attack. Otherwise, the real client would respond to the packets sent by the server and would interfere with the attack. This attack may seem difficult to complete, but there are programs on the Internet that automate this process so that anyone can accomplish this attack. The only defense is to remove non-critical services on vulnerable servers—or to implement some means of randomizing sequence numbers.

Hlen Field

The *Hlen* field is 4 bits in length. This field, which is also referred to as the *Offset field*, contains a value that indicates where the TCP header ends and the data field starts and is specified as a number of 32-bit words. This field is required because the inclusion of options can result in a variable length header. Because the minimum length of the TCP header is 20 bytes, the minimum value of the Hlen field would be five 32-bit words.

Code Bits Field

The *Code bits* field is also referred to as a *Flags* field because the field contains six bits, each of which is used as a flag to indicate whether a function is enabled or disabled. Two bit positions indicate whether the acknowledgment and urgent pointer fields are significant. The presence of the ACK bit can be used by packet filtering devices to determine whether a packet is part of a current TCP conversation, because only non-initial packets should have this bit set. However, crafting packets with this bit set which are not part of an existing TCP conversation is trivial. As a result, this check is by no means completely secure and would not prevent a determined attack.

   The purpose of the Urgent bit, or flag, is to recognize an urgent or prioritized activity, such as when a user presses the CTRL-BREAK key combination. The application will set the Urgent flag, which results in TCP immediately transmitting everything in its possession for the connection. The setting of the Urgent bit, or flag, also indicates that the urgent pointer field is in use. Here, the urgent pointer field indicates the offset in bytes from the current sequence number where the urgent data is located. Other bits, or flags, include a *Push* (PSH) bit that requests the receiver to immediately deliver data to the application and forgo any buffering, a *Reset* (RST) bit to reset a connection, a *Synchronization* (SYN) bit used to establish connections, and a *Finish* (FIN) bit, which signifies the sender has no more data and the connection should be released. Figure 4–2 illustrates the relationship of each of the six one-bit flags within the Code bit field.

Window Field

The *Window* field is 2 octets in length and provides TCP with the capacity to control the flow of data (flow control) between source and destination. This field is used to indicate the maximum number of blocks of data the receiving device can accept. A large value can significantly improve TCP performance, because the originator is then permitted to transmit a number of blocks without having to wait for an acknowledgment—while permitting the receiver to acknowledge the receipt of multiple blocks with one acknowledgment.

Because TCP is a full-duplex transmission protocol, both ends of a communications session can insert values in the Window field to control the flow of data. By reducing the value of the Window field, one end informs the other end to transmit less data. Thus, the use of the Window field provides a bi-directional flow control capability.

Checksum Field

The *Checksum* field is 2 octets in length and is included in the header as a mechanism for TCP to provide an error detection and correction capability. Instead of actually computing a checksum over the entire TCP header, the field is primarily concerned with ensuring that key fields are validated. To do so, the checksum calculation occurs over what is referred

Figure 4–2
The flags in the
Code bit field

URG	ACK	PSH	RST	SYN	FIN

```
URG:    Urgent pointer field significant.
ACK:    Acknowledgement field significant.
PSH:    Push function.
RST:    Reset the connection.
SYN:    Synchronize sequence numbers.
FIN:    Release the connection.
```

to as a *12-octet pseudo header*. This pseudo header includes the 32-bit source and destination address fields in the IP header, the 8-bit Protocol field, and a length field that denotes the length of the TCP header and data transported within the TCP segment. Thus, the checksum can be used to ensure that data arrived at its correct destination—and that the receiver has no doubt about the address of the originator nor the length of the header and application data transported by TCP.

Options and Padding Fields

The last two fields in the TCP header are the *Options* and *Padding* fields, which actually represent an Options field with—when necessary—a variable number of zeros added as pads to ensure that the header ends on a 32-bit boundary. The Options field is variable in length and is added as an even multiple of octets. This field specifies options required by the TCP protocol operating on a host, such as the protocol's segment size support, which indicates to the receiver the amount of data the originator is willing to accept. Table 4–2 lists the presently defined TCP option numbers. In examining the entries in Table 4–2, note that an option value of two indicates that a Maximum Segment Size field follows as the option field. Also note that this field is 4 octets in length. Concerning options zero and one, they are exactly 1 octet in length. All other options have a 1 octet value field, followed by a length field that transports the option.

Now that we have an appreciation for the TCP header, let's turn our attention to the second transport layer protocol supported by the TCP/IP protocol suite: the UDP.

Table 4–2

TCP option numbers

Number	Length	Meaning
0	—	End of Option List
1	—	No-Operation
2	4	Maximum Segment Size
3	3	WSOPT—Window Scale
4	2	SACK Permitted
5	N	SACK
6	6	Echo (obsoleted by option 8)
7	6	Echo Reply (Obsoleted by option 8)

continues

Table 4–2

Continued

Number	Length	Meaning
8	10	TSOPT—Time Stamp Option
9	2	Partial Order Connection Permitted
10	3	Partial Order Service Profile
11		CC
12		CC.NEW
13		CC.ECHO
14	3	TCP Alternate Checksum Request
15	N	TCP Alternate Checksum Data
16		Skeeter
17		Bubba
18	3	Trailer Checksum Option
19	18	MD5 Signature Option

TCP Alternate Checksum Numbers

Number	Description
0	TCP Checksum
1	8-bit Fletchers' algorithm
2	16-bit Fletchers' algorithm
3	Redundant Checksum Avoidance

The UDP Header

The *UDP* is the second transport layer protocol supported by the TCP/IP protocol suite. Through the use of UDP, an application can transport data in the form of IP datagrams without having to first establish a connection to the destination. Thus, UDP is a connectionless protocol. This concept also means that when transmission occurs via UDP, there is no need to release a connection, which simplifies the communications process. In turn, the result is a header that is greatly simplified and much smaller than TCP's header.

Figure 4–3
The UDP header

```
0                  16                  31
┌──────────────────┬──────────────────┐
│   Source Port    │ Destination Port │
├──────────────────┼──────────────────┤
│     Length       │     Checksum     │
└──────────────────┴──────────────────┘
```

Figure 4–3
The UDP header

Figure 4–3 illustrates the composition of the UDP header, which consists of 64 bytes followed by actual user data. In comparing the TCP and UDP headers, you will note the simplicity of the latter. Because UDP is a connectionless protocol that does not require the acknowledgment of datagrams—nor does it require a sequence of datagrams to be treated as an entity—the sequence and acknowledgment fields of UDP can be eliminated. Similarly, because UDP does not consider a sequence of datagrams as an entity, there is no need for a Window field. As a result of the best-effort, connectionless nature of UDP, a relatively small header is required for this transport layer protocol. Similar to TCP, an IP header will prefix the UDP header with the resulting message, which consists of the IP header, UDP header, and user data. This message is referred to as a *UDP datagram.*

The Source and Destination Port Fields

The Source and Destination Port fields are each 2 octets in length and function in a similar manner to their counterparts in the TCP header. In other words, the source port field is optional, and a value is either randomly selected or is filled with zeros when not used. The destination port, however, contains a numeral which identifies the destination application or process. Because UDP is commonly used by several Internet telephony products that do not use a standardized port number, you must determine the port that a specific product uses. Then, you will probably have to reprogram your organization's router access list and modify the configuration of any firewalls used by your organization. This action will enable UDP datagrams using ports previously blocked to transport Internet telephony data onto your private network via the Internet.

Length Field

The *Length* field indicates the length of the UDP datagram to include header and user data. This 2-octet field has a minimum value of eight that represents a UDP header without data.

Checksum Field

The Checksum field is 2 octets in length. The use of this field is optional, and this field is filled with zeros if the application does not require a checksum. If a checksum is required, the checksum is calculated based on the pseudo header. The pseudo header, a new, logically formed header, consists of the source and destination addresses and the Protocol field from the IP header. By verifying the contents of the two address fields through its checksum computation, the pseudo header assures that the UDP datagram is delivered to the correct destination network and host on the network. This function, however, does not verify the contents of the datagram.

Firewall and Router Access List Considerations

Because an IP header will prefix TCP and UDP headers, there are four addresses that can be used for enabling or disabling the flow of datagrams. Those addresses are the source and destination IP addresses contained in the IP header and the source and destination port numbers contained in the TCP and UDP headers. Both firewalls and routers include a packet filtering capability, which enables users to program access lists to permit or deny packets from flowing between two private networks from the Internet onto a private network (or in the reverse direction). Although routers are flexible and permit a high degree of user configuration capability, they do not look into the contents of data being transported—nor provide you with the capability to authenticate remote users, encrypt transmission, or perform proxy services. Thus, many organizations will program router access lists as a first line of defense and will use firewalls to enhance the security of their private network.

Note that Cisco has introduced a new feature known as *Context Based Access Control* (CBAC), which contains advanced security features. CBAC enables the router to make intelligent filtering decisions based on the data portion of the TCP/IP packet for certain applications. In some environments, CBAC provides the router with enough intelligence to establish a secure perimeter without using an additional firewall. We will discuss CBAC in detail later in this book.

CHAPTER 5

NetWare

Although many network managers and LAN administrators primarily work with the TCP/IP protocol suite, TCP/IP is not the only popular protocol used on LANs. During the 1980s and continuing through the mid–1990s, Novell's NetWare dominated the LAN market as the default network OS used by most businesses, government agencies, and colleges and universities. While the use of NetWare has decreased and the latest version of NetWare, Release 5, now primarily supports the TCP/IP protocol suite, we must note that tens of millions of LAN workstations still depend on NetWare's IPX and SPX protocols to transport data on an intra-LAN and inter-LAN basis. Thus, many readers will probably require information concerning security with respect to the use of classic NetWare transmission protocols.

Because knowledge of security measures is facilitated by a detailed understanding of NetWare, this chapter is focused on classical NetWare transport protocols. After first obtaining an overview of NetWare, we will turn our attention to IPX, NetWare's layer 3 protocol. This description will be followed by examining SPX, NetWare's layer 4 protocol.

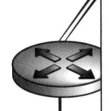

Overview

NetWare's design predates the development of the ISO OSI Reference Model. NetWare was developed as a layered protocol suite, however, and provides a great deal of flexibility for supporting different types of LANs. This flexibility results in its high degree of acceptance as a *network operating system* (NOS) during the early 1980s and continuing through today. As we examine the key components of NetWare, we will note that from a communications perspective, traffic for this network OS is provided by a layer 3 and a layer 4 protocol. As we will shortly note, the layer 3 protocol provides a connectionless, best-effort delivery service, while the layer 4 protocol provides a guaranteed delivery service.

General Structure

Figure 5–1 illustrates the general structure of classical NetWare in terms of a reference model. In actuality, NetWare does not directly support the physical and data link layers. Instead, NetWare is bound to a specific data link LAN protocol, such as Ethernet, Token Ring, or even ARCnet. Once NetWare is bound to a specific data link protocol, the program (by default) then supports the Physical layer used by the Data Link layer.

Network Layer Operation

At the Network layer, classical NetWare uses a proprietary protocol referred to as IPX. IPX represents a connectionless, unreliable protocol that operates on a best-effort basis. In other words, IPX does not guarantee delivery. Instead, IPX automatically resends a packet if the receiver does not respond to the preceding transmission within a predefined time interval.

Figure 5–1
The classical NetWare reference model

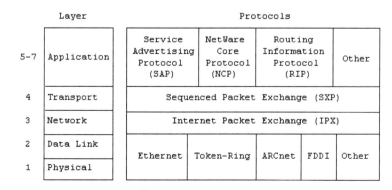

	Layer	Protocols			
5–7	Application	Service Advertising Protocol (SAP)	NetWare Core Protocol (NCP)	Routing Information Protocol (RIP)	Other
4	Transport	Sequenced Packet Exchange (SXP)			
3	Network	Internet Packet Exchange (IPX)			
2	Data Link	Ethernet	Token-Ring	ARCnet	FDDI	Other
1	Physical				

Transport Layer Operation

At the Transport layer, classical NetWare uses another proprietary protocol. This protocol is known as the *Sequenced Packet Exchange* (SPX). SPX is similar to TCP in that SPX provides a connection-oriented, guaranteed, sequenced delivery of packets. In addition, just like TCP, SPX includes a flow control mechanism which can reduce packet congestion during peak periods of network utilization. Both IPX and SPX can be considered to have evolved from the grandfather of networking protocols, the *Xerox Network System* (XNS).

SAPs, RIPs, and the NCP

In examining Figure 5–1, readers who may not be familiar with NetWare deserve a bit of explanation for a few entries. One entry is the *Service Advertising Protocol* (SAP), which actually represents an application that runs on NetWare servers. A SAP is generated about once a minute by each NetWare server as a broadcast packet. This packet contains the server's name, address, and the services offered. Each NetWare server copies all server names received via SAPs, as well as information concerning the type of server and its address to a special database that was originally referred to as the bindery. This process explains how a client on one network can note the presence of a particular type of server on the same network— or on another network—by querying any bindery to locate the address of a server that can provide a desired service. Although SAPs fill an important role, you should note that their effect upon the WAN can be far more detrimental than the effect on the level of utilization of a LAN. The reasoning behind this concept is that a WAN connection linking two LANs may provide an operating rate between one tenth and one-hundredth of the operating rate of the LANs that the WAN interconnects. Therefore, a large number of servers broadcasting SAPs may have a negligible effect upon the utilization level of a LAN, while their effect upon the utilization level of a WAN can be far more pronounced. This idea also explains why many routers that support classical NetWare provide a mechanism to selectively filter SAP broadcasts. Two additional entries in Figure 4–1 that warrant a bit of elaboration are the *NetWare Core Protocol* (NCP) and the *Routing Information Protocol* (RIP). NCP is responsible for providing file and print services to users of the OS, while RIP represents the mechanism which enables routers to update their routing tables. SAP, NCP, and RIP packets are formed by an appropriate header that is appended to an IPX header, while an SPX packet is formed by an SPX header being appended to an IPX header. Thus, IPX provides a common transport and delivery mechanism similar to the relationship of IP to TCP and UDP.

NetWare Addressing

NetWare is similar to other protocols because the program supports a mechanism to assign addresses to each station on the network. Where classical NetWare differs from other protocols is how the program provides Internet addressing. Each station on a NetWare network, commonly referred to as a *node,* is identified by a unique address that consists of three parts: a network address, node address, and socket number.

Network Address

The *network address* is a hex number containing from one to eight digits that identifies the network. Classical NetWare permits up to four *network interface cards* (NICs) to be installed in a server, with each card having a unique network address. Each card is expected to be connected to a separate cabling system. Figure 5–2 illustrates an example of the use of NetWare network addresses. In this example, a file server is used as a router to relay packets between network address A1 and network address B1.

Node Address

Each node on a NetWare network must have a unique address. That address can be up to 12 hex characters, or 48 bits, in length and is normally the layer 2 MAC address burned into the NIC. That address is commonly referred to as the *universally administrated address* and consists of a 3-byte vendor identifier, followed by a 3-byte number that uniquely identifies the adapter produced by the manufacturer. The IEEE assigns the vendor identifier, and the vendor becomes responsible for manufacturing NICs with unique numbers in the last six hex positions of the card's address that is burnt into the ROM.

Figure 5–2
Each NIC in a NetWare network is assigned a network address, which identifies a cabling system.

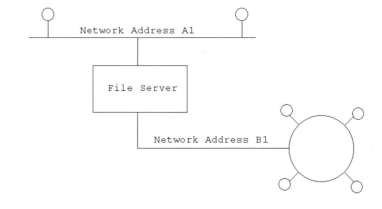

As an alternative to universally administrated addresses, some organizations assign their own 12-hex digit address to each adapter card via software. When a station boots up, the software-configured address overrides the universally administrated address. Setting the address via software results in the address being referred to as a locally administrated address. Regardless of the manner in which the 12-hex digit address is formed, the address serves to uniquely identify the station on the network.

One of the key advantages associated with the use of the MAC address as a node address is eliminating the need to have an Address Resolution Protocol to resolve layer 3 addresses to layer 2 addresses. Because NetWare uses a network address followed by a node address in its packets, once data arrives at a destination network, there is no need to discover the station's layer 2 address. That address is carried in the packet and eliminates the need for ARP.

Socket Number

The third part of NetWare's addressing scheme actually serves to identify the type of packet, permitting the multiplexing of different types of data to flow between two nodes. The *socket number* identifies a program running in a computer or a specific process within a program. As such, you could logically view the socket number as being similar to TCP and UDP port numbers. Of the three addresses, only the network and node addresses are used to deliver packets to the destination node. The socket number is only used by the destination node once the packet is delivered to the appropriate destination.

Now that we have an appreciation for the data transportation methods and addressing technique used by classical NetWare, let's turn our attention to the structure and composition of NetWare's communications protocols. Because we will literally follow the layer structure, let's first turn our attention to IPX.

IPX

NetWare's IPX represents a connectionless, best-effort delivery mechanism. In effect, IPX can be viewed as similar to UDP, but IPX operates at layer 3 instead of layer 4 of the ISO Reference Model. Because IPX does not wait for a connection to be established or for the acknowledgment of each transmitted packet, IPX is a relatively fast data delivery protocol. In addition, because IPX does not support the sequencing of packets, its header is relatively streamlined.

Packet Structure

Figure 5–3 illustrates the structure of an IPX packet, indicating the fields within the header of the packet. Note that an IPX packet consists of a 30-byte header that was originally followed by a data field that ranged from zero to a maximum of 546 bytes. While a data field of up to 546 bytes was sufficient during the 1980s, when most WANs consisted of analog lines, the migration to a digital backbone network structure and the use of fiber optics significantly lowered the transmission error rate on WANs. In turn, this lowered transmission error rate made the maximum packet length of 576 bytes to include the header inefficient for more modern digital transmission facilities. Therefore, Novell introduced an extended IPX packet. Under versions of NetWare beyond Release 3.1, the 576-byte IPX maximum length was removed by the use of NetWare's *Large Internet Packet Exchange* (LIPX). LIPX enables workstations and servers to communicate more efficiently, because the overhead of packets are reduced as their length increases.

Checksum Field

The *Checksum* field is two bytes in length and was included in IPX as a mechanism to provide compatibility with the packet header used by the XNS. Because LAN adapter cards perform a CRC check on the frame transporting IPX, this field is not necessary. Thus, under NetWare, the Checksum field is always set to a value of hex FFFF by IPX.

Figure 5–3
The IPX packet

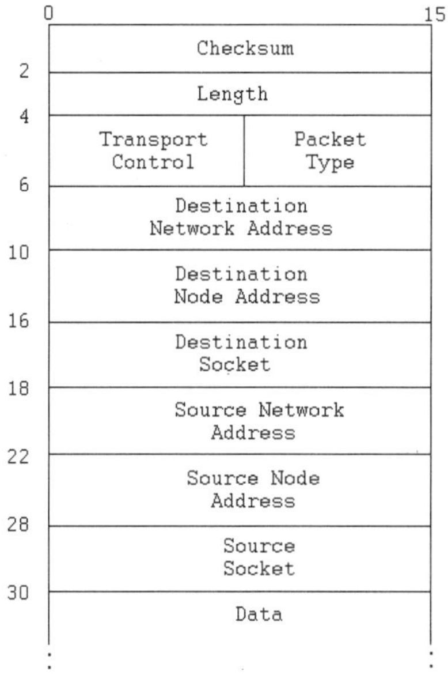

Length Field

The *Length* field is also two bytes in length. This field indicates the length of the entire IPX packet to include the header and data transported in the packet.

Transport Control Field

The *Transport Control* field is a one-byte field used to provide a mechanism to denote the number of networks a packet has traversed. Initially, IPX sets this field to a value of zero, and its value is incremented as the packet flows onto a new network. When the value in this field exceeds a maximum of 255, the packet is sent to the great bit bucket in the sky. Thus, you can see that the Transport Control field is similar to the TCP Time to Live field, because the field ensures that a packet does not wander through a series of interconnected NetWare networks until the end of time.

Packet Type Field

This one-byte field indicates the type of service offered or required by the packet. IPX commonly sets the Packet Type field value to either zero or four, while SPX uses a value of five. Those values provide compatibility with the Packet Type values specified by XNS, which can be viewed as a forerunner of NetWare. Table 5–1 indicates the Packet Type field values that were defined by Xerox.

Table 5–1

Packet Type field values defined by Xerox

Value	Description
0	Unknown Packet Type
1	Routing Information Packet
2	Echo Packet
3	Error Packet
4	Packet Exchange Packet
5	Sequenced Packet Protocol Packet
16–31	Experimental Packet
17	NCP

Destination Network Address Field

The *Destination Network Address* field represents the network address on which the destination node or station resides. This field is four bytes in length, and when set to zero, the field indicates that the destination node is on the same network as the source node.

Destination Node Address Field

The *Destination Node Address* field is six bytes in length and represents the physical, or hardware, address of the destination node. Similar to IP, a node address of all Fs indicates a broadcast address whereby the packet is read by all stations on the destination network.

Destination Socket Field

The *Destination Socket* field is two bytes in length. The value in this field identifies the socket address of the packet's destination process. In layman's terms, the value identifies the type of data being transported by the packet. Xerox originally reserved a series of socket numbers, and then Xerox assigned socket numbers to Novell for use by NetWare. Table 5–2 lists Xerox reserved and Novell assigned socket numbers.

Table 5–2

Xerox reserved and Novell assigned socket numbers

Socket Number	Description
Xerox Reserved	
1	Routing Information Packet
2	Echo Protocol Packet
3	Error Handler Packet
2Oh–3Fh	Experimental
1h–BB8h	Registered with Xerox
BB9h-	Dynamically Assignable
Xerox Assigned to Novell	
451h	File Service Packet
452h	Service Advertising Packet
453h	Routing Information Packet
455h	NetBIOS Packet
456h	Diagnostic Packet

Similar to Xerox, Novell also assigns socket numbers. Novell-assigned socket numbers begin at 8000h. Because the socket number identifies the type of data transported by an IPX packet, filtering on this field can be used to enable or disable the flow of specific types of packets between networks. For example, filtering socket values of 452h would filter SAP packets.

Source Network Field

The *Source Network* field is four bytes in length. The value in this field identifies the network on which the station transmitting the packet resides.

Source Node Field

The *Source Node* field contains the hardware address of the node transmitting the packet. This field is six bytes in length, enabling the field to hold the 48-bit MAC address of the transmitting node.

Source Socket Field

The last field in the IPX header is the *Source Socket* field. This field is two bytes in length and represents the socket address of the process transmitting the packet. Similar to TCP and UDP port usage, a NetWare server normally listens on a predefined socket number for specific types of client-server requests. The source socket value, however, can essentially have any value—meaning that for filtering purposes, the preferred action is to filter on the destination than on the source socket field value. Now that we have an appreciation for the fields with the IPX header, let's move up the protocol stack and investigate the composition of SPX and its utilization.

SPX

The SPX protocol represents the Transport layer protocol used by classical NetWare. Through the use of SPX, NetWare obtains the capacity to provide a guaranteed delivery of sequenced packets, as well as an error detection and correction capability. Thus, SPX in many ways can be considered Novell's equivalent to TCP in the TCP/IP protocol suite.

One common example of the use of SPX is for the transmission of *Remote Console* (RCONSOLE) session data. RCONSOLE provides a remote user with the capacity to perform file server operations as if the user were located at the server's console. Because each keystroke needs to be entered by a remote user to arrive in its correct sequence, SPX—by default—is used for RCONSOLE.

Although SPX has many benefits as opposed to IPX, the price of those benefits is similar to a comparison of TCP and UDP. In other words, SPX's guaranteed delivery of sequenced packets results in a higher level of overhead and is similar to the extra overhead of TCP versus UDP. Another difference is that SPX does not support broadcasts. If broadcasting were permitted, a connection would have to be established with each receiver first, and no messages could be transmitted if a receiver was not available. Now that we have a general appreciation for SPX, let's probe deeper and examine its packet structure to include the fields in its header.

Packet Structure

An SPX packet is formed by the addition of 12 bytes to the previously described IPX header. Figure 5-4 illustrates the SPX packet format to include its header. Note that the original SPX packet was similar to an IPX packet regarding its capacity to support a maximum length of 576 bytes. Therefore, the SPX packet has the capacity to support a data field up to 534 bytes, because the SPX header in effect consists of 12 additional bytes. Thus, 576-(30+12) results in a maximum data field of 534 bytes.

Figure 5–4

SPX packet format

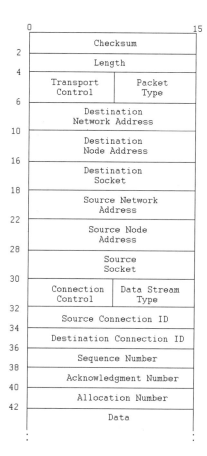

Because we previously examined the first 30 bytes in the IPX header, we will only focus our attention on the fields added by the SPX header and the certain IPX field changes when an SPX packet is formed.

Comparison to IPX

The two key differences between the first 30 bytes in an IPX header and the use of IPX for SPX transmission are the Packet Type and Destination Node field values. SPX uses a Packet Type field value of five, and the Destination Node field cannot contain a broadcast address of six bytes of hex FF. Other than those differences, the first 30 bytes in the IPX portion of the SPX header are used in the same manner as the fields in the IPX header. Therefore, let's turn our attention to the 12 bytes added by the SPX header.

Connection Control Field

The Connection Control field consists of four single-bit flags that are used by the SPX protocol to control the bi-directional flow of data across a connection. Figure 5–5 illustrates the position of each of the four defined flags in the Connection Control field and their hex values.

The *End-of-Message* flag is set by a client to signal to its partner that an end-of-connection condition has occurred. SPX ignores this flag and passes it on unaltered.

The *Attention* flag is set by a client if a packet needs immediate attention. Because the receiver should use this flag, SPX ignores the flag.

The Acknowledgment Required flag is set by SPX when an acknowledgment packet is required. Because SPX is responsible for acknowledgment requests and responses, this flag is used by the protocol.

The fourth flag bit in the Connection Control flag is the *System Packet* flag. SPX sets this bit when the packet being transmitted is a system

Figure 5–5
Connection Control field flags

```
bit position   8     7     6     5     4     3     2     1
             +-----+-----+-----+-----+-----+-----+-----+-----+
             |  S  | AR  |  A  | EOM |  U  |  U  |  U  |  U  |
             +-----+-----+-----+-----+-----+-----+-----+-----+
hex value     80h   40h   20h   10h   8h    4h    2h    1h
```

```
Legend:
    U      Undefined
    EOM    End-of-Message
    A      Attention
    AR     Acknowledgement Required
    S      System Packet
```

packet. This identification denotes to the receiving device that information carried in the packet is to be used by the protocol and as such is not delivered to clients.

Datastream Type Field

The *Datastream Type* field is a one-byte field whose value indicates the type of data contained in the packet. Table 5–3 indicates the potential values that can be contained in the Datastream Type field and what those values denote.

As indicated in Table 5–3, any Datastream Type field value from he×0 through hex FD is defined by the client. Thus, this field is used by the application and is ignored by SPX. The End-of-Connection field value is generated by SPX when a client issues a request to terminate an active connection and represents the last message delivered on the connection. In response, SPX generates a Datastream Type field value of hex FF for End-of Connection Acknowledgment, which is not delivered to the connected client.

Source Connection ID Field

The *Source Connection ID* field is a 16-bit field. This field contains a number generated by the node. That node number generates the SPX packet, and the SPX packet identifies the connection.

Destination Connection ID Field

The *Destination Connection ID* field is also a 16-bit field. The value in this field is assigned by SPX at the packet's destination and is used to de-multiplex incoming packets from different connections that arrive using the same socket value. This field is necessary, because any connections active at the same time on a host can use the same socket. Thus, the ID serves to differentiate one connection from another—although two or more connections could use the same socket number.

Table 5–3

Datastream Type
field values

Hex Value	Definition
0–FD	Client Defined
FE	End-of-Connection
FF	End-of-Connection Acknowledgment

Sequence Number Field

The *Sequence Number* field is another 16-bit field. This field contains a count of the number of packets exchanged in one direction on a connection with each node keeping its own count. The value of this field ranges from he×0 to hex FFF, wrapping to zero after the maximum value is reached.

Acknowledgment Number Field

The *Acknowledgment Number* field is also 16 bits in length. This field contains the Sequence Number of the next packet SPX expects to receive. If a packet is received with a Sequence Number less than the value of the Acknowledgment Number field value, the packet is considered in order. No retransmission is required.

Allocation Number Field

The last field in the SPX header before the Data field is the *Allocation* field. The value in this 16-bit field represents the number of listen buffers available in one direction on the connection. Because the unavailability of listen buffers would cause new packets to be lost, SPX can only transmit packets until the Sequence Number equals the value of the remote Allocation Number.

SAP, RIP, and NCP

Under classical NetWare, there are three other types of commonly used packets referred to as SAP, RIP, and NCP. Similar to SPX, SAP, RIP, and NCP packets are formed by the addition of specific headers behind the 30-byte IPX header.

SAP packets represent broadcasts from NetWare servers that contain information concerning the server type, its network, node, and socket address. RIP packets contain information that are used by routers to update their routing tables, while NCP packets are used for file and print services. Because the Packet Type field in the IP header can be examined to determine the specific type of header added to IPX, you do not need to filter information within each of those packets. We can filter those packets based on the value in the Packet Type field. Therefore, we will not probe deeper into the headers of those three packets.

6

Router Hardware and Software Overview

Building on our knowledge of the structure of the OSI Reference Model and the TCP/IP and NetWare protocol suites, we will now turn our attention to obtaining an overview of Cisco router hardware and software. In this chapter, we will first turn our attention to the basic hardware components of a Cisco router. This section will be followed by an examination of basic router software modules. Once the preceding task is accomplished, we will turn our attention to router operational modes and describe, discuss, and illustrate the use of different router functions.

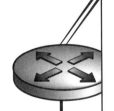

The overall purpose of this chapter is to acquaint readers with the general operation of Cisco routers and the manner in which they are configured. This chapter includes a number of examples of the use of EXEC commands, providing a review for readers who have familiarity with Cisco products—as well as giving necessary information concerning the configuration of the vendor's routers for people who might lack prior Cisco experience. In addition, when appropriate, certain guidelines and hints are included in this chapter and are based on the years of experience stemming from the authors' involvement in configuring and operating Cisco routers. Hopefully, these hints and guidelines might save you hours of puzzlement and make your router experience more pleasurable by being able to take advantage of lessons learned by the authors.

Basic Hardware Components

Cisco Systems manufactures a wide range of router products. Although those products differ considerably with respect to their processing power and number of interfaces they support, they use a core set of hardware components. Figure 6–1 illustrates a generic schematic that indicates the key components of a Cisco Systems router. While the CPU (or microprocessor), amount of ROM and RAM, and the number and manner in which I/O ports and media converters are used can differ from one product to another, each router will have the components indicated in the pre-

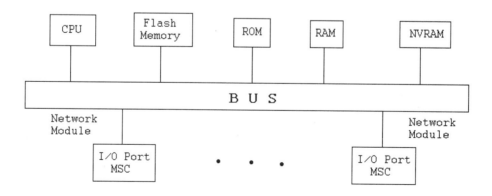

Figure 6–1
Media Specific Converter, basic router hardware components

viously referenced figure. By examining the function of each hardware component, we will obtain an appreciation for the manner in which the sum of the parts of a router come together to provide its functionality.

Central Processing Unit (CPU)

The *Central Processing Unit* (CPU), or microprocessor, is responsible for executing instructions that make up the router's *operating system* (OS)—as well as user commands entered via the console or via a Telnet connection. Thus, the processing power of the CPU is directly related to the processing capability of the router.

Flash Memory

Flash memory represents an erasable, reprogrammable type of ROM memory. On many routers, Flash memory represents an option that can be used to hold an image of the OS and the router's microcode. Because Flash memory can be updated without having to remove and replace chips, the cost of this option can easily pay for itself by saving on chip upgrades over a period of time. You can hold more than one OS image in Flash memory, providing there is enough space. This function is useful for testing new images. The Flash memory of a router can also be used to *trivial file transfer protocol* (TFTP) an OS image to another router.

ROM

ROM contains code that performs power-on diagnostics similar to the *power on self-test* (POST) that many PCs perform. In addition, a bootstrap program in ROM is used to load OS software. Although many routers require software upgrades to be performed by removing and replacing ROM chips on the router's system board, other routers might use different types of storage to hold the OS.

RAM

Random Access Memory (RAM) is used to hold routing tables, perform packet buffering, furnish an area for the queuing of packets when they cannot be directly output due to too much traffic routed to a common interface, and to provide memory for the router's configuration file when the device is operational. In addition, RAM provides space for caching ARP information that reduces ARP traffic and enhances the transmission capability of LANs connected to the router. When the router is powered off, the contents of RAM are cleared.

Nonvolatile RAM

Nonvolatile RAM retains its contents when a router is powered off. By storing a copy of its configuration file in NVRAM, the router can quickly recover from a power failure. The use of NVRAM eliminates the need for the router to maintain a hard disk or floppy to retain its configuration file. Therefore, no moving parts exist on a Cisco router, which means components last much longer. Most hardware failures in computer systems are due to the wear and tear on moving components, such as hard drives.

I/O Ports and Media-Specific Converters

The *Input/Output* (I/O) port represents the connection through which packets enter and exit a router. Each I/O port is connected to a *Media-Specific Converter* (MSC), which provides the physical interface to a specific type of media, such as an Ethernet or Token Ring LAN or an RS-232 or V.35 WAN interface. As data is received from a LAN, the layer 2 headers are removed as the packet is moved into RAM. When this action occurs, the CPU examines its routing table to determine the packet's output port and the manner in which the packet should be encapsulated.

The process just described is called *process switching* mode, because each packet must be processed by the CPU to consult the routing table and determine where to send the packet. Cisco routers also have a switching mode called *fast switching*. In fast switching mode, the router maintains a memory cache containing information about destination IP addresses and next-hop interfaces.

The router builds this cache by saving information previously obtained from the routing table. The first packet to a particular destination causes the CPU to consult the routing table. Once the information is obtained regarding the next-hop interface for that particular destination, however, this information is inserted into the fast switching cache. The routing table is not consulted for new packets sent to this destination. This action results in the router's capacity to switch packets at a much faster rate—resulting in a substantial reduction in the load on the router's CPU.

Variations exist on fast switching that make use of special hardware architectures included in some higher-end models, such as the 7200 and 7500 series. The principle is essentially the same, however, for all switching modes—a cache that contains destination address to interface mappings. The one exception to this situation is a switching mode called *netflow switching*, which caches not only the destination IP address but also the source IP address and the upper layer TCP or UDP ports. This switching mode is available only on higher-end router platforms. Lower-end routers, such as the 1600, 2500, 2600, 3600, and 4000 series, are only capable of normal fast switching.

A few specific points should be noted about fast switching. First, any change to the routing table or the ARP cache forces a purge of the fast switching cache. This function occurs so that during a topology change, the fast switching cache will be rebuilt. Additionally, the entries in the fast switching cache will vary depending on the contents of the routing table. The entry in the fast switching cache will match the corresponding entry in the routing table. For example, if the router has a route to the 10.1.1.0/24 network, the router will cache the destination 10.1.1.0/24. If the router only has a route to the 10.1.0.0/16 network, the router will cache the destination 10.1.0.0/16. If there is no entry in the routing table for the network or subnet, the router uses the default route and uses the default major network mask, so the router would cache the destination 10.0.0.0/8.

This pattern holds true if there is only one route to a particular destination. If there are multiple, equal cost, non-default paths, the router will cache the entire 32-bit destination. For example, if the destination IP address were 10.1.1.1 and the router had two routes to the 10.1.1.0/24 network, the router would cache the value 10.1.1.1/32 and match it to the first hop. The next destination on the 10.1.1.0/24 network, say 10.1.1.2/32, would be cached and matched with the second-next hop. If there were a third equal-cost path, the next destination on the 10.1.1.0/24 network would be cached with the third-next hop, and so on.

NOTE: Notice the caveat that this situation is true only for non-default routes. If the router must use the default route to send a packet, the router only caches the major network number and not the full 32-bit address as described earlier.

Essentially, the router uses a round-robin method to cache individual destinations to each successive hop, meaning that the router will load-share on a per destination basis. In other words, because the fast cache contains a mapping between an end destination and an interface, once the cache has been populated with an entry, all future packets for that destination will use the interface in the cache. The router will not place multiple interfaces in the fast switching cache for the same destination.

In process switching mode, the router load-shares on a per packet basis. Because there is no fast switching cache, each packet is sent in a round-robin fashion to each successive interface. While this action leads to a more evenly distributed network load, if there are multiple paths, the load on the router CPU is also increased—and slows down the rate at which the router can move packets. In most cases, you should leave fast switching turned on and live with the unequal distribution across multiple network paths.

The Router Initialization Process

When you power on a router, the router performs a sequence of predefined operations. Additional operations performed by the router depend on whether you previously configured the device. To obtain an appreciation of the router initialization process, let's examine the major events that occur when you power on the device.

Figure 6–2 illustrates in flowchart form the major functions performed during the router initialization process. When you apply power to the router, the router initially performs a series of diagnostic *power-on tests* (POST) which verify the operation of its processor, memory, and interface circuitry.

Once POST is completed, the bootstrap loader executes. The primary function of the loader is to initialize or place a copy of the OS image into main memory. To do so, however, the loader must first determine where the image of the OS is located. The image could be located on Flash memory, ROM, or even on the network.

To determine the location of the image of the OS, the bootstrap loader checks the router's configuration register. The configuration register's values can be set either by hardware jumpers or via software, depending on the router model. The settings of the register indicate the location of the OS and define other device functions, such as how the router reacts to the entry of a break key on the console keyboard—and whether diagnostic messages are displayed on the console terminal.

The configuration register in most current-model routers is a 16-bit value stored in NVRAM and is not a physical entity. In older model

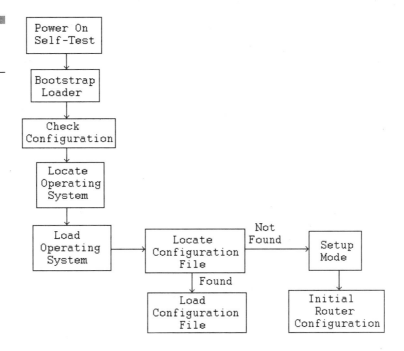

Figure 6–2
Router initialization process

routers such as the MGS and AGS+, the configuration register was a physical jumper with 16 pins. This idea is the origination of the term *register*. On both the software and the hardware configuration registers, the last four bits (pins in the case of the hardware register) indicate the boot field. The boot field tells the router where to locate its configuration file. The software register is displayed as a four-digit hexadecimal number, which looks similar to 0x2102. You can display the configuration register with the command show version. Each hexadecimal number represents four bits, so the first number reading from right-to-left is the *Boot* field. The boot field can range in value from zero to 15. In the earlier example, the boot field is two. Following the boot field is a table indicating how the router interprets the number in the boot field.

Table 6–1

The Meaning of the Boot Field Settings

Boot Field Value	Router Interpretation
0	RXBOOT Mode. The router must be manually booted using the b command.
1	Automatically boot from ROM
2-F	Examine the contents of the configuration file in NVRAM for boot system commands

In most cases, the boot register will be set to two, meaning that the router will look in the configuration file for boot commands. If none are found, the router will load the first image found in Flash memory. If there is no valid IOS image in Flash memory—or Flash memory cannot be found—the router attempts to load an image from a TFTP server by sending a TFTP request to the broadcast address requesting an IOS image.

Once the configuration register is checked, the bootstrap loader knows the location from which to load the OS image into the router's RAM and proceeds to do so. After the OS is loaded, the bootstrap loader looks for a previously created and saved configuration file in NVRAM. If the file is found, the file will be loaded into memory and executed on a line-by-line basis, resulting in the router becoming operational and working according to a predefined networking environment. If a previously created NVRAM file does not exist, the OS executes a predefined sequence of question-driven configuration displays referred to as a *Setup dialog*. Once the operator completes the Setup dialog, the configuration information will be stored in NVRAM and will be loaded as the default at the next initialization process. The router can be instructed to ignore the contents of NVRAM by setting the configuration register. If the second hexadecimal value from the right is set to four, 0x2142, the router will ignore the contents of NVRAM. This feature is used during password recovery on the router, so that an administrator can bypass the contents of the configuration file.

The following display illustrates the initial display generated by a Cisco 4500 router as power is applied, as the bootstrap is invoked, and as a previously defined configuration is loaded into memory. At the end of the display, take note of the prompt, which can easily scroll off a screen. On occasion, this problem results in a novice waiting a considerable period of time for something to happen—without realizing he or she needs to press the Return key to begin to access the system.

```
System Bootstrap, Version 5.2(7b) [mkamson 7b], RELEASE SOFTWARE
  (fc1)
Copyright (c) 1995 by cisco Systems, Inc.
C4500 processor with 8192 Kbytes of main memory
program load complete, entrypt: 0x80008000, size: 0x231afc
Self decompressing the image :
  ###############################################
###########################################################################
  #############
############################################################# [OK]
               Restricted Rights Legend
Use, duplication, or disclosure by the Government is
subject to restrictions as set forth in subparagraph
```

```
(c) of the Commercial Computer Software - Restricted
Rights clause at FAR sec. 52.227-19 and subparagraph
(c) (1) (ii) of the Rights in Technical Data and Computer
Software clause at DFARS sec. 252.227-7013.
                cisco Systems, Inc.
                170 West Tasman Drive
                San Jose, California 95134-1706
Cisco Internetwork Operating System Software
IOS (tm) 4500 Software (C4500-INR-M), Version 10.3(8), RELEASE
    SOFTWARE (fc2)
Copyright (c) 1986-1995 by cisco Systems, Inc.
Compiled Thu 14-Dec-95 22:10 by mkamson
Image text-base: 0x600087E0, data-base: 0x6043C000
cisco 4500 (R4K) processor (revision B) with 8192K/4096K bytes of
    memory.
Processor board serial number 73160394
R4600 processor, Implementation 32, Revision 2.0
G.703/E1 software, Version 1.0.
Bridging software.
X.25 software, Version 2.0, NET2, BFE and GOSIP compliant.
2 Ethernet/IEEE 802.3 interfaces.
1 Token Ring/IEEE 802.5 interface.
2 Serial network interfaces.
128K bytes of non-volatile configuration memory.
4096K bytes of processor board System flash (Read/Write)
4096K bytes of processor board Boot flash (Read/Write)
Press RETURN to get started!
```

Now that we have an appreciation for the basic hardware components of a router and its initialization process, let's turn our attention to router software. In doing so, let's obtain an understanding of the two key software components of a router and the relationship of router commands to the software components.

Basic Software Components

As briefly discussed in the prior section in this chapter, there are two key router software components: the OS image and the configuration file.

Operating System Image

The OS image is located by the bootstrap loader, based on the setting of the configuration register. Once the image is located, the image is loaded into the low-addressed portion of memory. The *OS image* consists of a series of routines that support the transfer of data through the device and manage buffer space, support different network functions, update routing tables, and execute user commands.

Configuration File

The second major router software component is the *configuration file.* This file is created by the router administrator and contains statements that are interpreted by the OS to tell it how to perform different functions built into the OS. Included in the configuration file, for example, can be statements that define one or more access lists and tell the OS to apply different access lists to different interfaces to provide a degree of control concerning the flow of packets through the router. Although the configuration file defines how to perform functions that affect the operation of the router, the OS actually does the work. The OS interprets and acts on the statements in the configuration file.

The configuration file contains statements stored in ASCII. As such, its contents can be displayed on the router console terminal or on a remote terminal. Once the configuration file is saved, the file is stored in the NVRAM and is loaded into upper-addressed memory each time the router is initialized. Figure 6–3 illustrates the relationship of the two key router software components with respect to router RAM.

Data Flow

We can obtain an appreciation for the use of configuration information by examining the flow of data within a router. In doing so, we will reference Figure 6–4, which illustrates the general flow of data within a router.

At the media interface, previously entered configuration commands inform the OS of the type of frames to be processed. For example, the interface could be Ethernet, Token Ring, FDDI, or even a WAN port such as an X.25 or Frame Relay serial interface. In defining the interface, you

Figure 6–3
Router software components

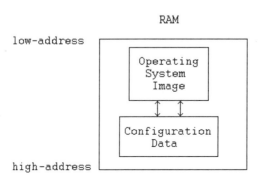

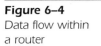

Figure 6–4
Data flow within
a router

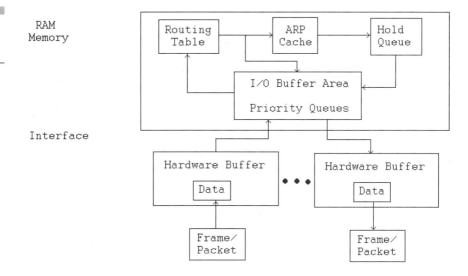

might be required to provide one or more operating rates and other parameters to fully define the interface.

Once the router knows the type of interface it must support, the router is able to verify the frame format of arriving data and correctly form frames for output via that interface or through a different interface. In addition, the router can check data integrity on received frames, because once the router knows the interface, it is able to use an appropriate *cyclic redundancy check* (CRC). Similarly, the router can compute and append an appropriate CRC to frames placed onto the media.

Within main memory, configuration commands are used to control the method by which routing table entries occur. If you configure static routing entries, the router will not exchange routing table entries with other routers. The ARP cache represents an area within memory which stores associations between IP addresses and their corresponding MAC layer 2 addresses. As data is received or prepared for transmission, the data might flow into one or more priority queues—where low priority traffic is temporarily delayed in favor of the router processing higher-priority traffic. If your router supports traffic prioritization, certain configuration statements are used to inform the router's OS of how to perform its prioritization tasks.

As data flows into the router, its location and status are tracked by a hold queue. Entries in the routing table denote the destination interface through which the packet will be routed. If the destination is a LAN and address resolution is required, the router will attempt to use the ARP cache to determine the MAC delivery address, as well as the manner in which the outgoing frame should be formed. If an appropriate address is not in cache, the router will form and issue an ARP packet to determine the necessary layer 2 address. Once the destination address and method of encapsulation is determined, the packet is ready for delivery to an outgoing interface port. Once again, the packet might be placed into a priority queue prior to being delivered into the transmit buffer of the interface for delivery onto the connected media. Now that we have an appreciation for the two key router software components, let's turn our attention to the manner in which we can develop the router configuration file.

The Router Configuration Process

The first time you take your router out of the box and power it on, or after you add one or more hardware components, you must use the *setup* command. This command is automatically invoked for either of the previously defined situations, or you can use the command later at the router's command interpreter prompt level (referred to as the EXEC). Prior to running setup or issuing EXEC commands, however, you should note the cabling needed to connect a terminal device to the router's system console port.

Cabling Considerations

The system console port on a router is configured as a *Data Terminal Equipment* (DTE) port. Because the RS-232 port on PCs and ASCII terminal devices are also configured as DTEs, you cannot directly cable the two together using a common, straight-through cable. Both the router's port and the terminal device transmit on pin 2 of the interface and receive data on pin 3. To correctly work with each other, you must obtain a "crossover cable" in which pin 2 at one end is crossed to pin 3 and the other end, and vice versa. The crossover table also ties certain control signals together, so it is actually a bit more than the reversal of pins 2 and 3. The cable is easily available to obtain, however, by simply specifying the term *crossover*. Once you install the correct cable, you should configure your terminal device to operate at 9600 baud, eight data bits, no parity, and one stop bit.

Console Access

You can use a variety of communications programs to access the router via its console port. Because Windows 95 and Windows 98 include the HyperTerminal communications program, we will briefly explore its use as a mechanism to configure a router.

Figure 6–5 illustrates the use of the HyperTerminal program for the creation of a new connection, which this author appropriately labeled "Cisco."

NOTE: Because you will directly cable your computer to the Cisco console port, you would configure the phone number entry for the use of a direct COM port. In the example shown in Figure 6–5, COM port 1 is shown selected.

Once you select the appropriate direct connect COM port and click the OK button, the HyperTerminal program will display a dialog box labeled Port Settings. Figure 6–6 illustrates the Port Settings dialog box for the COM1 port that was previously configured for the router connection we wish to establish.

In examining Figure 6–6, note that the Port Settings dialog box provides you with the capacity to define the communications settings to be

Figure 6–5

You must set the connection type to Direct when cabling a PC directly to the router console port.

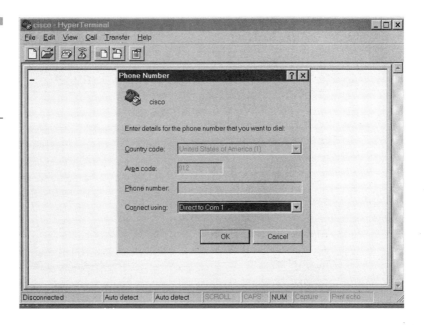

Figure 6-6
Through the Port
Settings dialog box,
you can configure
the communications
parameters to be
used by your
computer to match
those used by the
router console.

used between your PC and the router port. Because the router console port's default is 9600 bps, eight data bits, no parity, and one stop bit, the configuration in Figure 6–6 is set accordingly.

Setup Considerations

To facilitate the use of the *setup* facility, you should prepare for the use of the router. In doing so, you should make a list of the protocols you plan to route, determine the types of interfaces installed, and determine whether you plan to use bridging. In addition, because setup will prompt you to enter a variety of specific parameters for each protocol and interface, it is highly recommended that you consult the appropriate Cisco Systems router manuals to correctly determine these parameters. Included in the setup facility is the capacity to assign a name to the router, as well as assign both a direct connect and virtual terminal password. Once you complete the setup, you will be prompted to accept the configuration. Once the initial setup process is completed, you are ready to use the router's command interpreters.

The following display illustrates an example of the use of the router setup command to review—and, if desired—to modify one or more previously established configuration entries. The name of the router was assigned during a previous setup process such as CISCO4000, resulting in that name being displayed prior to a prompt character. The prompt character is a pound sign (#) that indicates we are in the router's privileged mode of operation (which we will shortly review). Note the enabled password is shown as "abadabado." That password must be specified after a person gains access to the router console port and enters the command *enable* to obtain access to privileged EXEC commands that alter a router's operating environment. In addition to the enable password, an administrator might also configure an enable secret password. The *enable secret* serves the same purpose as the standard enable password, except that the enable secret password is encrypted in the configuration file using MD5. When the configuration is displayed, only the encrypted version of the enable secret password will be seen. This feature is important to prevent anyone from determining what the enable secret password is by obtaining a copy of the router configuration. The regular enable password might also be encrypted by using the command *service password-encryption.* This command will also encrypt the passwords used for the *virtual terminal* (VTY), auxiliary, and console ports. The encryption used, however, is much weaker than the encryption used for the enable secret. Also, many free programs are available on the Internet to crack passwords encrypted in this manner in a few seconds. The authors recommend always using the enable secret password. If both the enable secret and the standard enable password are set, the enable secret password takes precedence.

To save on listing space, a portion of the router's setup configuration was eliminated from the following display (where the double rows of dots are shown).

NOTE: You can use the question mark at each line-entry level to obtain online assistance. Also note that once the configuration is completed, a command script is created by the router. This command script represents the latest configuration changes. You are then prompted to accept or reject the entire configuration.

```
CISCO4000#setup
            — System Configuration Dialog —
At any point you may enter a question mark '?' for help.
Refer to the 'Getting Started' Guide for additional help.
Use ctrl-c to abort configuration dialog at any prompt.
Default settings are in square brackets '[]'.
Continue with configuration dialog? [yes]:
First, would you like to see the current interface summary? [yes]:
Interface        IP-Address        OK?  Method    Status
    Protocol
Ethernet0        192.72.46.3       YES  NVRAM     up            down
Serial0          4.0.136.74        YES  NVRAM     down          down
Serial1          4.0.136.90        YES  NVRAM     down          down
TokenRing0       192.131.174.2     YES  NVRAM     initializing  down
Configuring global parameters:
  Enter host name [CISCO4000]:
```

The enable secret is a one-way cryptographic secret used
instead of the enable password when it exists.
    Enter enable secret [<Use current secret>]:
The enable password is used when there is no enable secret
and when using older software and some boot images.
    Enter enable password [abadabado]:
    Enter virtual terminal password [gobirds]:
    Configure SNMP Network Management? [yes]:
        Community string [public]:
    Configure IPX? [yes]:
    Configure bridging? [no]:
    Configure IP? [yes]:
        Configure IGRP routing? [no]:
        Configure RIP routing? [yes]:
Configuring interface parameters:
Configuring interface Ethernet0:
    Is this interface in use? [yes]:
    Configure IP on this interface? [yes]:
        IP address for this interface [192.72.46.3]:
        Number of bits in subnet field [0]:
        Class C network is 192.72.46.0, 0 subnet bits; mask is
    255.255.255.0
    Configure IPX on this interface? [yes]:
        IPX network number [110]:
Configuring interface Serial0:
    Is this interface in use? [yes]:
    Configure IP on this interface? [yes]:
    Configure IP unnumbered on this interface? [no]:
        IP address for this interface [4.0.136.74]:
        Number of bits in subnet field [22]:
        Class A network is 4.0.0.0, 22 subnet bits; mask is
    255.255.255.252
    Configure IPX on this interface? [no]:
. . . .
.   .   .   .   .   .
The following configuration command script was created:
hostname CISCO4000
enable secret 5 1soiv$pyh65G.wUNxX9LK90w7yc.
enable password abadabado
line vty 0 4
password gobirds
snmp-server community public
ipx routing
no bridge 1
ip routing
! Turn off IPX to prevent network conflicts.
interface Ethernet0
no ipx network
interface Serial0
no ipx network
interface Serial1
no ipx network
interface TokenRing0
no ipx network
!
interface Ethernet0
ip address 192.78.46.1 255.255.255.0
ipx network 110
. .   .   .   .

```
    .    .    .    .    .
router rip
network 192.78.46.0
network 200.1.2.0
network 4.0.0.0
network 192.131.174.0
!
end
Use this configuration? [Yes/no]:
```

Because the command interpreter is the key to entering router commands that control the manner in which the OS changes router functionality—to include applying access lists to interfaces—let's turn our attention to this object.

The Command Interpreter

The *command interpreter*, as its name implies, is responsible for interpreting router commands you enter. Referred to as the EXEC, the command interpreter checks each command—and, assuming the commands are correctly entered—performs the operation requested.

Assuming an administrator entered a password during the setup process, you must log into the router using the correct password prior to obtaining the capacity to enter an EXEC command. In actuality, there can be two passwords required to use EXEC commands, because there are two EXEC command levels: user and privileged. By logging into the router, you gain access to user EXEC commands that provide you with the capacity to connect to another host, provide a name to a logical connection, change the parameters of a terminal, display open connections, and perform similar operations that are not considered by Cisco Systems to represent critical operations. If you use the EXEC enable command to gain access to the use of privileged commands, you obtain the capacity to enter configuration information, turn privileged commands on or off, lock the terminal, and perform other critical functions. To use the EXEC enable command, you might have to enter another password if one was previously set with the enable-password configuration command.

User Mode Operations

Once you log into the router, you are placed into *user command mode*. In this mode, the system prompt appears as an angle bracket (>). If you previously entered a name for the router, that name will prefix the angle bracket. Otherwise, the default term "router" will prefix the angle bracket.

After you enter the user mode, typing the question mark (?) command results in the display of a list of user-level EXEC commands supported by the router you are using. The minitable below illustrates the use of these EXEC commands at the user level. In examining these commands, note that the command line entry CISCO4000>? indicates that during the setup process, the name CISCO4000 was assigned to the router.

atmsig	Execute ATM Signalling Commands
connect	Open a terminal connection
disable	Turn off privileged commands
disconnect	Disconnect an existing network connection
enable	Turn on privileged commands
exit	Exit from the EXEC
help	Description of the interactive help system
lock	Lock the terminal
login	Log in as a particular user
logout	Exit from the EXEC
name-connection	Name an existing network connection
pad	Open a X.29 PAD connection
ping	Send echo messages
ppp	Start IETF *Point-to-Point Protocol* (PPP)
resume	Resume an active network connection
show	Show running system information
slip	Start *Serial-line* IP (SLIP)
systat	Display information about terminal lines
telnet	Open a telnet connection
terminal	Set terminal line parameters
traceroute	Trace route to destination

tunnel	Open a tunnel connection
where	List active connections
x3	Set X.3 parameters on PAD

Privileged Mode of Operation

Because you can only configure a router through its privileged EXEC mode of operation, you can assign a password to this mode of operation. As previously noted, you would use the enable-password configuration command to do so, which means that you would first enter the privileged mode without password protection to set password protection.

To enter the privileged EXEC mode, you would enter the enable command at the angle bracket prompt. You would then be prompted to enter a password, after which the prompt would change to a pound sign (#)—which indicates that you are in the privileged EXEC mode of operation.

The following display illustrates the use of the question mark command at the privileged command level to display a list of commands supported at the privileged EXEC mode. In examining the entries in the display, note that the privileged mode command set includes all user EXEC commands previously listed in the previous display. In addition, the set includes the configure command, which provides you with the capacity to apply configuration parameters that affect the router on a global basis.

```
Password:
CISCO4000# ?
Exec commands:
  atmsig      Execute Atm Signalling Commands
  bfe         For manual emergency modes setting
  calendar    Manage the hardware calendar
  clear       Reset functions
  clock       Manage the system clock
  configure   Enter configuration mode
  connect     Open a terminal connection
  copy        Copy a config file to or from a tftp server
  debug       Debugging functions (see also 'undebug')
  disable     Turn off privileged commands
  disconnect  Disconnect an existing network connection
  enable      Turn on privileged commands
  erase       Erase flash or configuration memory
  exit        Exit from the EXEC
  help        Description of the interactive help system
  lock        Lock the terminal
```

```
login               Log in as a particular user
logout              Exit from the EXEC
mbranch             Trace multicast route down tree branch
mrbranch            Trace reverse multicast route up tree branch
name-connection  Name an existing network connection
no                  Disable debugging functions
pad                 Open a X.29 PAD connection
ping                Send echo messages
ppp                 Start IETF Point-to-Point Protocol (PPP)
reload              Halt and perform a cold restart
resume              Resume an active network connection
rsh                 Execute a remote command
send                Send a message to other tty lines
setup               Run the SETUP command facility
show                Show running system information
slip                Start Serial-line IP (SLIP)
start-chat          Start a chat-script on a line
systat              Display information about terminal lines
telnet              Open a telnet connection
terminal            Set terminal line parameters
test                Test subsystems, memory, and interfaces
traceroute          Trace route to destination
tunnel              Open a tunnel connection
undebug             Disable debugging functions (see also 'debug')
verify              Verify checksum of a Flash file
where               List active connections
write               Write running configuration to memory,
network, or terminal
x3                  Set X.3 parameters on PAD
```

The following display illustrates the use of the configure command once you are in privileged EXEC mode, followed by the question mark command to display a list of configuration commands supported by the router used at a particular point in time. In examining this display, note that you first use the enable command to enter the privileged level of the EXEC and a password to obtain the pound sign prompt. After you enter the configure command at the privileged mode prompt, EXEC prompts you for the source of the configuration commands to be entered. The default is to type commands from the console. Pressing the Return key results in the use of this method of configuration.

```
CISCO4000#configure
Configuring from terminal, memory, or network [terminal]?
Enter configuration commands, one per line.  End with CNTL/Z.
CISCO4000(config)#?
Configure commands:
  aaa                         Authentication, Authorization and
  Accounting.
  access-list                 Add an access list entry
```

```
       alias                       Create command alias
       arp                         Set a static ARP entry
       async-bootp                 Modify system bootp parameters
       autonomous-system           Specify local AS number to which we
       belong
       banner                      Define a login banner
       boot                        Modify system boot parameters
       bridge                      Bridging Group.
       buffers                     Adjust system buffer pool
       parameters
       cdp                         Global CDP configuration
       subcommands
       chat-script                 Define a modem chat script
       clock                       Configure time-of-day clock
       config-register             Define the configuration register
       default-value               Default character-bits values
       dialer-list                 Create a dialer list entry
       dlsw                        Data Link Switching global
       configuration commands
       dnsix-dmdp                  Provide DMDP service for DNSIX
       dnsix-nat                   Provide DNSIX service for audit
       trails
       downward-compatible-config  Generate a configuration compatible
       with older
                                       software
   -More-
```

Table 6–2 provides a summary of configuration command entry methods and their operational results. Entries in this table summarize the relationship between the use of different command entry methods and the use of different types of storage for both accessing and storing configuration commands. Cisco changed the format of these commands beginning in Version 10.3 of the router OS. Both forms of the commands are still accepted by the router in the most current releases, although at some point it is assumed that the older version of the commands will be phased out.

Configuration Command Categories

Configuration commands can be categorized into four general categories: *global*, which defines system-wide parameters; *interface*, which defines WAN or LAN interfaces; *line*, which defines the characteristics of a serial terminal line; and *router subcommands*, which are used to configure a routing protocol.

Table 6–2

Configuration
Command Entry
Methods

Command	Operational Result
Configure terminal	To configure router manually from the console
Configure memory	To load a previously created configuration from NVRAM
Configure network	To load a previously created configuration from a network server via TFTP
Write terminal	Display the current configuration in RAM
Write network	Share the current configuration in RAM with a network server via TFTP
Show configuration	Display the previously saved configuration in NVRAM
Write erase	Erase the contents of NVRAM
Reload	Loads the contents of NVRAM into RAM and occurs on power on automatically

Global Configuration Commands

Global configuration commands are used to define system-wide parameters to include access lists. The earlier display, which previously showed the use of the configure command, also illustrates a list of global commands applicable to the router used by the authors.

As you probably surmised by now, you can obtain help information about a specific command by entering the command followed by the question mark. The next display illustrates the use of the question mark to obtain information about the access list command.

```
CISCO4000(config)# access-list ?
  <1-99>       IP standard access list
  <100-199>    IP extended access list
  <1000-1099>  IPX SAP access list
  <1100-1199>  Extended 48-bit MAC address access list
  <200-299>    Protocol type-code access list
  <700-799>    48-bit MAC address access list
  <800-899>    IPX standard access list
  <900-999>    IPX extended access list
```

In examining this display, note that the online help for access lists provides a general review of the number range for different access lists supported by the router. In Chapter 7, we will examine access lists in considerable detail, so at this point in time we will simply note that they are numbered and are used to enable or disable the flow of packets across a router's interface.

Interface Commands   -

A second category of router commands is *interface* commands. Interface commands define the characteristics of a LAN or WAN interface and are preceded by an interface command. The next display illustrates the use of the interface serial 0 command, followed by the question mark command, to display a partial list of interface configuration commands that can be applied to the serial 0 interface.

```
CISCO4000(config)#interface serial 0
CISCO4000(config-if)#?
Interface configuration commands:
  access-expression          Build a bridge boolean access
                             expression
  arp                        Set arp type (arpa, probe, snap)
                             or timeout
  backup                     Modify dial-backup parameters
  bandwidth                  Set bandwidth informational
                             parameter
  bridge-group               Transparent bridging interface
                             parameters
  carrier-delay              Specify delay for interface
                             transitions
  cdp                        CDP interface subcommands
  clock                      Configure serial interface clock
  compress                   Set serial interface for
                             compression
  custom-queue-list          Assign a custom queue list to an
                             interface
  dce-terminal-timing-enable Enable DCE terminal timing
  delay                      Specify interface throughput delay
  description                Interface specific description
  dialer                     Dial-on-demand routing (DDR)
                             commands
  dialer-group               Assign interface to dialer-list
  down-when-looped           Force looped serial interface down
  dte-invert-txc             Invert transmit clock
  dxi                        ATM-DXI configuration commands
  encapsulation              Set encapsulation type for an
                             interface
  exit                       Exit from interface configuration
                             mode
  frame-relay                Set frame relay parameters
 -More-
```

Through the use of the interface command, you can assign a network to a particular port and configure one or more specific parameters required for the interface. For example, interface ethernet 0 informs the router that port 0 is connected to an Ethernet network.

Line Commands

Line commands are used to modify the operation of a serial terminal line. The following display illustrates the use of the line command, followed by the question mark command, to display a list of lines that can be configured.

```
CISCO4000(config)#line ?
  <0-6>     First Line number
  aux       Auxiliary line
  console   Primary terminal line
  vty       Virtual terminal
```

Router Commands

The fourth category of privileged commands is *router subcommands*. Such commands are used to configure IP routing protocol parameters and follow the use of the router command. The top portion of the next display illustrates the use of the router command, followed by the question mark command, to display a list of router subcommands supported by the router used at this point in time.

```
CISCO4000(config)#router ?
  bgp        Border Gateway Protocol (BGP)
  egp        Exterior Gateway Protocol (EGP)
  eigrp      Enhanced Interior Gateway Routing Protocol (EIGRP)
  igrp       Interior Gateway Routing Protocol (IGRP)
  isis       ISO IS-IS
  iso-igrp   IGRP for OSI networks
  mobile     Mobile routes
  ospf       Open Shortest Path First (OSPF)
  rip        Routing Information Protocol (RIP)
  static     Static routes

CISCO4000(config)#router rip
CISCO4000(config-router)#?
Router configuration commands:
  default-metric          Set metric of redistributed routes
  distance                Define an administrative distance
  distribute-list         Filter networks in routing updates
  exit                    Exit from routing protocol
                          configuration mode
  help                    Description of the interactive help
                          system
  maximum-paths           Forward packets over multiple paths
  neighbor                Specify a neighbor router
  network                 Enable routing on an IP network
  no                      Negate or set default values of a
                          command
  offset-list             Add or subtract offset from IGRP or RIP
                          metrics
  passive-interface       Suppress routing updates on an interface
  redistribute            Redistribute information from another
                          routing protocol
  timers                  Adjust routing timers
  validate-update-source  Perform sanity checks against source
                          address of routing updates
```

NOTE: You can "drill down" to obtain information about a particular router command by entering that command and then entering the question mark command, as illustrated in the lower portion of the previous display.

Now that we have a general appreciation for the basic hardware and software components of a router and its EXEC command modes, let's conclude this chapter by focusing our attention on router security management issues.

Abbreviating Commands

We should note here that you often do not need to type the entire word for the router to accept a command. Generally, three or four letters of the command are enough for the router to discern which command is being requested and to perform the desired action.

For example, the command `Router# show interface serial 0` could be abbreviated as `Router# sh int s0`, which is certainly much easier to type (see Table 6–3). When in doubt, try abbreviating the command to the first three letters. If the first three letters are not enough for the router to determine the command you are requesting, you will get an "ambiguous command" error at the router prompt. You can then use the router's context-sensitive help program by typing the first three letters with a question mark at the end. The router will display all of the commands that match the first three letters, and then you can add as many characters as necessary to distinguish the command you want.

Table 6–3

Router Shortcut Commands

<ctl>+<p> or Up arrow key	recalls the previous command
<ctl>+<a>	moves to the beginning of the line
<ctl>+<e>	moves to the end of the line
<esc>+<b>	moves back one word
<ctl>+<f>	moves forward one character
<ctl>+<b>	moves back one character
<esc>+<f>	moves forward one word
show history	shows recently used commands

Remember, the question mark is your friend. By using the built-in, context-sensitive help menu, even a Cisco novice can determine the correct syntax of a command. Listed next are a few other tricks which can greatly assist an administrator when entering configuration commands.

Security Management Considerations

Regardless of the manner in which you intend to use a router, there are several key security-related areas you must consider. Those areas include establishing passwords to secure access to your router and the development of appropriate access lists to govern the flow of acceptable data through the router.

Password Management

You can control access to your router, to the use of privileged EXEC commands, and even to individual lines through the use of passwords. To do so, you would use one or more of the commands listed in Table 6–4.

The following display illustrates the use of the configure, line, and password commands to change a previously established password—which controls access from the console terminal. Note that this new password contains a numeric character, which is used to separate two conventional alphabetic portions of a password. In general, you should definitely consider using a mixture of numbers, letters, and symbols in your passwords to minimize the potential of a hacker employing a successful dictionary attack.

Table 6–4

Security Management Commands

Command	Operational Effect
line console 0	Establishes a password on the console terminal
line vty 0 4	Establishes a password for Telnet connections
enable-password	Establishes a password for access to the privileged EXE mode
enable secret	Establishes an enable secret password using MD5 encryption
service password-encryption	Protects the display of passwords from the use of the *idsplay* command

```
CISCO4000#configure
Configuring from terminal, memory, or network [terminal]?
Enter configuration commands, one per line.  End with CNTL/Z.
CISCO4000(config)#line vty 0 4
CISCO4000(config-line)#login
CISCO4000(config-line)#password bad4you
CISCO4000(config-line)#exit
CISCO4000(config)#exit
```

Access Lists

A second area of security management involves controlling the flow of packets through the router. To do so, you can configure one or more access lists and apply those lists to one or more router interfaces. Because the focus of Chapter 7 is access lists, let's turn to that chapter to obtain the details associated with this important topic.

7

Cisco Router Access Lists

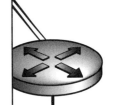

In the previous chapters, we have reviewed the operation of many protocols. As we will see, an understanding of the inner workings of these protocols and their address structure is critical to the proper construction and implementation of Cisco access lists. In this chapter, we will begin our discussion by defining Cisco access lists and examining their role in securing Cisco networks. We then examine the Cisco methodology for constructing and maintaining Cisco access lists. Once we have a basic understanding of how access lists are constructed, we will begin our discussion of IP access lists and provide detailed examples showing their use. We will also make a distinction between traditional IP access lists and next-generation IP access lists. Next-generation IP access lists provide significant enhancements beyond the capability of traditional IP access lists.

Cisco Access List Technology

We will begin by discussing why access lists are important to Cisco security. There are many facets to security and one of the most important is the capability to control the flow of data packets within a network. Specifically, preventing packets from entering a network by examining information within the packet header is critical. This capability is typically termed "packet filtering" and is one of the most important uses of Cisco access lists although, as we shall see, it is not the only use.

Packet filtering allows you to control data flows in your network based on source and destination IP addresses and the type of application used. For example, packet filtering allows you to prevent packets from entering your network if the packets are part of a telnet session that originated from certain address ranges. Additionally, you can prevent all packets from a certain IP address range from entering your network, regardless of the application used. These kinds of functions are especially useful when applied to routers.

In many cases, routers serve as a boundary between administrative domains. The term "administrative domain" is used to indicate a general grouping of network devices such as workstations, servers, routers, and network links that are maintained by a single administrative group. Many times the term "autonomous system" is used to serve the same designation, but autonomous system has a very specific meaning in computer networks, so we will use administrative domain instead.

Different administrative domains normally have different security policies, and there is usually limited access between data networks in separate administrative domains. In most cases, an administrative domain makes up a company's corporate network, although some large companies may have many administrative domains.

One of the functions served by routers is to tie these separate administrative domains together. Routers serve this function, for example, as a connection point between a corporate LAN and the Internet or between two or more corporate networks. In these situations, routers are uniquely suited to filter packets because every packet between the two administrative domains must pass through the router. Additionally, a router is usually necessary to enable data network connectivity between geographically separated organizations, so no additional equipment or software is needed to enable the security functions of packet filtering.

Although special hardware can be installed in many server platforms to provide WAN connectivity between separate organizations, these solutions typically do not scale very well. Servers usually do not offer the same range of protocols and physical interfaces as a Cisco router. Although an adequate solution can be built from various server hardware and software for small organizations, many organizations prefer an "off the shelf" solution. All the functionality for creating a complex security perimeter solution is contained within the Cisco IOS; no add-on software packages or hardware components need to be purchased.

Cisco uses the term *Internetwork Operating System* (IOS) to designate the operating system used by Cisco routers. The operating system on Cisco routers provides many of the same features of more traditional operating systems, like Unix and Windows, but it also provides many specialized features. It controls the system hardware such as memory and interfaces, and also takes care of executing necessary system tasks like moving packets and building dynamic information such as the routing and ARP tables. When an administrator issues commands at a router prompt to modify a routers' configuration, the commands interface with the IOS.

One of the most powerful features of the Cisco router IOS is its capability to intelligently filter packets flowing between data networks. This capability is provided through the creation and application of access lists.

Access Lists Defined

An access list is an ordered list of statements denying or permitting packets based on matching criteria contained within the packet. Let's examine this definition in greater detail. An access list is an ordered list. In other words, the order in which the statements are created in an access list is very important. One of the most common mistakes made when creating access lists is entering the access list statements in an incorrect order.

Access list statements can either permit or deny packets. Additionally, it should be pointed out now that there is always an implicit "Deny All" statement at the end of a Cisco access list. A packet that is not explicitly permitted will be rejected by the implicit Deny All statement at the end of the access list. Another common mistake when creating access lists is forgetting this fact.

The criteria used to permit or deny packets is based solely on information contained within the packet itself. Usually, this information is restricted to information contained within the layer 3 or layer 4 header. Therefore, with few exceptions, access lists cannot use information above layer 4 to filter packets. Although application-specific commands may be contained in the data portion of the packet, an access list is not capable of filtering based on this information. For example, an access list is not capable of filtering specific FTP commands. The one caveat to this is the use of *Context-Based Access Control* (CBAC), which has the capability to filter packets based on well-known application layer information. CBAC will be covered in detail in Chapter 8, "Advanced Cisco Router Security Features."

The above discussion is not meant to imply that the only function of access lists is packet filtering. This is most certainly not the case. Cisco access lists are used for many purposes other than packet filtering. In fact, anytime a list of permitted addresses and/or protocols is needed to define which packets are to be included in a process, an access list is used. Some of the other situations in which access lists can be used are as follows:

- **Dial on Demand**: Access lists are used to define which packets are permitted to cause a dial connection to occur. This is commonly called defining interesting packets.
- **Queuing Features**: Access lists define which types of packets are allocated to different types of outgoing queues so that some classes of packets are given priority over others.
- **Routing Update Filters**: Access lists prevent certain network routes from being advertised or accepted by routing protocols.
- **Router Access**: Access lists control telnet and SNMP access to the router itself. This is in contrast to filtering packets that pass through the router.

As can be seen from this list, access lists play an integral role in many features used in Cisco routers, but not all of these features are related to security. In addition to examining the use of access lists for packet filtering, we will briefly examine the use of access lists to control access to the router and their use in filtering routing protocol updates. Many sources also provide information on these and other uses of access lists on the Cisco web site. The remainder of this chapter will concentrate on the use of access lists for packet filtering.

Creating Access Lists

We now turn our attention to the creation and operation of access lists. The basic syntax of an access list is:

```
Access-list [1-1199] [permit|deny] [protocol|protocol-keyword]
   [source source-wildcard|any] [source port] [destination
   destination-wildcard|any] [destination port] [precedence
   precedence#] [options]
```

We will discuss each of these fields in detail next. Actual commands are in bold, and the other statements are English equivalents of the command syntax. Each section of the command is separated on its own line with a number to facilitate discussion. In practice, each access list entry normally appears on a single line in the router configuration.

```
Access-list
[access list number 1-1199]
[permit or deny]
[some protocol]
[source address and mask]
[source port number or range]
[destination address and mask]
[destination port number or range]
[options]
```

A few words need to be said about the above command structure. First, not all the fields are required. Only fields 1, 2, and 4 are required in every type of access list. Most access lists also include fields 3 and 6. Each field is discussed below:

```
[access list number 1-1199]
```

The actual number that is used varies, depending on the type of access list used. Different types of access lists use different numbers. An IP access list, for example, uses a different number than an IPX access list. There are many different types of access lists.

```
[permit or deny]
```

A permit or deny statement is always required. This is how you specify whether the packets that match an access list entry are to be allowed or denied access.

```
[some protocol]
```

Quite a few different protocols can be filtered using an access list. A short list includes IP, IPX, AppleTalk, DECnet, VINES, and XNS. It is also possible to filter on MAC layer addresses. Within most protocol stacks, there are usually additional protocols that can be filtered. For example, filters can also be created for TCP, UDP, and ICMP, all of which use IP at the network layer.

```
[source address and mask]
```

The source address and mask of the packets is always required. The source address is normally the layer 3 address of the packet, unless the access list is a MAC layer filter. The mask portion tells the router how much of the address to match when filtering packets. The concept is similar to a subnet mask. For instance, you may want to match all packets originating from the 10.10.0.0 255.255.0.0 subnet. The mask allows you to tell the router to match only the first two octets of the address. If no mask is specified, an exact match is assumed. If 10.10.0.0 is typed, the access list entry would only match packets with a source address of 10.10.0.0 (a very unlikely source address). Although the principle is the same, the syntax of this mask is different than a network mask. We cover this topic in greater detail later. In addition to the use of an actual address, many protocols also support the use of the "any" keyword.

```
[source port number or range]
```

This field is used when filtering on layer 4 information. It allows you to specify a particular higher-layer port. If the access list protocol is TCP, for example, you could specify a source TCP port of 25 (SMTP). You can also use symbols like GT for "greater than," LT for "less than," and RANGE to create specific ranges of port numbers.

```
[destination address and mask]
```

This field has the same parameter structure as the source address and mask.

```
[destination port number or range]
```

This field has the same parameter structure as the source port number or range.

```
[options]
```

This field allows a variety of additional fields to be matched in the access list entry. The contents of the field vary depending on the type of access list. A typical option for a TCP access list would be "established," indicating the access list entry would examine the packet to see if the ACK or RST bit is set. The "log" option is also common, indicating that matches of the access list entry should be logged to the router's buffer or a syslog server. Other options include filtering on TOS and IP precedence.

We will cover each of these fields for particular IP access lists later in this chapter. Access lists for other protocols will be discussed in later chapters.

Access List Details

The code below is a portion of a sample access list configuration for a Cisco router applied to the serial 0 interface. Only the relevant portions of the configuration are shown.

```
interface Serial0
ip address 170.10.10.1 255.255.255.0
ip access-group 101 in
!
access-list 101 permit tcp any any established
access-list 101 permit udp any gt 1023 host 160.10.2.100 eq 53
access-list 101 permit ip any host 160.10.2.101
access-list 101 permit icmp any any echo-reply
```

Figure 7–1 shows the router this sample configuration is taken from.

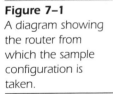

Figure 7–1
A diagram showing the router from which the sample configuration is taken.

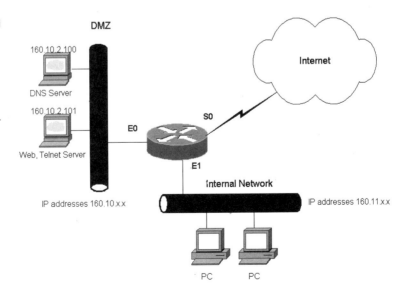

For the moment, try not to be too concerned about interpreting what this access list is doing; we will cover this topic in greater detail later. Instead concentrate on examining how the access list statements have been created and how the access list has been applied.

Notice that the access list has been created in one section and there is a separate command for applying the access list to the serial interface. Also notice that the access list is applied to the serial interface in a particular direction. The direction indicates whether packets are examined as they *arrive* (in) or *leave* (out) an interface on the router.

The English translation of this access list is included below. Each access list entry appears on a separate line in bold.

```
Access-list 101 permit tcp any any established
```

This permits TCP from any host to any host if the ACK or RST bit is set, which indicates it is part of an established connection. Note that the first packet in a TCP conversation does not have the ACK bit set. Essentially, the established keyword is designed to prevent TCP conversations from being initiated from the untrusted side of a router while allowing packets that are part of an already established TCP conversation to go through.

```
Access-list 101 permit udp any gt 1023 host 160.10.2.100 eq 53
```

This permits UDP from any host with a client source port (ports below 1024 are reserved for servers) to host 160.10.2.100 with destination port DNS (53).

```
Access-list 101 permit ip any host 160.10.2.101
```

This permits IP from any host to host 160.10.2.101.

```
Access-list 101 permit icmp any any echo-reply
```

This permits ICMP from any host to any host if the packet is a response to a ping request (echo-reply).

```
Access-list 101 deny ip any any
```

This denies all other packets (this line is implicit and does not appear unless explicitly typed).

Some of the the access list syntax may be unfamiliar right now. In later sections, we will cover the syntax of different types of IP access lists in greater detail.

Applying Access Lists

For those unfamiliar with IOS commands, the block of code below displays the commands to actually create the access list shown earlier in the sample access list configuration code and apply it to the interface.

```
2514# config term
2514(config)# access-list 101 permit tcp any any established
2514(config)# access-list 101 permit udp gt 1023 any host
   160.10.2.100 eq 53
2514(config)# access-list 101 permit ip any host 160.10.2.101
2514(config)# access-list 101 permit icmp any any eq echo-reply
2514(config)# interface serial 0
2514(config-if)# ip access-group 101 in
2514(config-if)# exit
2514(config)# exit
2514#
```

Notice that the access list entries in the code here are entered in the same order in which they appear in the earlier configuration code. This is no accident. New access list entries are always added to the bottom of the existing access list; there is currently no mechanism for adding entries into a specific position in the access list without deleting and recreating the entire access list.

This is extremely important because, as we mentioned earlier, access lists are ordered lists. They are evaluated from the top down. Once a matching entry is found, the access list processing function exits and no more entries are considered. The following flowchart shown in Figure 7–2 illustrates this process.

The access list code contains several points of interest. First, notice that only TCP/IP protocols are used in this example, yet numerous protocols other than those in the TCP/IP suite can be specified. Table 7–1 shows the types of access lists that can be created for various protocols. The number range on the right side of the table specifies the access list number range that is used when creating an access list of the specified type.

Figure 7–2

A logical flowchart illustrating how packets are matched against the entries in an access list.

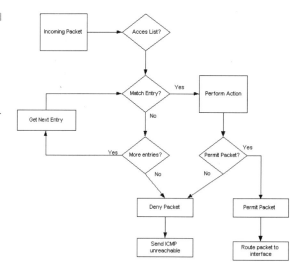

Table 7–1

Access Lists Protocols and Their Number Ranges

Protocol	Range
IP	1–99
Extended IP	100–199
Ethernet type code	200–299
Ethernet address	700–799
Transparent bridging (protocol type)	200–299
Transparent bridging (vendor code)	700–799
Extended transparent bridging	1100–1199
DECNet and extended DECNet	300–399
XNS	400–499
Extended XNS	500–599
AppleTalk	600–699
Source-route bridging (protocol type)	200–299
Source-route bridging (vendor code)	700–799
IPX	800–899
Extended IPX	900–999
IPX SAP	1000–1099

Table 7–1

Continued

Protocol	Range
Standard VINES	1–100
Extended VINES	101–200
Simple VINES	201–300

When an access list is created, a number is assigned to the access list within a specific range. This number is used in all subsequent references to the access list. For example, in the configuration code, we used access list number 101. Looking in Table 7–1, we see that this could either be an Extended IP access list or an Extended VINES access list. In this case, it is an Extended IP access list, which we can tell by looking at the actual access list commands. Notice further in the configuration code that this number is used to reference the access list when it is applied to the serial 0 interface.

This brings us to the next point of interest regarding our sample configuration. Notice that there is a separate command beneath the serial 0 interface referencing access list 101. This command is how we indicate to the router that the access list will check packets either arriving or leaving this interface. If no commands apply the access list to an interface, creating the access list serves little purpose with regard to packet filtering. We could, however, create an access list for use with one of the other technologies mentioned earlier, in which case it would not be applied to an interface. For the most part, we will not cover other uses of access lists in this book.

Until the access list is applied to an interface, no packet filtering occurs. To reiterate, simply creating an access list is only the first step. To actually enable packet filtering using the created access list, the access list must be applied to an interface.

It has already been stated that the command applying the access list to an interface is what indicates to the router that packets arriving or leaving the interface are subject to filtering. The direction of the filtering can be selected by using the keyword "in" or "out." Notice in the sample configuration code the use of the keyword "in." This tells the router to apply the access list filter to packets arriving inbound on the serial 0 interface. This corresponds to packets arriving from outside administrative domains and applies to packets arriving from the Internet. If we specify "out" as the keyword, we would be filtering packets that are leaving the serial 0 interface. This corresponds to packets originating from the Ethernet E0 interface in Figure 7–1, which means we would be filtering our own packets as they leave our administrative domain. Although this is certainly possible and sometimes desirable, it would not be what we want in this particular example.

A key point is that an outbound access list does not filter packets originated by the router itself. Even if a packet originated by the router matches a deny entry in an outbound access list, the packet will not be filtered. Essentially, packets originated by the router itself are not subject to outbound access list restrictions. Inbound packets destined for the router are subject to an inbound access list. This difference is important. If we were running a routing protocol on the serial interface of the router in Figure 7–1, we would need to explicitly allow routing updates in our access list. Otherwise, the implicit Deny All in the inbound access list would deny the routing updates.

One additional point worth noting is that an interface may have both an inbound and outbound access list for each protocol supported, but it may not have more than one of each for any particular protocol. We could have an Extended IP access list outbound, for example, on the serial 0 interface in our configuration, but we could not have an additional Extended IP access list inbound. Figure 7–3 shows a visual representation of this.

Figure 7–3

An interface cannot have more than one access list of the same type applied in the same direction.

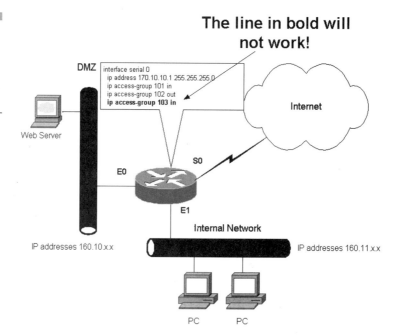

The next block of code shows what occurs on the router when you try to apply more than one access list of the same type to an interface.

```
2514#config terminal
Enter configuration commands, one per line. End with CNTL/Z.
2514(config)#interface serial 0
2514(config-if)#ip access-group 101 in
2514(config-if)#exit
2514#write terminal

Building configuration . . .

Current configuration:
!
hostname 2514
!
interface Serial0
 ip address 170.10.10.1 255.255.255.0
ip access-group 101 in


2514#config terminal
Enter configuration commands, one per line. End with CNTL/Z.
2514(config)#interface serial0
2514(config-if)#ip access-group 102 in
2514(config-if)#exit
2514#write terminal

Building configuration . . .

Current configuration:
!
hostname 2514
!
interface Serial0
ip address 170.10.10.1 255.255.255.0
ip access-group 102 in
```

Notice that the application of access list 102 to the serial interface overrides the previous application of access list 101.

Named Access Lists

You may have noticed that since each access list type has a limited range of acceptable numbers that can be used, it is possible, though not likely, that one could run out of acceptable numbers to use. If, for example, one needed to create more than 100 Extended IP access lists, the restriction of using only numbers 100 through 199 would be a limiting factor. Named access lists provide an alternative. (Note that named access lists are available in IOS version 11.2 and higher.)

As the title implies, named access lists are exactly that, access lists that are referenced by a name instead of by a number. In addition to allowing an unlimited number of access lists of a particular type to be created, named access lists provide other features as well. Specifically, they allow you to delete specific entries in an access list. In numbered access lists, this is not possible. If an administrator desires to delete an entry in the access list, the entire list must be deleted and then recreated, omitting the undesired entry. As we noted earlier, any additions to an access list are automatically added to the end of the list. Named access lists do not change this property.

Not all types of access lists can be referenced by name instead of number. Table 7–2 is a list of the access list types that can be referenced by name.

The name designator for a named access list can use virtually any alphanumeric character including: [,], {, }, _, -, +, /, \, ˚, &, $, #, @, !, and ?. The one caveat to this is that the name must begin with a standard alpha character, a–z or A–Z. Names are case-sensitive, so "TEST" and "test" are different, unique names. The largest name the authors attempted to create was one containing 100 characters and the creation was successful. Realistically, 25 characters should be more than sufficient for creating a meaningful access list name designation. Below is an example of a named extended IP access list and is the equivalent of the access list presented previously in the sample configuration code.

```
Interface serial 0
 Ip access-group test in
 !
ip access-list extended test
 permit tcp any any established
 permit udp any host 160.10.2.100 eq 53
 permit ip any host 160.20.2.101
 permit icmp any any echo-reply
```

Table 7–2

Protocols That Can Be Used with Named Access Lists

Protocol
Apollo Domain
IP (All forms)
IPX (All forms)
ISO CLNS
NetBIOS IPX
Source-route Bridging NetBIOS

Except for the lack of an access list number preceding each list entry, note that code above looks identical to the numbered access list example in the access list configuration sample. If we wanted to delete one of the entries in the list, we could do so, as shown in the code here:

```
2514# show access-list test
Extended IP access-list test
  permit tcp any any established
  permit udp any gt 1023 host 160.10.2.100 ep 53
  permit ip any host 160.10.2.101
  permit icmp any any echo-reply
2514# config term
2514(config)# ip access-list extended test
2514(config-int)# no permit icmp any any echo-reply
2514(config-int)# exit
2514(config)# exit
2514# show access-list
Extended IP access-list test
  permit tcp any any established
  permit udp any gt 1023 host 160.10.2.100 eq 53
  permit ip any host 160.10.2.101
2514#
```

This would not be possible with a numbered access list, as shown in the next block of code, which shows an attempted deletion of a specific entry using a numbered access list:

```
2514# show access-list 101
access-list 101 permit tcp any any established
access-list 101 permit udp any gt 1023 host 160.10.2.100 ep 53
access-list 101 permit ip any host 160.10.2.101
access-list 101 permit icmp any any echo-reply
2514# conf term
2514(config)# no access-list 101 permit icmp any any echo-reply
2514(config)# exit
2514# show access-list 101
2514#
```

Notice that the entire access list has been deleted.

Editing Access Lists

Although named access lists allow an administrator to selectively delete entries in an access list, they do not allow the selective addition of entries. If an administrator needs to add entries into the access list in specific positions, the entire list must be deleted and recreated with the new entries. Although this process sounds very time-consuming, the use of the TFTP protocol can greatly reduce the administrative burden.

The TFTP protocol enables an administrator to load commands from a text file saved on a remote device running the TFTP service. TFTP daemons are available for both Windows and Unix platforms. In fact, a TFTP daemon for Windows platforms is available on the Cisco web site at:

```
http://www.cisco.com/public/sw-center/sw-other.shtml
```

To see how this can be advantageous when managing access lists, let's return to our example in Figure 7–1. Suppose that we wanted to add an access list entry to the access list denying network 175.100.1.0/24 access to the destination IP address 160.10.2.101. Notice that this is the same destination IP address referenced in the current third line of the access list. Because the third line permits all IP addresses access to this host, it is necessary to add the deny entry before the existing third entry for it to have any affect. We could accomplish this by creating a text file on the machine functioning as our TFTP server, which is listed below. In this example, we assume that the access list is currently applied to the serial 0 interface as in the access list configuration sample and in Figure 7–1.

```
Acl.txt
interface serial 0
no ip access-group 101 in
no access-list 101
exit
access-list 101 permit tcp any any established
access-list 101 permit udp any gt 1023 host 160.10.2.100 eq 53
access-list 101 deny ip 175.100.1.0 0.0.0.255 host 160.10.2.101
access-list 101 permit ip any host 160.10.2.101
access-list 101 permit icmp any any echo-reply
interface serial 0
ip access-group 101 in
```

We place the code shown above on our TFTP server in a directory called /tftp/upload and then issue the commands displayed below. Assume for the purposes of this example that the IP address of our TFTP server is 10.1.1.1. Typed entries are shown in bold.

```
2514# config net
Host or network configuration file [host]? host
Address of remote host [255.255.255.255]? 10.1.1.1
Name of configuration file [router-conf]? Acl.txt
Configure using acl.txt from 10.1.1.1? [confirm]
Loading acl.txt from 10.1.1.1 (via e0): !
[OK-21/128975  bytes]
2514#
```

Several points are worth noting from the above code. First, notice that the commands are the *exact* commands that would be entered into the command line of the router if we were entering them at the router prompt; this is required. If the syntax of the commands is incorrect, the operation will fail. For this reason, we recommend creating a standard access list template that you verify is correct. Then all that is necessary is to change the appropriate access list entries to create additional files. It is recommended that you keep a separate file for every access list in use on your network. This makes it easy to manipulate any access list should you need to do so in the future. The initial investment in time up front will pay off down the road.

The second point to note is that the access list is first removed from the serial interface before deleting and the recreating each of the entries. This is *highly* recommended. According to the Cisco literature, if a nonexistent access list is applied to an interface, the effect will be the same as if no access list were applied to the interface. Although in some instances the authors have found this to be true, in other cases we have found that leaving an access list applied to an interface while deleting and recreating the access list can have unpredictable results, including blocking legitimate packets. If the access list happened to be applied to the interface where communication between the router and the TFTP server occurs, the results could be disastrous. It is always safer to remove the access list before editing and re-application.

Of course, no packets would be blocked for the short duration when the access list is removed from the interface. The process of transferring the configuration file via TFTP is usually extremely quick, normally only a few seconds, and it is extremely unlikely that an attack could transpire during this small window of time. For the truly paranoid, however, the interface could be administratively shutdown prior to this procedure and then enabled by adding "shutdown" prior to editing the access list and "no shutdown" after editing the list without removing the access list from the interface. Of course, if the interface is being used to transfer the configuration file to the router, this is not an option.

Access List Processing Revisited

The TFTP procedure described in the previous section is necessary because of the top-down processing of access lists. If we simply added a deny entry to the access list, it would be automatically placed at the end of the list. The deny would never be reached because any packets matching the criteria "source network 175.100.1.0, destination address 160.10.2.101" would be matched by the statement "any network, destination address 160.10.2.101" higher in the list. We illustrate this in Figure 7–4.

Figure 7–4
An example showing
how access list
statements should be
ordered.

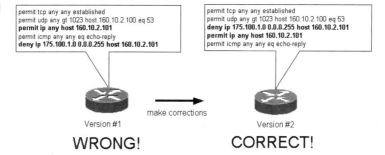

```
permit tcp any any established
permit udp any gt 1023 host 160.10.2.100 eq 53
permit ip any host 160.10.2.101
permit icmp any any eq echo-reply
deny ip 175.100.1.0 0.0.0.255 host 160.10.2.101
```

```
permit tcp any any established
permit udp any gt 1023 host 160.10.2.100 eq 53
deny ip 175.100.1.0 0.0.0.255 host 160.10.2.101
permit ip any host 160.10.2.101
permit icmp any any eq echo-reply
```

make corrections

Version #1

Version #2

WRONG!

CORRECT!

Notice the difference between the access list in version #1 and version #2 in Figure 7–4. Pay particular attention to the entries in bold. In version #1, the last entry will never be reached because the previous entry in bold matches all the packets matched by the last entry. This situation is remedied in version #2 of the access list, and the new entry is placed before the original entry.

Placement of Entries in an Access List

Figure 7–4 serves to point out a valuable rule when configuring access lists: Configure the access list so that the most specific entries are listed first.

If we examine Figure 7–4, we can see that the added entry is more specific than the original. What do we mean by this? Well, let's examine the protocol first. In this case, they are both IP. If one had been TCP instead of IP, however, the TCP entry would be more specific. All TCP packets are also IP packets, but not all IP packets are TCP packets. Thus, entries matching on IP packet are more general than packets matching on TCP packets. The same holds true for UDP and ICMP packets as well. Although all UDP and ICMP packets are also IP packets, not all IP packets are UDP or ICMP.

As a point of analogy, imagine a security guard in a building whose job it is to stop (filter) all people from entering the building carrying tan briefcases. Assume there is another guard whose job it is to stop (filter) all people carrying briefcases of any kind. The security guard that stops people carrying tan briefcases has a more specific job than the guard who stops people carrying just any old briefcase. In this scenario, if the guard stopping people carrying tan briefcases is placed deep in the building and the guard stopping people with any briefcase is placed at the entrance, no people carrying tan briefcases will ever reach the second guard. He has no job to perform because all the people with briefcases will be stopped at the entrance. In this analogy, the tan briefcases would be TCP packets and the generic briefcases would be IP packets.

Returning to our comparison of the two entries in Figure 7–4, we next look at the source address. The original entry states it will match any address in the source address. The new entry states it will match packets from the 175.100.1.0/24 network, which is certainly more specific than the original with regard to source address. Also, if we examine the destination address, we see they are the same. Thus, we know that the new packet is more specific because the *Internet protocol* (IP) is the same, the source address is more specific, and the destination address is the same.

If the destination address for the new packet had been a different host, the decision would have been arbitrary. If the destination address for the new packet was less specific than the original, such as the entire 160.10.2.0/24 subnet, the decision would also have been arbitrary because the two access list entries would block different types of packets. It is only important to follow the rule of placing more specific entries first in the access list when there is in fact an entry that matches at least some of the packets that would be matched by another access list entry. Here we illustrate several examples of this principle:

```
Address 10.0.0.0/8   IS a subset of 'any'
Address 10.16.0.0/16   IS a subset of 10.0.0.0/8
Address 10.10.1.0/24   IS NOT a subset of 10.16.0.0/16
Protocol number 25 IS a subset of 'less than 1024'
Protocol number 25 IS NOT a subset of 'range 100-115'
```

In general, we can see that address range #1 is a subset of address range #2 if it falls completely within the range of address range #2. All subnets of 10.16.0.0 are also subnets of 10.0.0.0. In the same way, we can see that all subnets of 10.10.1.0 are not subnets of 10.16.0.0. The examples later in this chapter will serve to reinforce the concepts presented in this section.

Representing Address Ranges—Using Wildcard Masks

We turn now to a discussion of one of the most misunderstood access list topics, wildcard masks. Cisco access lists provide a way to specify a network range in a permit or deny statement through the use of wildcard masks, which are very similar to subnet masks. Recall that a subnet mask is used to determine how many bits of an IP address represent the subnet portion. Essentially, the subnet mask determines which bits are relevant to determine the subnet mask. A binary 1 in the subnet mask indicates that the corresponding bit in the IP address is part of the subnet range. A binary 0 in the subnet mask indicates that the corresponding bit in the IP address is part of the host range.

Similarly, a wildcard mask is used to determine which bits are relevant when examining packets to determine if they match a specific access list entry. When using a wildcard mask, a binary 0 represents a "match" condition and a binary 1 represents a "don't care" condition. That is, if a binary 0 appears in a bit in the wildcard mask, the corresponding bit in the IP address portion of the access list entry must be matched. If a binary 1 appears in a bit in the wildcard mask, the corresponding bit in the IP address can be either 1 or 0. The binary 1 in the wildcard mask indicates we "don't care" what the corresponding bit in the IP address is.

Although IP addresses are normally represented in a decimal format, it is important to convert the IP address and mask to binary in order to fully understand the process that occurs. A brief illustration should serve to illustrate the use of wildcard masks. Assume that we wanted to accept all IP packets from subnet 10.10.0.0 255.255.0.0 to the host using IP address 160.10.2.100 and wanted to block all other IP packets. Our first attempt to create the access list is shown here:

```
2514(config)#access-list 101 permit ip 10.10.0.0 0.0.0.0
  160.10.2.100 0.0.0.0
2514(config)#exit
2514#sh access-list 101
Extended IP access list 101
 permit ip host 10.10.0.0 host 160.10.2.100
```

Notice that we have created the access list using the wildcard mask 0.0.0.0. When the "show access list" command is issued, the router displays this as a "host" entry, meaning that the source network address 10.10.0.0 is matched exactly. In the above code, only IP packets with a source address of 10.10.0.0 are allowed access to IP address 160.10.2.100. Note that all other source addresses are denied, including 10.10.1.1, 10.10.1.2, and so on. This is not what we wanted. We wanted to allow *all* hosts on the 10.10.0.0/16 network, not host 10.10.0.0.

Based on the example code above, we want to create a wildcard mask that matches the first two octets "10.10" but doesn't care about the last two octets "0.0." In other words, we want to create an access list that allows any value to appear in the last two octets. Earlier we stated that in a wildcard mask, a binary 0 indicates a match condition and a binary 1 indicates a don't care condition. Applying this logic we create the access list:

```
2514(config)#access-list 101 permit ip 10.10.0.0 0.0.255.255
  160.10.2.100 0.0.0.0
2514(config)#exit
2514#sh access-list 101
Extended IP access list 101
 permit ip 10.10.0.0 0.0.255.255 host 160.10.2.100
```

Notice the entry in bold shows the new wildcard mask that we have created. The last two octets contain all binary 1 values (equivalent to decimal 255), indicating that any value may appear in the last two octets. This corresponds to matching IP addresses between 10.10.0.0 and 10.10.255.255, which is the result we were looking for.

A point of interest is that because the entire last two octets are specified as binary 1 values in the wildcard mask, we could specify *any* values for these two octets in the address portion and would achieve the same results. For example, we could specify the access list entry:

```
2514#config terminal
2514(config)#access-list 101 permit ip 10.10.0.0 0.0.255.255 host
   160.10.100
2514#show access-list 101
Extended IP access list 101
 permit ip 10.10.0.0 0.0.255.255 host 160.10.100.1


2514#config terminal
2514#(config)#$ 102 permit ip 10.10.250.129 0.0.255.255 host
   160.10.100.1
2514(config)#exit
2514#show access-list 102
Extended IP access list 102
 permit ip 10.10.0.0 0.0.255.255 host 160.10.100.1
```

Pay particular attention to the entries in bold. Notice that in access list 102 we entered 10.10.250.129 for the source IP address. However, when we issue a "show access list 102" command, the result is identical to access list 101. No matter what value is entered in the IP address portion of the access list, if the corresponding bit in the wildcard mask is a binary 1, the IOS automatically converts that bit in the IP address portion of the access list entry to a binary 0. Because a binary 1 in the wildcard mask means we "don't care" about the corresponding bit in the IP address, it doesn't matter whether the bit in the IP address is a binary 1 or a binary 0. The IOS displays the "don't care" bit positions as a binary 0 in the IP address portion to avoid confusion.

Note that we have not needed to convert our decimal numbers to binary because we have used numbers that are either all binary 1's (decimal 255) or all binary 0's (decimal 0). In the next section, we will use numbers that necessitate converting our decimal values to binary.

Wildcard Mask Examples

Several examples of wildcard masks are illustrated below.

NOTE: In the examples that follow, it is assumed that we already know
which subnet we are trying to filter and are trying to determine the
wildcard mask.

```
Network address: 175.100.10.0/24
Network mask: 255.255.255.0
```

Question: What is the wildcard mask?

Answer: Convert the network mask to binary. Invert the bits so that a
binary 1 becomes a 0 and a binary 0 becomes a 1. The result is the wildcard mask.

```
255.255.255.0 = 11111111.11111111.11111111.00000000
------------------------- invert
    0.0.0.255 = 00000000.00000000.00000000.11111111
```

As we can see, the wildcard mask is 0.0.0.255. We can verify this by performing the access list match operation on the original network address:

```
    0.0.0.255 = 00000000.00000000.00000000.11111111
175.100.10.10 = 10111001.01100110.00001010.00001010
------------------------- apply match
 175.100.10.x = 10111001.01100110.00001010.xxxxxxxx
```

We have applied the wildcard match algorithm that states that a binary
0 is a "match" condition and a binary 1 is a "don't care" condition. Any
value may appear in the bits where an x is shown, indicating that any host
on the 175.100.10.0 subnet will be matched by the access list entry.

Let's examine a more complicated example:

```
Network address: 175.100.10.0/19
Network mask: 255.255.224.0
```

Question: What is the wildcard mask?

```
255.255.224.0 = 11111111.11111111.11100000.00000000
------------------------- invert
   0.0.31.255 = 00000000.00000000.00011111.11111111
```

Now that we computed the wildcard mask, let's verify its composition:

```
0.0.31.255    = 00000000.00000000.00011111.11111111
175.100.0.0   = 10111001.01100110.00000000.00000000
-------------------------- apply match
175.100.0.x   = 10111001.01100110.000xxxxx.xxxxxxxx
```

Again, the x values indicate where any value can occur. For example, the range of addresses matched by this wildcard mask would be

```
Begin: 175.100.0.0    = 10111001.01100110.00000000.00000000
End: 175.100.31.255   = 10111001.01100110.00011111.11111111
```

along with all values in-between.

Up to this point, we have known the subnet we wished to filter in our examples. We now examine a situation in which only a range of subnets are known and will attempt to determine the wildcard mask.

In this example, assume that we want our access list entry to match only the following subnets:

```
175.100.8.0/24
175.100.9.0/24
175.100.10.0/24
175.100.11.0/24
175.100.12.0/24
175.100.13.0/24
175.100.14.0/24
```

Instead of listing each subnet individually in its own access list entry, we would like to specify a single access list entry that matches all these subnets.

We begin by examining the beginning and ending subnet numbers in binary format. We will place a series of x's to indicate where the host bits are, which are not relevant for determining the wildcard mask.

```
175.100.8.0   = 10111001.01100110.00001000.xxxxxxxx
175.100.14.0  = 10111001.01100110.00001110.xxxxxxxx
```

We know that the first two octets are the same for each of the subnets listed and that the last octet is used for host addresses, so we can concentrate on the third octet only.

Our first reaction might be that we don't care about the lowest-order three bits of the third octet. Using this logic, our network mask would be

```
0.0.7.255     = 00000000.00000000.00000111.11111111
```

If we look closely, however, we see that not only does this match subnets 175.100.8.0/24 through 175.100.8.14.0/24, but it also matches 175.100.15.0/24 . We do not want to match the 175.100.15.0/24 subnet, so the lowest order bit in the third octet should not be included.

NOTE: The bits increase in order from right to left. Each bit indicates 2 raised to the *n*th power where n equals the bit position minus 1. The first bit is the farthest bit on the right of the octet in position 1, so the value is 2 to the power of 0 (1−1=0), or 1. The second bit is the second bit from the right of the octet and the value is 2 to the first power (2−1=1), or 2. The numbers increase as powers of 2 from right to left: 4, 8, 16, 32, 64 and 128. If you add all these numbers together, you get 255, which is why the decimal equivalent of all binary 1's for an octet is 255.

This looks simple enough to fix. We decide to match the lowest-order bit in the third octet but not the bits in the second and third positions. The following mask is the result:

```
0.0.6.255 = 00000000.00000000.00000110.11111111
```

This looks a little better. The subnet 175.100.15.0/24 will not be matched by this wildcard mask. However, now we have another problem. By placing a binary 0 in the lowest order bit in the third octet, we are saying that this bit must "match" the bit in the address we specify in the access list entry. The address to be used is the beginning address in the range we are attempting to summarize.

```
Access-list 101 permit ip 175.100.8.0 0.0.6.255 any
175.100.8.0 = 10111001.01100110.00001000.00000000
```

We can see that the lowest-order bit in the third octet of the IP address portion is a binary 0. This particular bit corresponds to 2 raised to the 0 power, a 1. Because only packets whose IP addresses match this bit will be allowed, the following subnets would be denied:

```
175.100.9.0  = 10111001.01100110.00001001.00000000
175.100.11.0 = 10111001.01100110.00001011.00000000
175.100.13.0 = 10111001.01100110.00001101.00000000
175.100.15.0 = 10111001.01100110.00001111.00000000
```

Notice that all these subnets have a binary 1 in the lowest-order bit of the third octet. This bit does not match the first bit specified by our address:

```
175.100.8.0 = 10111001.01100110.00001000.00000000
```

Therefore, all the IP packets from odd numbered subnets, including 175.100.15.0, would be denied. Again, this is not what we want.

NOTE: This example is, however, useful to remember if you ever have to filter strange address ranges like "all even subnets" or "all odd subnets."

We have two ways of solving our problem:

1. Explicitly deny the addresses that fall outside of our range.
2. Determine the correct ranges needed and summarize only the specific addresses we wish to match.

In this particular case, the first option is the easiest of the two. All we need to do is create an explicit deny statement for the 175.100.15.0/24 subnet and then allow the remaining addresses in the range:

```
Access-list 101 deny ip 175.100.15.0 0.0.0.255 any
Access-list 101 permit ip 175.100.8.0 0.0.7.255 any
```

Although the second access list entry would permit subnet 175.100.15.0/24, we are explicitly denying this entry, so no packets matching that subnet will ever be allowed by the second entry.

In this particular case it was fairly easy to spot which subnet needed to be denied. Many instances occur in which it is not as obvious. In most cases, the range is larger and the number of individual subnets that would have to be denied make finding the correct ranges a more attractive option.

Determining the correct subnet ranges can be done in many ways. Appendix A of this book contains an algorithm developed by the authors. This algorithm is used to produce the following wildcard mask ranges for the subnet range 175.100.8.0/24 through 175.100.14.0/24 (a much more complicated example is also included in Appendix A):

```
Access-list 101 permit ip 175.100.8.0 0.0.3.255 any
Access-list 101 permit ip 175.100.12.0 0.0.1.255 any
Access-list 101 permit ip 175.100.14.0 0.0.0.255 any
```

The first access list entry permits subnets 175.100.8.0/24 through 175.100.11.0/24, the second entry permits subnets 175.100.12.0/24 through 175.100.13.0/24, and the last entry permits subnet 175.100.14.0/24.

The example in Appendix A summarizes the subnet range 175.100.38.0/24 through 175.100.92.0/24 , as shown.

```
Access-list 101 permit ip 175.100.38.0 0.0.1.255 any
Access-list 101 permit ip 175.100.40.0 0.0.7.255 any
Access-list 101 permit ip 175.100.48.0 0.0.15.255 any
Access-list 101 permit ip 175.100.64.0 0.0.15.255 any
Access-list 101 permit ip 175.100.80.0 0.0.7.255 any
Access-list 101 permit ip 175.100.88.0 0.0.3.255 any
Access-list 101 permit ip 175.100.92.0 0.0.0.255 any
```

We can select an entry at random and show that the values fall within the specified range. We choose the fourth entry:

```
Access-list 101 permit ip 175.100.64.0 0.0.15.255 any


175.100.64.0 = 10111001.01100110.01000000.00000000
  0.0.15.255 = 00000000.00000000.00001111.11111111
               10111001.01100110.0100xxxx.xxxxxxxx
```

Because the lowest four order bits of the third octet are "don't care" bits, this represents numbers 64 through 79, which as we can see falls within the range 38 through 92. Similar checks can be performed on each entry to determine that they all fall within the specified range.

Additional Wildcard Mask Example

For the curious, we will present an example using a standard network mask in an access list. Note that the example below is *not* something you would normally want to do. If you see a configuration like the one below in the real world, it is probably a mistake.

This is the same example presented above, except that the network mask 255.255.224.0 is used instead of the wildcard mask:

```
255.255.224.0 = 11111111.11111111.11100000.00000000
175.100.10.0 = 10111001.01100110.00001010.00000000
----------------------- apply match
    x.x.10.0 = xxxxxxxx.xxxxxxxx.xxx01010.00000000
```

The x positions indicate where any value can occur, so the range is:

```
Begin: 0.0.10.0   = 00000000.00000000.00001010.00000000
End: 255.255.234.0 = 11111111.11111111.11101010.00000000
```

and all values in-between.

Note that the last octet must always be zero and the values in the second octet range between 10 and 234. This type of match is only useful if you attempt to filter a certain range of hosts or subnets originating from *any* network. In most cases, this would not be useful. Most often the use of a traditional network mask of this type in an access list is an error on the part of the administrator and is not intentional.

Wildcard Mask Shortcuts

You may have already noticed that there is a shortcut to determining what the wildcard mask is from the subnet mask without converting to binary. All you need to do is subtract the subnet mask number in decimal for each octet from 255 and the result is the wildcard mask. For example:

```
Network mask = 255.255.224.0
Wildcard mask = ?
1st octet = 255-network mask = 255-255 = 0
2nd octet = 255-network mask = 255-255 = 0
3rd octet = 255-network mask = 255-224 = 31
4th octet = 255-network mask = 255-0 = 255
Wildcard mask:
1st octet = 0
2nd octet = 0
3rd octet = 31
4th octet = 255
Result = 0.0.31.255
```

Use of this method is a quick and easy way to determine the wildcard mask. However, it is essential that the reader understand *why* it works, not just *how*.

Wildcard Masks Concluded

In later chapters, we will return to the concept of wildcard masking again as we continue to discuss access lists. The central point to remember is that a binary 0 is a compare and a binary 1 is an unconditional match when implementing wildcard masks. This will become increasingly important to remember as we examine other protocols with other addresses formats. It is also crucial that you have a firm grasp of binary representation for the network address and wildcard mask. The examples presented in the remainder of this chapter will serve to reinforce these concepts.

Packet Filtering Technology

Before we continue a detailed discussion of IP access lists, it is important to say a few words about packet filtering technology. In concept, a packet filter is fairly simple. It provides a method that specifies which packets are permitted access through a device and which packets are denied by examining information contained within the packet. Typically, a packet filter is an ordered list of statements allowing or denying packets based on various criteria. We have seen several examples earlier in this chapter using Cisco access lists as packet filters.

The criteria used to permit or deny packets are normally layer 3 address and/or layer 4 port information. Most packet filters are not capable of examining information above layer 4, although some implementations do understand higher-layer information for standard applications such as FTP, SMTP, Unix R-commands, and so on.

Traditionally, Cisco IP packet filters have been capable of interpreting packet information only up to layer 4. In the most current revisions of Cisco router code, new types of IP access lists enable the filtering of higher-layer information for many common applications. We will refer to these IP access lists as next-generation access lists and will be examined in much greater detail in Chapter 8, "Advanced Cisco Router Security Features."

The Role of Packet Filters

Packet filtering provides an important role in securing many networks and many devices can implement packet filters. In addition to Cisco routers, many other vendors offer software that allows you to add packet filtering capabilities to nearly all operating systems. By applying this software to a traditional host operating system such as Unix or Windows NT, users can create a firewall. The term firewall is often used in computer network security to define a system placed between trusted resources and untrusted resources that restricts access between the two. A firewall would likely be placed between your internal data network and the Internet.

A packet filter allows you to specify certain criteria that a packet must meet to be permitted through a network device. Packets that do not meet the designated criteria are denied, and packets that are not explicitly denied or permitted are denied by default. The implicit deny of what is not permitted is an important security feature and one that is employed by nearly all modern packet filtering systems. The implicit deny can be overridden, but it is normally on by default. As we have seen, Cisco access lists implement this feature.

Packet Filters Defined

A packet filter can be thought of as the expression of a security policy in computer language. For example, a security policy might be expressed in English language by the following statements:

```
Allow inbound Web traffic to our Web server
Allow all outbound traffic
(implicit deny of everything else)
```

An adaptation of this policy to a language that a computer can understand might look something like the following:

```
Permit IP inbound from any to Web-server protocol equal http
Permit IP inbound from any to any equal return-traffic
Permit IP outbound from any to any
(implicit deny all)
```

NOTE: The term "any" functions as a wildcard, representing any IP address.

A point worth noting is that in our pseudo-language we have specified an entry that has no corollary in the English language security policy. Line 2 is necessary to permit the return traffic for sessions initiated from the inside. If this line is not added, return traffic would not be permitted through our packet filter. Packets could flow to the outside world, but we would not be able to accept any response, which would not be very useful because network conversations are essentially bidirectional. Even when a host is only receiving data, in the majority of cases the sending station will need to obtain acknowledgments from the receiving station that the data sent has been received and understood. In this regard, a network conversation between hosts is much like a telephone conversation. Even if only one person is speaking, the listener must occasionally say something to acknowledge they have heard and understood what the speaker is saying.

As we have seen, Cisco access list language is very similar to our computer language example. One major difference between the Cisco implementation and the above pseudo-language is the requirement to use the layer 3 address instead of the device name. This policy implemented in Cisco ACL language would be

```
Access-list 101 permit TCP any host a.b.c.d eq http
Acccss-list 101 permit TCP any any established
(implicit deny all)
interface serial 0
IP access-group 101 in
```

NOTE: The `a.b.c.d` is used merely as placeholder to indicate where an actual IP address would reside. (In an actual implementation, an IP address would be used.)

Note a few things from this example. First, there is no statement permitting outbound packets; it's not necessary because Cisco access lists are applied in a particular direction on an interface. The direction is important because it refers to the direction of packets from the routers' perspective. In this example, the packets are arriving at the serial 0 interface from another router, so they are arriving "inbound." If the packets are leaving the routers serial 0 interface, the access list would be applied "outbound." In the above example, because the ACL is applied inbound, it does not affect any traffic in the outbound direction (traffic leaving the serial interface).

Also notice the use of the keyword "established." This keyword is the Cisco method for allowing return traffic. It checks for the existence of an ACK or RST flag in the TCP packet. Recall from Chapter 4, "TCP and UDP," that these flags are used by TCP for flow control purposes. If one of these bits is turned on, it usually means that the packet is part of an ongoing conversation. We use the caveat "usually" because it is fairly easy for an attacker to write code to manipulate this flag and send packets with the ACK or RST bit turned on that are not part of a legitimate ongoing conversation. As such, the use of the established keyword is by no means a foolproof method for determining whether a packet is part of an existing conversation or not.

Stateless and Stateful Packet Filtering

It is worth noting at this point that traditional Cisco ACLs examine each packet as if it is a stand-alone entity and cannot determine if the packet is actually part of an ongoing TCP/UDP conversation. Traditional ACLs have no mechanism for checking to see if an inbound TCP packet with the ACK bit set is actually part of an existing conversation. This type of packet filtering is called "stateless" because the router does not maintain information on the status or state of existing conversations. We will see in later sections that context-based ACLs *do* maintain information about the state of existing TCP/UDP conversations and are thus able to determine whether a packet is part of an existing conversation or not. Let's examine Figure 7–5.

Figure 7–5
A firewall
maintaining
information about
the state of existing
TCP/IP conversations

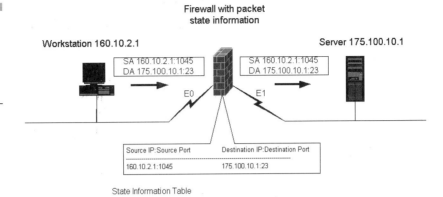

State Information Table

The firewall shown in Figure 7–5 maintains information about the state of existing connections. Once the initial three-way handshake is completed between host 160.10.2.1 and the telnet server 175.100.10.1, the router places an entry into a state table recording the source and destination addresses and ports. Incoming packets are checked to insure that they are part of the existing session. Information about both TCP and UDP conversations are recorded in the state table.

A traditional access list does not maintain information about the state of existing connections. It is only capable of checking for the presence of the ACK or RST bit to attempt to determine if incoming packets are part of a legitimate conversation by using the established keyword. No check of this type would be possible with UDP conversations because UDP is a connectionless protocol and no flags in the protocol header indicate whether it is part of an existing connection or not. We will further discuss this and other limitations of packet filter technology in the next section.

Packet Filter Limitations

In this section, we will discuss four packet filter limitations:

- IP address spoofing
- Stateless packet inspection
- Limited information
- Human error

IP Address Spoofing

The first limitation that should be noted is the need to filter by address. This means that packet filters are vulnerable to someone impersonating an address so that the packets sent from their machine appear to have originated from a machine you trust. Unfortunately, this is a fairly easy procedure. The upside is that in order to actually complete a connection, the originator of the packets must be able to know in advance what the responses will be from the end-station. Return packets will not be sent to the original impersonator's machine but to the legitimate machine whose network address the attacker is impersonating. The difficulty of carrying out this process often depends on the attacker's ability to guess what sequence numbers will be used during the initial TCP three-way handshake (and this in turn depends on the manner in which the operating system of the attacked host implements the underlying TCP stack).

Recall from Chapter 4, "TCP and UDP," that there is an initial handshake process that must take place between hosts before a TCP conversation can occur. It is during this phase that the attacker would have to guess the initial sequence number sent in reply to the SYN request from the attacker's machine. Because the SYN-ACK reply is routed to the legitimate owner of the spoofed IP address, the attacking machine would never see the reply. This necessitates guessing the initial sequence number contained in the SYN-ACK packet so that the ACK sent from the attacker's machine would contain the correct information to complete the three-way handshake. This may sound difficult, but numerous programs on the Internet can automate this process successfully.

Additionally, a *denial of service* (DoS) attack is somewhat easy to accomplish by spoofing the originating address. In a DoS attack, an attacker does not attempt to actually complete a connection with the attacked host, but instead merely sends special packets to the host in an attempt to temporarily disrupt the host's capability to function. The attacker will generally spoof the originating address in these packets, so it is nearly impossible to trace them back to the actual attacker's machine. Preventing this kind of attack with traditional packet filters is very difficult.

The Cisco IOS provides mechanisms to block the more common DoS attacks, and we will cover these in detail in Chapter 8, "Advanced Cisco Router Security Features." (Note that this limitation applies to protocols other than IP as well, but IP is by far the most common protocol used in attacks due to its widespread use on many networks, especially the Internet).

Stateless Packet Inspection

As noted earlier, another limitation of traditional access lists is that they are incapable of detecting whether a packet is truly part of an existing upper-layer conversation. Normally the access list examines each packet as a stand-alone entity. As mentioned above, traditional access lists *do* provide a mechanism for checking individual packets to determine if *it is* part of an existing conversation through the use of the established keyword. However, this check is easily spoofed by a skilled attacker and will only deter the most casual offenders. Additionally, the established keyword check is only useful for the TCP protocol and is unavailable for UDP conversations.

Limited Information

Another limitation of traditional access lists is their limited capability to examine information above the IP layer. Extended access lists have the capability to look at certain information in the layer 4 headers, but only in a very simplistic sense. Traditional access lists have no way of examining information above layer 4 and are incapable of securely handling protocols that use unpredictable layer 4 information, such as FTP. Both of these limitations are addressed by next-generation access lists. We will examine the new access list enhancements developed by Cisco in Chapter 8.

Human Error

Last but not least, we can add human error to the list of potential access list problems. Human error isn't exactly an access list limitation, but it's certainly worth mentioning. Many times, errors in the creation or application of an access list lead to security holes. The most common human errors, although not the only ones, are:

- Failure to create access list entries in the correct order
- Failure to apply the access list to an interface in the correct direction
- Failure to apply the access list to an interface
- Failure to add new access list entries in the correct order

It is important that you be aware of these potential pitfalls as you develop a greater understanding of Cisco access lists. In the next section, we discuss a few key principles to keep in mind when configuring Cisco access lists.

Configuration Principles

We will conclude this section by examining the key details that are important to remember when configuring Cisco access lists.

TOP-DOWN PROCESSING   Cisco access lists are evaluated in a sequential fashion beginning with the first entry. As soon as a match is encountered, the access list processing is completed and no more entries are considered. Therefore, it is important to put more specific entries toward the top of the access list.

IMPLICIT DENY ALL   There is always an implicit "deny all" entry at the end of the access list. Thus, any packet that does not explicitly match one of the access list entries will automatically be denied. This behavior can be overridden by placing an explicit "permit all" as the last entry in the list.

NEW ENTRIES ARE ADDED TO THE BOTTOM   Any new access list entries are automatically added to the bottom of the list. This fact is important to remember when attempting to make modifications to an existing access list. If modifications are necessary for an entry in an access list, it may be necessary to delete and recreate the entire access list. This process can be mediated by creating the access list off-line in a text file and using TFTP to upload any changes to existing access lists.

SEPARATE CREATION AND APPLICATION PROCESSES   The actual application of an access list is done on an interface or subinterface basis. The creation of an access list is done before an the list is applied to an interface. Access lists reside in the configuration file and not be applied to any interface. Similarly, an access list that has not been defined can be applied to an interface (see next paragraph).

UNDEFINED ACCESS LISTS   If an access list that has not been created is referenced in the configuration, the effect will be the same as if the access list contained a "permit all" entry. In other words, all traffic will be permitted. We have found this principle does not always hold true, however. We *strongly* recommend that you never apply an access list to an interface unless the access list has been created. We also recommend removing the access list from the interface before making any changes to the access list.

These principles will be discussed further as we illustrate specific examples throughout this chapter.

Traditional IP Access Lists

Traditional IP access lists are available in two varieties: standard and extended. Standard access lists allow filtering by source address only and are thus very limited in functionality. Extended access lists allow filtering by source address, destination address, and upper-layer protocols. We examine standard access lists first.

Standard Access Lists

The basic format of a standard IP access list is:

```
Access-list [1-99] [permit|deny] [ip address] [mask] [log]
```

NOTE: The log keyword is available only in IOS 11.3 and later versions.

Each access list is given a unique number that is used to inform the IOS of the type of access list you are defining. This number is also used in all subsequent references to the access list. Standard IP access lists are defined within the range 1–99. In IOS version 11.2, named access lists were introduced, allowing you to define names for your access lists. These lists were created so you can delete specific entries in the access list without recreating the entire list. Additional entries, however, are still added to the end of the access list.

Standard IP access lists allow filtering by source IP address only. In the examples that follow, we will use the following diagram as a reference point, as shown in Figure 7–6.

Suppose in Figure 7–6 that we want to allow only clients with node addresses .10 and .11 on segment 1 to have access to servers on segment 2. How would we accomplish this? Our initial configuration is shown here:

```
Interface ethernet 1
 Ip access-group 1 out

Ip access-list 1 permit 160.10.1.10 0.0.0.0
Ip access-list 1 permit 160.10.1.11 0.0.0.0
```

Notice a few things from this example. First, the access list includes only two entries. Since by default everything else is denied, this might have the unintended side effect that all other IP packets are blocked to servers on segment 2. The network mask of these entries is all zeroes, indicating an

Figure 7–6
A Cisco routing
example

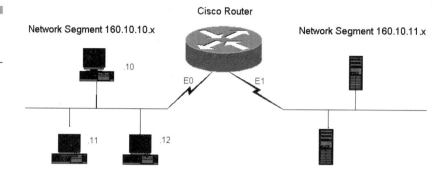

Cisco Router

Network Segment 160.10.10.x

Network Segment 160.10.11.x

.10

E0   E1

.11   .12

exact match (this is the default, so we could have avoided typing the wild-card mask in this example). Also notice how the access list is applied to the outgoing interface on *Ethernet1* (E1). The access list could have been applied to interface *Ethernet0* (E0) as an inbound access list, but this would have the undesired effect of blocking outbound traffic from *all* other hosts on segment 1; no hosts other than those specified to be permitted in the access list would be able to send packets outside of segment 1.

To see why this is so, imagine how the packets arrive at the router. A host on segment 1 with an IP address 160.10.1.12 sends a packet to the router interface E0. From the routers' perspective, this packet is incoming from the E0 segment, so it is "inbound." Therefore, it would apply the access list criteria to the packet that would then be denied by the implicit "deny all."

Keeping these ideas in mind, let's modify this access list a bit. In this modification, we assume that other network segments need access to the servers on segment 2. The modification is shown here:

```
Interface ethernet 1
 Ip access-group 1 out

Ip access-list 1 permit 160.10.1.10.0.0.0.0
Ip access-list 1 permit 160.10.1.11.0.0.0.0
Ip access-list 1 deny 160.10.1.0.0.0.0.255
Ip access-list 1 permit any
```

The small modifications change things quite a bit. First, we now have an explicit deny statement for every address on network 160.10.1.0. This may seem like a contradiction. Won't this have the effect of blocking the two nodes we wanted to allow access? The answer is no, and the reason is due to the top-down processing of access lists. Recall that earlier this was one of our configuration principles. Access lists are not "compiled," like program code, and combined. Each entry in the access list is read sequentially, from top to bottom for each packet that is processed on an interface. Once a match is reached, the remaining access list entries are ignored. This is why the order of the entries in an access list is so critical and why you should put the more specific entries first. Recall our discussion of this topic earlier in this chapter. Once the match is made for the node addresses 160.10.1.10 or 160.10.1.11, the search is completed and none of the remaining access list entries are examined.

Notice also that now we have added an explicit "permit any" to the end of this access list. This permit statement negates the normal implicit "deny all." This feature should be used with great caution. It assumes that explicit deny entries have been created for any packets you want to prevent from transiting a router interface. Because the default "deny all" has been overridden, if a packet is not explicitly denied, it would be permitted access through the router interface.

Due to the sheer volume of addresses, it is usually much easier (and more secure) to use explicit permits for the packets you know you want to allow access and deny everything else. Modifications can be made to the access list later to add additional permit entries if needed. This example is used simply to illustrate what *can* be done with an access list, not necessarily what *should* be done.

It is worth noting at this point, as you may have already noticed, that standard IP access lists are not very flexible. Because they only allow you to specify a filter by source IP address, in many cases they do not provide the necessary granularity that is required. It's a bit like trying to squash a gnat with a sledgehammer. For this reason, we will not spend much more time on standard IP access lists and will move on to the much more flexible extended IP access lists.

However, before moving on, we will point out three cases where the use of standard access lists is actually more beneficial than extended access lists:

- Limiting virtual terminal access
- Limiting SNMP access
- Routing protocol filters

LIMITING VIRTUAL TERMINAL ACCESS   Often you'll want to limit the IP addresses that are allowed to remotely access your router. This is prudent, because if someone were able to guess the user access password, they could run simple dictionary attacks against the enable password indefinitely. Once the enable password is gained, the entire router is compromised. One way in which you could limit virtual terminal access would be to apply an extended access list to every interface permitting telnet access to only a select few addresses. This quickly becomes cumbersome, however, and there is a much simpler and cleaner way. In this example, let's return to Figure 7–6 and assume we want to allow only the host 160.10.1.10 virtual terminal access to the router. A simple solution is the following:

```
Access-list 1 permit 160.10.1.10 0.0.0.0
Line vty 0 4
 Access-class 1 in
```

This prevents any host other than 160.10.1.10 from accessing the router remotely, without having to apply access lists to every interface. We can also limit the capability to telnet from the router once someone has gained virtual terminal access by applying an access list outbound to the virtual terminal ports:

```
Access-list 1 deny any
Line vty 0 4
Access-class 1 out
```

This prevents a terminal line connection to any other destination. What purpose would this serve? Well, if telnet access is gained, an attacker might not be able to compromise the enable password (assuming a good password were chosen), but they could use the router as a "jumping-off point" to attack other hosts within the network. Because a router is normally a trusted device in your network, this could be a very effective way to further compromise your internal hosts. Of course, selective access could be allowed to hosts on a certain network:

```
Access-list 1 permit 160.10.1.0 0.0.0.255
Line vty 0 4
Access-class 1 out
```

This allows terminal line connections to devices on the 160.10.1.0 network.

LIMITING SNMP ACCESS *Simple Network Management Protocol* (SNMP) is often used in a data network to manage network devices such as servers and routers. SNMP uses a very simple authentication scheme called a *community string*. The community string is essentially a password that allows an SNMP-speaking device to read and write information to an SNMP-capable device, such as a router. There are two SNMP modes, *Read-Only* (RO) and *Read-*

Write (RW). Each SNMP mode uses a different community string. Although this protocol is very useful to network administrators, it is also very dangerous. If you must enable SNMP access on your routers, it is often useful to limit the IP addresses that are allowed SNMP access. Below is an example limiting both read and write access to station 160.10.1.10:

```
Access-list 1 permit 160.10.1.10 0.0.0.0
Snmp-server community public RO 1
Snmp-server community private RW 1
```

ROUTING PROTOCOL FILTERS Another good use of standard access lists is to filter certain network ranges when redistributing routes between different routing protocols. Many times it is necessary to perform "mutual redistribution" when you need to redistribute some routes from one routing protocol into another routing protocol and a different set of routes from the second protocol into the first protocol. The danger here is that if filtering is not used, a route can get redistributed from the first protocol into the second protocol and back into the first protocol. This will obviously confuse routers about where particular routes are being originated. A simple example should suffice to drive the point home. In Figure 7–7, the router is receiving information about network 141.10.0.0 via the RIP routing protocol. The router is also running OSPF and receiving information about network 150.10.0.0 via that routing protocol.

The router in Figure 7–7 needs to announce both of these routes via both protocols. The initial configuration is quite simple. First, we need to redistribute from RIP into OSPF:

```
Router rip
Network 141.10.0.0

Router ospf 1
Network 150.10.0.0 0.0.255.255 area 0
Redistribute rip
Default metric 100
```

Figure 7–7
A router redistributing between the RIP and OSPF routing protocols

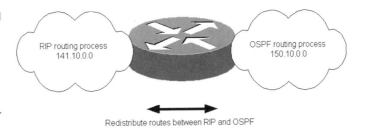

RIP routing process
141.10.0.0

OSPF routing process
150.10.0.0

Redistribute routes between RIP and OSPF

This allows the router to announce the RIP-derived 141.10.0.0 route via OSPF. However, now we must announce the 150.10.0.0 route via RIP:

```
Router rip
Network 141.10.0.0
Redistribute OSPF 1
Default-metric 3

Router ospf 1
Network 150.10.0.0 0.0.255.255 area 0
Redistribute rip
Default-metric 100
```

This configuration looks correct, but there is a problem. We previously redistributed the network 141.10.0.0 into OSPF from RIP. Now we are redistributing all OSPF routes into RIP and the 141.10.0.0 network will get distributed into RIP as an OSPF learned route. At this point, things become very confused.

The solution is to use a standard access list to specify which routes are to be allowed to be distributed into each routing protocol. Note in the following example that an access list is applied on each routing protocol:

```
Access-list 1 permit 141.10.0.0 0.0.255.255
Access-list 2 deny 141.10.0.0 0.0.255.255
Access-list 2 permit any
Router rip
Network 141.10.0.0
Redistribute OSPF 1
Default-metric 3
Distribute-list 1 out OSPF 1

Router ospf 1
Network 151.10.0.0 0.0.255.255 area 0
Redistribute RIP
Default-metric 100
Distribute-list 2 out RIP
```

In this example, we are allowing *only* network 141.10.0.0 to be distributed from RIP into OSPF. Notice that the second access list is the exact opposite of the first. It permits all routes *except* 141.10.0.0 to be distributed from OSPF into RIP. Much more complicated examples are possible, but this should give you an idea of how standard access lists are useful when mutual redistribution between routing protocols is needed. We turn next to extended IP access lists.

Extended IP Access Lists

Extended IP access lists provide much greater functionality and flexibility than standard IP access lists. Extended access lists provide the capability to filter by source address as in standard access lists, but they can also filter by destination address and upper layer protocol information. Very complex packet filters can be built with extended access lists. Extended access lists are numbered from 100–199 and their format is

```
Access-list [100-199] [permit|deny] [protocol|protocol-keyword]
    [source source-wildcard|any] [destination destination-
    wildcard|any] [precedence precedence#] [tos tos] [log]
```

A list of possible protocols includes

- IP
- TCP
- UDP
- ICMP
- IGMP
- GRE
- IGRP
- EIGRP
- IPINIP
- OSPF
- NOS
- Integer in the range 0 through 255

To match any Internet protocol, use the keyword IP. Some of the protocols, such as TCP, UDP, and ICMP, have more options that are supported by alternate syntax. We will examine the more common protocols in this section. Extended access lists allow you to filter by IP precedence and type of service fields as well, although few organizations actually use these features. Additionally, you can log access list matches by using the optional LOG keyword at the end of an access list entry. Log entries will be sent to whatever logging facility you have enabled on the router.

Let's begin our discussion of extended IP access lists with a typical Internet design. As illustrated in Figure 7–8, we have a Cisco router with three interfaces: one Serial connection to an *Internet Service Provider* (ISP), one Ethernet *Demilitarized Zone* connection (DMZ) and one Ethernet connection to an internal network.

The first step is to define our security policy. Without defining which applications we wish to permit access into and out of our network, we do not have a starting point to create our access list.

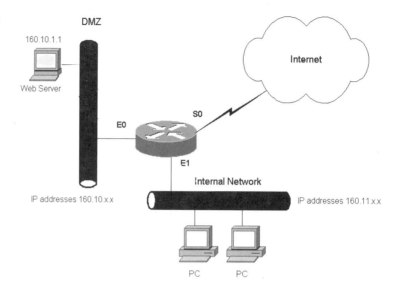

Figure 7–8
A sample Internet-connected router

We'll start with a very simple security policy:

```
Permit Internet access to our Web server for HTTP
Permit 160.11.x.x network all access out
Permit return traffic inbound
(implicit deny all)
```

We now have a simple policy definition. In the above policy, return traffic indicates traffic that is inbound from the Internet in response to a TCP/IP conversation initiated from inside hosts. Recall that TCP/IP conversations are two-way, so we must allow legitimate responses from hosts on the Internet to conversations initiated by hosts on our inside network.

The next factor that must be determined is the interface on which to place the access list and the direction we wish to filter. The general rule of thumb when determining which interface to place an access list on are

■ Place standard access lists as close to the destination as possible.
■ Place extended access lists as close to the source as possible.

The logic for these rules is fairly straightforward. A standard access list uses only the source address to determine whether a packet is to be permitted or denied. If a standard access list is placed too close to the source, packets that we would wish to include would be blocked. In Figure 7–9, we wish to prevent workstation A from accessing server number 3.

The arrows show four possible interfaces where we could place the access list. It is apparent that if we place the access list on either interface

Figure 7–9
In this example, we have four potential interfaces on which we could place the access list.

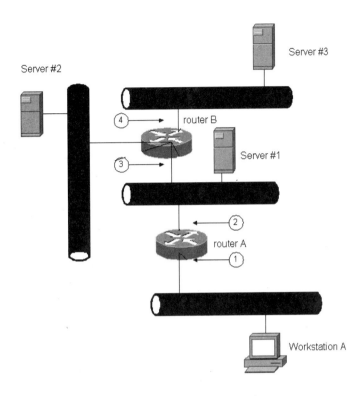

on router A, we will prevent workstation A from accessing not only server 3, but also server 1 and 2. This is more restrictive than we wished. We see that we must place the access list on router B, but which interface? If we place the access list at the interface labeled 3, we block access to server 2 as well as server 3, so again this is more restrictive than we wished. We see then that the access list should be placed on the interface labeled 4 as an outbound access list (the packets to be filtered are flowing out interface 4 towards server 3).

An extended access list, however, typically uses both source and destination IP addresses. Additionally, the access list often specifies the source and destination port as well, but let's return to the sample network shown in Figure 7–8. We stated that we wished to allow inbound traffic to our Web server if it is the HTTP protocol. How do we accomplish this?

Filtering the TCP Protocol

First, we must understand the characteristics of the HTTP protocol. We know that HTTP uses TCP as its transport protocol. We also know that HTTP uses TCP port 80. For HTTP, this is all the information that is necessary to create an appropriate access list entry. HTTP is what is called a "single channel" protocol, meaning that all packets originated by the HTTP server are identified by TCP port 80 and all information originated by the HTTP client is identified by whichever TCP port higher than 1023 the client has chosen for the connection.

Some protocols, such as FTP, use multiple port numbers to communicate between a server and a client. The port numbers used by these protocols is often dynamically chosen, making it difficult to create static filters. These protocols are called "multi-channel" and provide unique problems when creating access lists, as we shall see.

HTTP Services

Returning to our HTTP example, let's create an access list entry permitting inbound traffic if the destination address is our Web server and the TCP port is 80:

```
Access-list 101 permit TCP any 160.10.1.1 0.0.0.0 eq 80
```

Notice the use of the TCP keyword in this access list entry. As stated above, we know that HTTP uses the TCP protocol as its transport, so we know that we should use the TCP keyword. The use of TCP allows us to specify the destination port of 80.

The general format of a TCP access list entry is shown below:

```
Access-list [100-199] [permit|deny] TCP [source source-
   wildcard|any] [source port] [destination destination-
   wildcard|any]
[destination port] [precedence precedence#] [tos tos] [log]
   [established]
```

Not all the fields are necessary. The precedence and tos fields are used infrequently. The log keyword would allow us to log information about all packets matching this access list entry to either a syslog server or to the router's buffer. We discussed the use of the keyword "established" earlier. It is not used in this example because we are allowing connections initiated from the Internet access to our Web server. The initial packets inbound from the Internet hosts would not have the ACK or RST bit set, so if we used the established keyword, no Internet hosts would be able to establish communication with our Web server.

Inbound Traffic

We also stated that we want to include inbound packets if they were part of a conversation initiated by our internal hosts. In this case, we will use the `established` keyword to check inbound packets for the presence of the ACK or RST bit:

```
Access-list 101 permit TCP any 160.11.0.0 0.0.255.25 established
```

Note that in this entry we did not specify any port numbers. We do not know what protocols the hosts on our network will be using, so it is difficult to specify port numbers. However, we do know that ports are chosen by our client workstations randomly from the port range 1024–65535. Because we know that our client ports should always be in this range, we could modify our access list entry as shown below:

```
Access-list 101 permit tcp any 160.11.0.0 0.0.255.255 gt 1023
   established
```

This ensures that no packets inbound to our internal network will be accepted unless the destination port is higher than 1023. Because the vast majority of server ports are less than 1023, this provides additional security. An attacker could spoof the ACK or RST bit in a packet, allowing the packet to slip past the access list entry, but the destination port would have to be higher than 1023. This prevents spoofed packets from interfering with devices running services such as FTP, DNS, and so on that run on ports below 1024.

FTP Services

Suppose now that we decide to allow FTP services on our DMZ as well as HTTP. It sounds simple enough. Based on our HTTP example, all we need to know is the port number used by FTP, right? We know that FTP uses TCP port 21, so we create an access list entry as shown:

```
Access-list 101 permit TCP any 160.10.1.1 0.0.0.0 eq 21
```

Outside clients can reach the FTP server, however, but their session hangs when they issue any commands. Why? Well, we must understand the way the FTP protocol operates. Although it is true that FTP uses TCP port 21, it also uses TCP port 20. Port 21 is used for the transfer of FTP commands, while port 20 is used to transfer data. To complicate matters, instead of the client simply opening an additional connection to port 20, the server initiates the connection from port 20 to the clients' randomly chosen port above 1023. The client then sends the port information to the server over the established data channel. Therefore, we need to modify our access list to account for the use of this additional port number:

```
Access-list 101 permit TCP any 160.10.1.1 0.0.0.0 eq 21
Access-list 101 permit TCP any 160.10.1.1 0.0.0.0 eq 20
```

A point worth noting is that since we are allowing access from outside FTP clients to our FTP server, the access list entries are fairly simple. What if our internal clients attempted to contact FTP servers on the Internet? Recall that earlier we used the following access list entry to permit return traffic to our internal hosts:

```
Access-list 101 permit tcp any 160.11.0.0 0.0.255.255 gt 1023
    established
```

Will this entry permit our clients to use the FTP protocol? Unfortunately, the answer is no. To see why, remember that we stated previously that the FTP server initiates the return connection to the clients. This would mean that FTP servers on the Internet would initiate a new connection back to our FTP clients. Although the destination port number would be greater than 1023, the ACK or RST bit would not be set. Consequently, the packet would fail to pass the established keyword check and would be denied. We must add a new access list entry:

```
Access-list 101 permit tcp any eq 20 160.11.0.0 0.0.255.255 gt
    1023
Access-list 101 permit tcp any 160.11.0.0 0.0.255.255 gt 1023
    established
```

Note the use of 20 as the source port and the lack of the established keyword in this example. Although we show the new access list entry prior to the previous entry, we could have placed the new entry after the previous entry. Recall our earlier discussion regarding the placement of access list entries. We see that the new entry appears to be more specific than our previous entry, yet the previous entry used the established keyword and the new entry does not. Therefore, the new entry does not match a subset of packets matched by the previous entry.

Many protocols use multiple ports in a manner similar to FTP. As stated earlier, these applications are called "multi-channel". Creating filters for these applications is very challenging with traditional access lists. When we examine next-generation access lists in Chapter 8, "Advanced Cisco Router Security Features," we will see that context-based access control provides features to deal securely with many multi-channel protocols.

Let's now examine the access list in its entirety up to this point. Figure 7–8 can be referenced as a reminder.

```
Interface serial 0
 Ip access-group 101 in

Access-list 101 permit tcp any 160.10.1.1 eq 80
Access-list 101 permit tcp any 160.10.1.1 eq 21
Access-list 101 permit tcp any 160.10.1.1 eq 20
Access-list 101 permit tcp any eq 20 160.11.0.0 0.0.255.255 gt
  1023
Access-list 101 permit tcp any 160.11.0.0 0.0.255.255 gt 1023
  established
```

So far, our access list has dealt only with applications using TCP as their transport. Let's now turn to an application that uses UDP as its transport protocol.

Filtering the UDP Protocol

Recall from Chapter 4, "TCP and UDP," that UDP is a connectionless protocol. Therefore, there is no SYN-ACK negotiation and no bits in the UDP header to determine whether a packet is part of an existing UDP conversation. As a consequence, UDP presents new challenges when attempting to create appropriate access list entries.

Let's return to our example and add to our existing requirements the need for our inside network clients to access a *Domain Name Service*(DNS) server on the Internet. DNS provides the means to map host names to IP addresses. Most client-initiated conversations typically reference servers by name, so the capability to correlate host names to IP addresses is critical. For the purposes of this example, we'll assume that we have no DNS server in-house and must use a DNS server provided by our ISP. For the purposes of this example, assume that the IP address of our ISP's DNS server is 157.100.1.1.

We know that the DNS application uses UDP port 53, so we create the following access list entry:

```
Access-list 101 permit udp 157.100.1.1 0.0.0.0 eq 53 any gt 1023
```

Note that in this example we again rely on the principle that the client ports will be randomly chosen ports above 1023. This ensures that even if an attacker spoofed their source address and source port to make it appear that their packets were originating from our ISP's DNS server, they would not be able to send packets to any of our servers on port numbers below 1024. Also notice that there is no established keyword. Because no ACK or RST bits are checked in the UDP header, use of the established keyword is prevented.

There are several applications that use UDP as their transport protocol. By far the most useful is DNS. With the exception of DNS, it is usually not necessary to provide these services over insecure connections such as the Internet.

Filtering the ICMP Protocol

Most people who use TCP/IP networks use the *Internet Control Message Protocol* (ICMP) everyday, although they may not be aware of it. ICMP is unique in that it is used by a wide variety of applications. Two of the most widely used applications, ping and traceroute, for instance, rely on the ICMP protocol to function. ICMP is responsible for signaling errors in the network and providing information about problems encountered with the use of other protocols.

For example, ICMP is used by Cisco routers to send "destination unreachable" messages in response to packets that are blocked by an access list. The ICMP messages "echo-request" and "echo-reply" are used by the ping application to test network connectivity. ICMP's "*time to live* (TTL) exceeded" messages are used by the traceroute program to determine the network path from one host to another. Applications also use ICMP responses to determine the maximum MTU size that a particular path through a network will support.

As you can see, ICMP provides a tremendous amount of information to other network services and applications. Without ICMP, many of the services used by administrators everyday would not function very well or would not work at all. However, it is for this very reason that attackers utilize ICMP to gather valuable information about your network, information that most administrators would prefer to keep secret.

Filtering ICMP is a bit different than filtering other TCP/IP protocols due to the fact that many ICMP messages are sent outbound in response to other protocols. That is, to filter the effects of ICMP, most often you will need to filter ICMP in both directions. In most cases, the only types of ICMP packets that are useful to allow into your network are the following items:

- **Echo-request:** used by ping
- **Echo-reply:** used by ping
- **Packet-too-big:** used by programs to determine path MTU
- ***Time to Live* (TTL) exceeded:** used by traceroute
- **Destination unreachable:** used to allow sessions to timeout more quickly

Not all of these are needed in both directions. Returning to our sample network, we may want to allow stations on our internal network to ping devices on the Internet, but not vice versa. Similarly, we would also like to allow internal stations to perform a traceroute to devices on the Internet, but prevent hosts on the Internet from running the traceroute program on our internal hosts. Both of these situations are very common requirements because ping and traceroute allow outsiders to gain information about the hosts on your internal network. We will add the following access list entries to our configuration:

```
Interface serial 0
 Ip access-group 102 out
 Ip access-group 101 in
Access-list 102 permit icmp 160.11.0.0 0.0.255.255 any echo-
    request
Access-list 102 permit icmp 160.11.0.0 0.0.255.255 any packet-too-
    big
Access-list 101 permit icmp any 160.11.0.0 0.0.255.255 echo-reply
Access-list 101 permit icmp any 160.11.0.0 0.0.255.255 packet-too-
    big
Access-list 101 permit icmp any 160.11.0.0 0.0.255.255 time-
    exceeded
```

Notice that we are allowing only three kinds of ICMP messages inbound:

■ **Echo-reply**: a response to echo-request via ping

■ **Packet-too-big**: a message used by internal hosts to determine network path MTU size

■ **Time-exceeded**: a message used by traceroute from internal hosts

Notice also that we have created a new access list that filters ICMP packets outbound. This access list allows only echo-request and packet-too-big. Our complete access list is shown here:

```
Interface serial 0
 Ip access-group 101 in
 Ip access-group 102 out

Access-list 102 permit icmp 160.11.0.0 0.0.255.255 any echo-
    request
Access-list 102 permit icmp 160.11.0.0 0.0.255.255 any packet-too-
    big

Access-list 101 permit icmp any 160.11.0.0 0.0.255.255 echo-reply
Access-list 101 permit icmp any 160.11.0.0 0.0.255.255 packet-too-
    big
Access-list 101 permit icmp any 160.11.0.0 0.0.255.255 ttl-
    exceeded
```

```
Access-list 101 permit icmp any 160.10.1.1 eq 80
Access-list 101 permit icmp any 160.10.1.1 eq 21
Access-list 101 permit icmp any 160.10.1.1 eq 20
Access-list 101 permit icmp any eq 20 160.11.0.0 0.0.255.255 gt
   1023
Access-list 101 permit icmp any 160.11.0.0 0.0.255.255 gt 1023
   established
Access-list 101 permit udp 157.100.1.1 0.0.0.0 eq 53 any gt 1023
```

Notice the order of the access list entries in list number 101. Because ICMP, TCP, and UDP entries are all different protocols, the placement of each section of entries is somewhat arbitrary. In general, if there are sections of different protocols, it is best to place those entries that will be referenced the most toward the top. This will lower the amount to time it takes to process the access list for a particular packet.

It appears that we have successfully created and applied our access lists, yet once we place the access list entries in place, no traffic can get to the Internet! Why? Well, let's examine access list 102 in the previous example. It filters ICMP packets outbound to the Internet and looks OK, except for one thing. We are not allowing any packets other than ICMP. Remember, there is always an implicit "deny all" at the end of each access list, so without adding a few more permit statements, everything except ICMP is being blocked. We will see in the next section how to add permit entries for generic IP packets.

Filtering IP Packets

We now see that we must allow IP packets from our internal network to have access to the Internet by adding a few access list entries to access list number 102 in the previous example. We'll do so below:

```
Access-list 102 permit ip 160.10.0.0 0.0.255.255 any
Access-list 102 permit ip 160.11.0.0 0.0.255.255 any
```

The addition of these entries to access list number 102 will allow packets from both the DMZ segment and our internal network segment to have access to the Internet. As an added layer of security, it is always prudent to add what is called "anti-spoofing" access list entries to an inbound access list. The purpose of anti-spoofing entries is to block IP packets that have a source address of an internal network or a source address that is invalid. A list of invalid source addresses include unregistered addresses, loopback addresses, and multicast addresses. No legitimate packets should ever contain a source address of any of these types. Attackers frequently use these address ranges as the source address of their packets to prevent administrators from tracing them to the originating source machine.

Here are the additions to our access list that will block the IP addresses:

```
Access-list 101 deny ip 160.10.0.0 0.0.255.255 any
Access-list 101 deny ip 160.11.0.0 0.0.255.255 any
Access-list 101 deny ip 10.0.0.0 0.255.255.255 any
Access-list 101 deny ip 172.16.0.0 0.31.255.255 any
Access-list 101 deny ip 192.168.0.0 0.0.255.255 any
Access-list 101 deny ip 127.0.0.0 0.255.255.255 any
Access-list 101 deny ip 224.0.0.0 31.255.255.255 any
```

The anti-spoofing entries should be placed before all other entries in our inbound access list. This ensures that only packets with valid IP addresses will be examined by our remaining entries.

Finally, it is always prudent to block packets originating from the DMZ. This step is taken so that if a host in the DMZ becomes compromised, an attacker cannot use the compromised host as a "jumping-off point" to further compromise hosts on the internal network. If possible, access from hosts on the DMZ to hosts on the internal network should be blocked entirely. However, in most cases this is not an option.

Often an administrator needs to perform system maintenance tasks on the machines in the DMZ from their personal workstation on the internal network. Otherwise, the Web server on the DMZ will serve internal users as well as Internet users. At a minimum, hosts on the DMZ segment should not be allowed to initiate connections to either the internal network or the Internet. Below is an additional access list blocking initiated connections:

```
Interface ethernet 0
 Ip access-group 103 in
Access-list 103 permit tcp 160.10.0.0 0.0.255.255 any established
Access-list 103 deny ip 160.10.0.0 0.0.255.255 160.11.0.0
   0.0.255.255
Access-list 103 permit tcp 160.10.1.1 0.0.0.0 eq 20 any
```

Let's examine a few characteristics of this access list. The first entry permits any packets from the 160.10.0.0 subnet if they are part of an established connection. The packets could be destined for either the Internet or our internal network. The second entry blocks all other IP packets from the DMZ segment to our internal network. The last entry permits packets initiated from our DMZ server to the Internet if the source port is 20. This is necessary to allow FTP connections to our server from the Internet.

Notice that the second entry is an IP protocol entry and the last is a TCP entry. In most cases, the TCP entries are placed prior to the IP entries. In this case, however, if we had placed entry 3 before entry 2, we would allow packets from the DMZ server with port 20 access to our internal network. We do not want to allow any packets from the DMZ to our internal network unless they are part of an established connection.

Our final access list configuration is shown here:

```
Interface serial 0
 Ip access-group 101 in
 Ip access-group 102 out
!
interface ethernet 0
 ip access-group 103 in
!
access-list 103 permit tcp 160.10.0.0 0.0.255.255 any established
access-list 103 deny ip 160.10.0.0 0.0.255.255 160.11.0.0
  0.0.255.255
access-list 103 permit tcp 160.10.1.1 0.0.0.0 eq 20 any
!
access-list 102 permit icmp 160.11.0.0 0.0.255.255 any echo-
   request
access-list 102 permit icmp 160.11.0.0 0.0.255.255 any packet-too-
   big
access-list 102 permit icmp 160.10.0.0 0.0.255.255 any echo-
   request
access-list 102 permit icmp 160.10.0.0 0.0.255.255 any packet-too-
   big
access-list 102 deny icmp 160.11.0.0 0.0.255.255 any
access-list 102 deny icmp 160.10.0.0 0.0.255.255 any
access-list 102 permit ip 160.11.0.0 0.0.255.255 any
access-list 102 permit ip 160.10.0.0 0.0.255.255 any
!
access-list 101 deny ip 160.10.0.0 0.0.255.255 any
access-list 101 deny ip 160.11.0.0 0.0.255.255 any
access-list 101 deny ip 10.0.0.0 0.255.255.255 any
access-list 101 deny ip 172.16.0.0 0.15.255.255 any
access-list 101 deny ip 192.168.0.0 0.0.255.255 any
access-list 101 deny ip 127.0.0.0 0.255.255.255 any
access-list 101 deny ip 224.0.0.0 31.255.255.255 any
access-list 101 permit icmp any 160.11.0.0 0.0.255.255 echo-reply
access-list 101 permit icmp any 160.11.0.0 0.0.255.255 packet-too-
   big
access-list 101 permit icmp any 160.11.0.0 0.0.255.255 ttl-
   exceeded
access-list 101 permit icmp any 160.10.0.0 0.0.255.255 echo-reply
access-list 101 permit icmp any 160.10.0.0 0.0.255.255 packet-too-
   big
access-list 101 permit icmp any 160.10.0.0 0.0.255.255 ttl-
   exceeded
access-list 101 permit tcp any 160.10.1.1 eq 80
access-list 101 permit tcp any 160.10.1.1 eq 21
access-list 101 permit tcp any 160.10.1.1 eq 20
access-list 101 permit tcp any eq 20 160.11.0.0 0.0.255.255 gt
  1023
access-list 101 permit tcp any 160.11.0.0 0.0.255.255 gt 1023
   established
access-list 101 permit udp 157.100.1.1 0.0.0.0 eq 53 any gt 1023
```

Other Protocols

Obviously, many additional protocols have not been covered by the access list examples in this chapter; it's simply not possible for us to cover all the protocols that you may encounter in your own network. This chapter's discussion, however, should provide a solid foundation that you can adapt to your own particular environment. Applications will normally use one of the protocols presented and the examples in this chapter can be adapted to incorporate them.

Discovering Protocols

On a final note, a common problem encountered when attempting to create access list entries for protocols is the lack of information about the ports in use. This problem can be alleviated through the creative use of access lists. In the example below, we have created an access list that permits all protocols but logs information regarding the matches. In this manner, the log entries can be examined to determine which ports the applications are using and then appropriate access list entries can be created:

```
Interface serial 0
 Ip access-group 101 in
 Ip access-group 102 out
!
Logging buffered
!
Access-list 101 permit tcp any any log
Access-list 101 permit udp any any log
Access-list 101 permit ip any any log
!
Access-list 102 permit tcp any any log
Access-list 102 permit udp any any log
Access-list 102 permit ip any any log
```

In practice, you will probably only want to log one protocol at a time to avoid consuming too many resources. The command "show log" displays detailed information about each packet that matches the access list entries. If possible, it is advisable to narrow the log entries to particular IP address ranges.

In this section, we have seen how to create complex access lists using IP, TCP, UDP, and ICMP. We have also seen examples of the limitations in using traditional access lists, including the inability to maintain information about the state of existing connections. In the next chapter, we examine powerful access list features, including the capability to maintain information about the state of existing connections. Next-generation IP access lists and additional IP security features will also be discussed in Chapter 8, "Advanced Cisco Router Security Features."

Advanced Cisco Router Security Features

In this chapter, we will examine many of the more advanced security features available on Cisco routers. Cisco has introduced many significant enhancements for traditional IP access lists, including the capability to maintain information about the state of existing connections. In addition to access list enhancements, we will discuss other features that might be used to provide greater security on your network, such as TCP intercept and Network Address Translation.

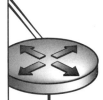

Next Generation Access Lists

In this section, we examine several enhancements for traditional Cisco access lists. We will first examine dynamic access lists, which provide the capacity to create dynamic openings in an access list through a user authentication process. We will then look at time-based access lists, which enable you to configure different security policies based on factors such as the time of day or days of the week. After examining time-based access lists, we will cover reflexive access lists, which will create dynamic openings in an access list on an as-needed basis as connections are opened through the router. We will complete our coverage of next generation access lists by examining *Context Based Access Control* (CBAC), which is capable of creating dynamic openings in an access list such as reflexive access lists—but supports a much greater variety of applications.

Dynamic Access Lists

Dynamic access lists are the first type of enhanced access list we will examine. These access lists are also referred to as *lock-and-key security.* *Dynamic access lists* permit dynamic entries to be inserted into traditional, standard, or extended IP access lists. Dynamic entries in the access list are created by users through an authentication process. Users open a Telnet session to the Cisco router to authenticate themselves. Once the user is authenticated, the router closes the Telnet session and places a dynamic entry in the inbound access list, which permits packets originating from the IP address of the user's workstation. This principle is illustrated in Figure 8–1.

Entries are dynamically removed after either the idle-timeout or maximum-timeout period expires. Users might be authenticated against a user database contained on the router itself or against a TACACS+ or Radius database. An administrator might also specify a generic password to authenticate all users. An example configuration using dynamic access lists is shown below. Only relevant portions of the configuration are shown.

```
Username test password temp
!
Interface serial 0
   Ip address 160.12.1.1 255.255.255.0
   Encapsulation ppp
   Ip access-group 101 in
!
```

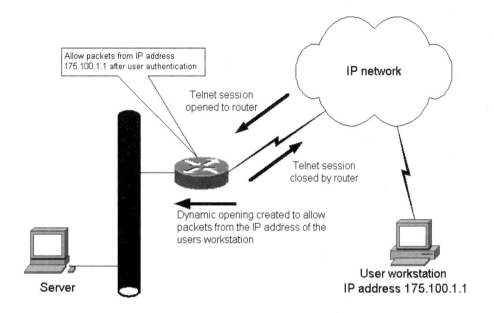

Figure 8–1
A user opens a Telnet session to the router and must authenticate. Once the user is authenticated, a dynamic entry will be opened in an access list—enabling packets from the IP address of the users workstation.

```
access-list 101 permit tcp any host 160.12.1.1 eq telnet
access-list 101 dynamic testlist timeout 10 permit ip any any
!
line vty 0 4
  login local
  autocommand access-enable host timeout 5
```

The code below shows what a user would see when the user initiates a Telnet session to the router.

```
telnet 160.12.1.1
Trying 160.12.1.1 ... Open


User Access Verification

Username: test
Password:
[Connection to 160.12.1.1 closed by foreign host]
```

Notice that the router closes the connection immediately after authentication. A dynamic entry has been added to the access list. The code below shows the output from "show access list" before and after user authentication.

```
Before:
router#sh access-list
Extended IP access list 101
    permit tcp any host 160.12.1.1 eq telnet
    Dynamic test Max. 10 mins. permit ip any any timeout 5 min.

After:
router#sh access-list
Extended IP access list 101
    permit tcp any host 160.12.1.1 eq telnet (24 matches)
    Dynamic test Max. 10 mins. permit ip any any timeout 5 min.
        permit ip host 175.100.1.1 any idle-time 5 min.
router#
```

Notice that a dynamic access list entry has been created. The entry is identical to the static access list entry in the router configuration, except for the fact that the source address has been changed from "any" to "175.100.1.1." The other properties of the dynamic entry have been inherited from the main access list entry. Specifically, the protocol is IP, and the destination is any. We could have specified other protocols, such as TCP, or more specific destination IP addresses if we wished.

Several points of interest exist in the configuration code. Notice that the username "test," which is how we create a user database on the router, is defined. Another option would have been to add a generic password to the virtual terminal lines that all users could use to authenticate themselves. Using a generic password is not recommended. While it might make administration easier, generic passwords also make it easier for an attacker to create openings on the router. When both a user ID and a password are used, both must be guessed to gain access.

Next, notice the entries for access list 101. The first entry is necessary to enable users to telnet to the router for authentication. The use of the "dynamic" keyword in the second entry signals the use of dynamic access lists. The timeout defined in the access list statement is a maximum timeout period and is optional.

Notice that the permit statement allows all IP packets. The dynamic entry created will provide IP packets from all authenticated hosts access to any IP addresses, as seen in the above code. We could have modified this access list entry to permit only certain protocols, ports, and destinations, like any other extended access list entry—only the source IP address would be replaced in the dynamic entry. This situation means that all users would have the same access. No method exists to create different access list entries based upon different users.

Finally, notice the use of the "autocommand" keyword beneath the vty line in the sample configuration using dynamic access lists. This command enables the creation of dynamic entries in the access list after a user has authenticated via a Telnet session to the router. The timeout parameter listed with the "autocommand" statement is an idle timeout and is also optional. One of the timeout parameters should be used; otherwise, dynamic entries will never time out and will remain active until the next router reload.

Notice that by using this configuration, you prevent an administrator from managing the router remotely through a normal Telnet session. All Telnet sessions opened to the router would be treated as if you were attempting to establish dynamic access list entries. This feature creates a problem when an administrator needs to manage a router remotely. To enable normal Telnet access to the router for management purposes, the following changes would need to be made to the configuration:

```
line vty 3 4
login local
password cisco
rotary 1
```

The use of the "rotary 1" command enables normal Telnet access to the router on port 3001. An administrator would need to specify the use of port 3001 when attempting to access the router via a Telnet session, as in the following example:

```
telnet 160.12.1.1 3001
```

Next, we present some tips to follow when configuring dynamic access lists.

- Do not assign the same name to a dynamic access list that used on another access list.
- Define at least the idle timeout or the absolute timeout. If both are defined, the idle timeout should be less than the absolute timeout.
- If possible, limit the openings that are created by dynamic access list entries to particular protocols and particular destination IP addresses.

Limitations

Although dynamic access lists provide a significant enhancement for traditional IP access lists, they also come with their own set of limitations.

First, there is no way for an administrator to provide different users with different kinds of access. Notice in our sample configuration that there is no match between username and individual dynamic entries.

Also, enabling external hosts to open dynamic entries in an access list is a potential security risk, due to the danger of outside parties sniffing the network and capturing login information. A normal Telnet session passes login information "in the clear," meaning an attacker can passively (and easily) collect this information. This task would normally be accomplished by compromising a machine located at an ISP's premises and installing sniffer software. Although this situation might not sound likely, it happens quite often.

For this reason, we recommend that serious thought be given to enabling users to create dynamic entries on a router by accessing the router through an Internet connection. If dynamic access lists are used, we strongly urge that only small openings be enabled, such as to particular host IP addresses and a particular protocol. If a hacker were to sniff the user ID and password during the login process of a legitimate user, the hacker would be able to create the same openings in your router as that user. They could then use this opening as an entry into your network for further attacks. We recommend that you use caution when implementing dynamic access lists.

Time-Based Access Lists

Time-based access lists are a new feature available in IOS Version 12.0 and are available on all platforms. Prior to the introduction of this feature, there was no program in Cisco routers that would enable an administrator to establish different security policies based on the time of day. Time-based access lists provide this capacity, as well as the capability to establish different policies based on days of the week (and absolute criteria, such as calendar day and year). Time-based access lists also provide greater flexibility when using access lists to implement many other Cisco features, such as policy-based routing, queuing, and dial-on-demand. In this section, we will demonstrate the use of time-based access lists for use only with packet filtering.

Essentially, only two steps are necessary to implement time-based access lists:

▪ Defining a time range

▪ Referencing the time range in an access list entry

The following syntax is used to create a time range. Actual keywords are in bold.

```
time-range [time-range-name]
absolute [start time date] [end time date]
```

and/or

```
periodic days-of-the-week hh:mm to [days-of-the-week] hh:mm
```

The "time" parameter is entered in the format *hh:mm,* where *hh* is the hour of day in 24-hour format, and *mm* is the minute of the hour. For example, 5 a.m. is entered as 05:00, and 5 p.m. is entered as 17:00. The days of the week can be listed individually, separated by a space: Monday Tuesday Wednesday Thursday Friday Saturday Sunday. You can also use the keyword "daily" to represent Monday through Sunday, the keyword "weekday" to represent Monday through Friday, and the keyword "weekend" to represent Saturday and Sunday.

Once the time-range has been created, the range might be referenced through the use of the optional keyword "time-range" in a traditional access list entry. An example is shown here:

```
Time-range deny-http
  Periodic weekdays 8:00 to 17:00
!
time-range allow-snmp
  periodic weekend 9:00 to 11:00
!
access-list 101 permit tcp any any eq www time-range deny-http
access-list 101 permit udp any any eq snmp time-range allow-snmp
```

If desired, we could also create a time-range referencing an absolute time period:

```
Time-range allow-telnet
  Absolute start 8:00 31 january 1999 end 8:00 15 february 2001
!
access-list 101 permit tcp any any eq telent time-range allow-
  telnet
```

Time-based criteria can be also be used with traditional numbered and named access lists, as well as dynamic access lists.

Limitations

Obviously, using time-based access lists depends on the router having the correct time. Cisco routers can use the NTP to synchronize their clocks to a dependable time source. Here's a simple example of the use of NTP:

```
clock timezone PST -8
clock summer-time PDT recurring
ntp update-calendar
ntp server 161.10.1.1
interface ethernet 0
  ntp broadcast
```

We could specify that a router has the authoritative clock through the use of the command *ntp master*. More coverage of NTP is beyond the scope of this book. The NTP protocol and its use in a Cisco router network is covered in detail in documents on the Cisco Web site at http://www.cisco.com.

Reflexive Access Lists

Reflexive access lists were introduced in IOS Version 11.3 and are available on all router platforms. Reflexive access lists provide a way to maintain information about the state of existing connections. Recall our earlier discussion in Chapter 6, "Cisco Router Access Lists," about the difference between stateful and stateless packet filtering. Also recall that traditional access lists have no method for determining whether a packet is part of an existing connection. Reflexive access lists provide an enhanced method to remedy this shortcoming by creating dynamic, temporary openings in an access list—similar to dynamic access lists.

A reflexive access list is triggered when a new IP traffic session is initiated from inside your network to an external network. The reflexive access list generates a new, temporary opening. The new entry permits traffic to enter the network if the traffic is part of the original session. The temporary entry created has the following characteristics:

- The entry is always a permit entry.
- The entry specifies the same protocol as the original outbound packet (i.e., TCP, UDP, ICMP, or IP).
- The new entry swaps the source and destination IP addresses.
- The new entry swaps the source and destination upper-layer port numbers (for ICMP, type numbers are used).
- The entry exists until either the session is closed or the idle timeout is reached. Only TCP conversations will be actively closed through the monitoring of FIN or RST bits in incoming packets. Other protocols such as UDP must reach the idle timeout.

Essentially, reflexive access lists create "mirror image" or "reflected" entries in an existing access list, and these entries enable packets which are part of an existing connection to pass through the access list. For example, suppose a user initiated an outbound Telnet session from IP address 160.10.1.100 to IP address 175.100.10.1 using source TCP port number 1045. The original outbound packet has the following characteristics:

Source IP address: 160.10.1.100

Source TCP port: 1045

Destination IP address: 175.100.10.1

Destination TCP port: 23 (Telnet)

Reflexive access lists would create a "reflected" access list entry enabling inbound return traffic:

```
permit tcp 175.100.10.1 eq 23 160.10.1.100 eq 1045
```

Notice that this entry is a mirror image of the outbound packets. The source and destination IP addresses and the source and destination port numbers have been exchanged. This entry is the reverse image of the original outgoing packets, as if the original packets were viewed in the reflection of a mirror.

Limitations

Reflexive access lists are powerful, but they suffer from one major drawback. Many protocols do not use a simple, one data, "channel" connection. In this context, "channel" means a single, fixed port number. For example, as we saw in Chapter 6, FTP uses multiple source ports during a conversation. FTP also relies on the server's capacity to initiate a connection to the originating host.

Reflexive access lists do not account for this property of some applications and are therefore not capable of handling them. As a rule of thumb, reflexive access lists are only capable of handling *single channel* applications. These are applications that only use a single, static port that does not change over the duration of the conversation. Many applications that use multiple port numbers, or "channels," rely on the capability of the server to actively establish a connection with the originating client.

NOTE: This feature, and not the use of multiple ports per se, precludes their use with reflexive access lists. If multiple outgoing connections were necessary, reflexive access lists would just generate multiple "reflected" entries.

For example, there is a version of the FTP protocol called *passive mode FTP* (PASV). In this mode, the server does not perform an active open to the originating client. Instead, the client exchanges port information over the traditional command channel and then performs an additional open to the server on an agreed upon port. In this case, because both sessions are outbound from the client, reflexive access lists would simply create an additional "reflected" entry, and the data conversation would succeed.

Examples

The use of reflexive access lists is best illustrated with an example. In Figure 8–2, we show a sample network diagram. We also show the use of reflexive access lists to monitor all outbound TCP, UDP, and ICMP traffic in the code below. Only relevant portions of the configuration are shown.

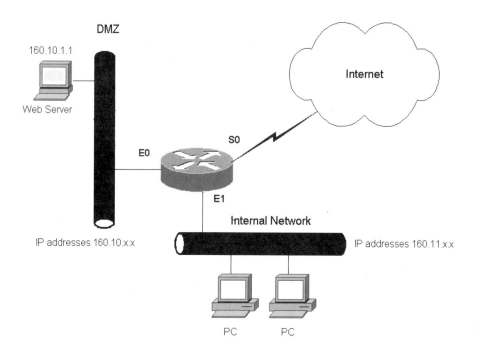

Figure 8–2
A sample network configuration

```
interface serial 0
  ip access-group infilter in
  ip access-group outfilter out
!
ip reflexive-list timeout 120
!
ip access-list extended outfilter
  permit tcp any any reflect my_packets
  permit udp any any reflect my_packets
  permit icmp any any reflect my_packets
!
ip access-list extended infilter
  deny ip 10.0.0.0 0.255.255.255 any
  deny ip 172.16.0.0 0.31.255.255 any
  deny ip 192.168.0.0 0.0.255.255 any
evaluate my_packets
```

Examine the configuration above. The first step is to create an extended named access list, which will include a permit statement for all the protocols we wish to enable to create "reflected" entries. The use of named access lists is required. In the earlier example, we have created a named access list called "outfilter." Within the body of this named access list, we have created entries for TCP, UDP, and ICMP. Notice that the entries are all permit entries. Also notice the use of the keyword "reflect." This keyword signals the use of reflexive access lists. Also notice the use of the name "my_packets" for each of the entries. This name is used later to reference the reflexive access list entries.

As shown in the code above, the reflexive access list entries are "nested" beneath a traditional named access list called "infilter." Although it isn't shown, the named access list "outfilter" could contain other non-reflexive access list entries. If the access list entries contain both reflexive and non-reflexive entries, the order placement is crucial. Only packets that reach the reflexive access list entries will be enabled to create "reflected" entries. If a packet matches an entry higher in the named access list, the packet will not be evaluated by the reflexive entries. As an example, here's a modified version of our "outfilter" access list:

```
ip access-list extended outfilter
  permit ip any any
  permit tcp any any reflect my_packets
  permit udp any any reflect my_packets
  permit icmp any any reflect my_packets
```

Notice the addition of an entry permitting all IP packets. Notice, too, that this entry does not use the keyword "reflect," indicating that the entry is not a reflexive access list entry. Because all IP packets would be matched by this entry, none of our remaining reflexive access list entries would ever be matched—so no "reflected" entries would ever be created in our inbound access list "infilter."

An additional point worth noting is that non-reflexive access list entries could be interwoven with reflexive access list entries within the same named access list. No requirement exists that all of the reflexive entries appear contiguously. This characteristic provides a great deal of flexibility when creating reflexive access lists. Certain protocols and IP address ranges can be included as reflexive access list entries, and others might not be included. Here's a simple example to illustrate this point:

```
ip access-list extended outfilter
  permit ip 160.100.10.1 any
  permit tcp any any reflect my_packets
  permit udp any any reflect my_packets
  deny icmp 160.100.10.0 0.0.0.255 any echo-reply
  permit icmp any any reflect my_packets
```

Let's return now to our original example showing the use of reflexive access lists to monitor all outbound TCP, UDP, and ICMP traffic. Notice that the reflexive access list "my_packets" is referenced by the named access list "infilter." The command "evaluate my_packets" signals the placement of the dynamic entries that will be created by the reflexive access list "my_packets." Notice that there are other access list entries preceding the "evaluate" command. These entries will be considered prior to any entries created by our reflexive access list "my_packets."

We could also create additional access list entries after the "evaluate" command. These entries would be examined after any entries created by our reflexive access list "my_packets." As with all other access lists, the order is critical. Once a matching access list entry is found, no other entries are considered. In the code sample below, we show the output of "show access list" command before and after an inside client initiates an outbound Telnet session. The Telnet session has the following characteristics:

Source IP address: 160.10.1.100

Source TCP port: 1045

Destination IP address: 175.100.10.1

Destination TCP port: 23 (Telnet)

```
Before:
router#sh access-list
Extended IP access list infilter
  deny ip 10.0.0.0 0.255.255.255 any
  deny ip 172.16.0.0 0.31.255.255 any
```

```
        deny ip 192.168.0.0 0.0.255.255 any
        evaluate my_packets
extended IP access list outfilter
   permit tcp any any reflect my_packets
   permit udp any any reflect my_packets
   permit icmp any any reflect my_packets
```

```
After
router#sh access-list
Extended IP access list infilter
   deny ip 10.0.0.0 0.255.255.255 any
   deny ip 172.16.0.0 0.31.255.255 any
   deny ip 192.168.0.0 0.0255.255 any
   evaluate my_packets
extended IP access list outfilter
   permit tcp any any reflect my_packets
   permit udp any any reflect my_packets
   permit icmp any any reflect my_packets
```
reflexive IP access list my_packets
 permit tcp host 175.100.10.1 eq telnet host 160.10.1.100 eq 1045
  (10 matches) (time left 110 seconds)

Notice that the reflexive access list "my_traffic" now appears with a new entry.

One final point regarding reflexive access lists is the use of a timeout variable. We mentioned earlier that only TCP traffic is actively closed. A TCP reflexive access list entry will be closed immediately after receipt of a packet, with the RST bit set and within five seconds of the detection of two FIN bits. Because UDP and ICMP do not have similar options in their headers, an idle timeout is necessary to determine when entries for these kinds of protocols should be deleted. The default idle timeout is 300 seconds. In the configuration sample of reflexive access lists to monitor all outbound TCP, UDP, and ICMP traffic, we changed the global timeout to 120 seconds with the global command `ip reflexive-list timeout 120`. The timeout value can also be set independently for each reflexive access list entry by using the keyword "timeout."

```
ip access list extended outfilter
permit tcp any any reflect my_packets
permit udp any any reflect my_packets timeout 60
permit icmp any any reflect my_packets
```

The configuration change described earlier sets the timeout for UDP entries to 60 seconds.

While reflexive access lists are powerful and provide a significant enhancement for traditional access lists, they are still limited by their lack of knowledge about the behavior of multi-channel applications. In the next section, we discuss CBAC, which is capable of understanding the behavior of many multi-channel applications and is much more flexible than reflexive access lists.

Context Based Access Control (CBAC)

CBAC was originally introduced in IOS Version 11.2 in a special release called the *Firewall Feature Set*, or simply FFS. The original release was available only on the 1600- and 2500-series platforms. In release 12.0, Cisco included CBAC support for the 1700-, 2600- and 3600-series router platforms. CBAC is similar in concept to reflexive access lists, because CBAC provides the capacity to dynamically create openings through a filtering router when a connection is initiated from within the protected network. CBAC includes additional intelligence, however, that enables it to filter—based on application-layer protocol information—to learn about the state of a UDP or TCP session. This feature enables support of applications that involve multiple channels created through client/server negotiation, such as FTP. As noted previously, reflexive access lists are not capable of handling these kinds of applications. CBAC is much more than an access list enhancement; rather, it is a comprehensive set of security tools. In addition to providing application-layer filtering capabilities, CBAC provides the following items:

- Java blocking
- Denial-of-service prevention and detection
- Real-time alerts and audit trails

We will examine each of these features in detail in the following sections.

Overview

CBAC works in a manner similar to reflexive access lists. Outgoing sessions are inspected, and temporary openings are created to enable the return traffic. The difference is that CBAC is capable of examining and securely handling a variety of applications based on upper-layer information. Reflexive access lists, like traditional access lists, are not capable of examining information higher than layer 4. A list of the applications for which CBAC provides intelligent filtering is shown in Table 8–1.

CBAC works by examining packets as they leave specified interfaces. The information contained in the packet, such as IP addresses and port numbers, is installed in a packet "state information" table. The *state table* is used by CBAC to create temporary openings in an access list for return

Table 8–1

A List of the Applications Which CBAC Is Capable of Handling Securely

CU-SeeMe (White Pine version)	RPC (Sun version)
FTP	SMTP
H.323 (Netmeeting, ProShare, etc.)	SQL*Net
Java	StreamWorks
Unix R-commands (rlogin, rexec, etc.)	TFTP
RealAudio	VDOLive
"single-channel" TCP (i.e., Telnet)	"single-channel" UDP (i.e., DNS)

traffic. CBAC examines application-layer information for certain protocols to insure that appropriate return traffic is provided access. For example, CBAC would monitor an outgoing FTP session and would permit the resulting data connection to be initiated from the FTP server to the originating client. CBAC is aware of the behavior of the FTP application and can intelligently create necessary openings in the router access lists. CBAC performs similar functions for the other protocols listed earlier. We examine this process in detail in the next section.

The Process

This section details the process that CBAC follows to monitor outbound traffic sessions and create appropriate inbound access list entries.

1. An outgoing packet reaches the router. The packet is evaluated against an outgoing access list. The access list should enable all traffic to be inspected by CBAC. (Denied traffic is simply dropped.)

2. CBAC inspects the packet and records information about the packet in the state table. The information recorded includes the source and destination IP addresses and port numbers.

3. CBAC creates a temporary opening in an access list for the return traffic. The openings created will vary, depending on the application used.

4. A return packet reaches the router. The return packet is permitted by the access list and is inspected by CBAC. CBAC will modify the state table and inbound access list as necessary.

5. All future inbound and outbound packets that are part of this conversation are inspected by CBAC, so that the state table and access list might be modified accordingly.

6. When the connection is completed, the entries in the state table and the inbound access list are removed.

Notice that for CBAC to operate, both an access list defining which packets are to be inspected by CBAC and an access list where the entries are actually created are needed. We show a detailed example of this principle later in this section.

Caveats

- CBAC only inspects TCP and UDP packets. Other IP traffic (such as ICMP) should be filtered with traditional IP access lists.

- Packets with the router as the source or destination address are not inspected by CBAC.

- If both encryption and CBAC are configured, CBAC will not have the capacity to accurately inspect the contents of the encrypted packets. In this scenario, the only multi-channel protocols that CBAC will be able to inspect are StreamWorks and CU-SeeMe. CBAC should be configured to inspect only these applications and generic TCP and UDP sessions.

- CBAC uses approximately 600 bytes of memory per connection to maintain the state table. Additionally, a small amount of additional processing occurs during the inspection process.

Configuration

To configure CBAC, you must perform the following tasks:

1. Choose an interface where you will configure CBAC.
2. Configure access lists on the interface.
3. Configure timeouts and thresholds.
4. Define the inspection rules.
5. Apply the inspection rules.

We will cover each of these topics in detail.

Choose an Interface

The first step is to decide whether to configure CBAC on an "internal" or "external" interface. An *internal* interface is an interface on the router where client sessions originate. This side is often called the "trusted" or "clean" side of the router. This interface will be on the router closest to the devices you are attempting to protect. An *external* interface is an interface on the router where client sessions exit the router. This side is often called the "untrusted" or "dirty" side of the router. This interface will be the one closest to the devices you are attempting to filter.

If there are more than two interfaces, the extra interfaces are normally used as a *demilitarized zone* (DMZ). A DMZ is a segment that provides services to both the internal and external interfaces. For example, a Web server used by both internal and external clients would be placed on the DMZ. The purpose of the DMZ is to provide services to external clients —while still limiting inbound traffic to the internal network. This way, if a host on the DMZ is compromised, hosts on the internal network are still protected. If a device on the internal side of the router were compromised, there would be no way the router could prevent further compromise of internal hosts. A good source for more discussion on the design of secure perimeters is *Building Internet Firewalls* by Chapman and Zwicky.

If there is only an internal and external interface, it is most common to configure CBAC on the external interface. This way, any traffic attempting to enter the network will be inspected by CBAC. If there are one or more DMZ segments, CBAC can be configured on either the interface closest to the originating hosts or on the interface closest to the destination hosts. We will show an example where CBAC is configured closest to the originating hosts. Traffic might be initiated from external and internal clients to hosts on the DMZ. Any traffic attempting to enter the internal network, however, would be blocked. CBAC is intelligent enough to create openings in an access list on an interface other than the interface where inspection is defined. As we will see, if CBAC is configured to inspect traffic arriving at an inside interface, CBAC can create openings in an inbound access list on the outside interface of the router for the return traffic.

If CBAC is configured in two directions, CBAC should be configured for one direction first and then configured independently for the second direction. When configuring CBAC in complex situations, you should configure CBAC on the interface where the traffic originates. CBAC will take care of creating the necessary openings for the return traffic. We will see an example of this complex situation later.

Because the configuration of CBAC on a router with a DMZ interface is more complex than on a router with only two interfaces, we will provide an example of the former. We will use the network diagram in Figure 8–3 as a reference.

Notice that FTP, DNS, and SMTP services are available on the server in the DMZ. We will return Figure 8–3 later in this section.

Configure Access Lists

For CBAC to operate, access lists must be configured for both outbound and inbound traffic. In this context, outbound refers to traffic that is originating from a trusted side of the router to an untrusted side of the router. Inbound refers to traffic that is originating from an untrusted side of the router to a trusted side of the router. The outbound access list spec-

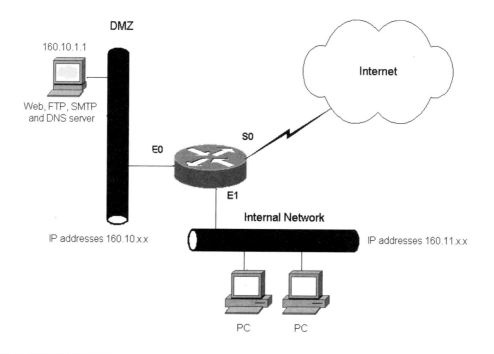

Figure 8–3
A sample network configuration

ifies traffic that you wish to be inspected by CBAC. This access list might be either a standard or extended IP access list. The inbound access list is the access list where temporary openings will actually be created and managed by CBAC. This access list must be an extended IP access list.

NOTE: In this context, an access list filtering inbound traffic could be applied either inbound (on the untrusted interface of the router) or outbound (on the trusted interface of the router). In the example in this section, we will configure multiple inbound and outbound access lists to accommodate CBAC in two directions.

Configure Timeouts and Thresholds

CBAC uses configurable timers to determine the duration of inactive sessions. Also, as stated earlier, CBAC provides a means to prevent *Denial of Service* (DoS) attacks. CBAC does this task by monitoring the number and frequency of half-open connections. For TCP, a half-open session is a session that has not completed the initial three-way handshake. For UDP, a half-open session is a session for which the firewall has detected no return traffic. Each of the applicable commands is listed in Table 8–2 with its default value.

Note that CBAC counts both UDP and TCP when determining the number and rate of half-open sessions. Also keep in mind that half-open sessions are only monitored for connections configured for inspection by CBAC. Later in this chapter, we will look at a feature called TCP intercept that can be used to monitor all TCP connection requests.

Define Inspection Rules

The definition of inspection rules is simple for most protocols. For all protocols except RPC and Java, the format is the following:

```
ip inspect name inspection-name protocol [timeout seconds]
```

Example:

```
ip inspect name firewall ftp
ip inspect name firewall smtp timeout 60
```

For RPC, the format is slightly different:

```
ip inspect name inspection-name rpc program-number number [wait-
    time minutes] [timeout seconds]
```

Table 8–2

Commands Used
to Configure
Timeout Values
Associated with
the Use of CBAC

Ip inspect tcp synwait-time *seconds*	30 seconds	Length of time to wait for TCP session to establish
Ip inspect tcp finwait-time *seconds*	five seconds	Length of time TCP is managed after FIN-exchange
Ip inspect tcp idle-time *seconds*	3600 seconds	TCP idle timeout
Ip inspect udp idle-time *seconds*	30 seconds	UDP idle timeout
Ip inspect dns-timeout *seconds*	five seconds	DNS lookup idle timer
Ip inspect max-incomplete high *number*	500 sessions	Max number of half-open connections before CBAC begins closing connections
Ip inspect max-incomplete low *number*	400 sessions	Number of half-open connections causing CBAC to stop closing connections
Ip inspect one-minute high *number*	500 sessions	Rate of half-open sessions per minute before CBAC begins closing connections
Ip inspect one-minute low *number*	400 sessions	Rate of half-open sessions per minute causing CBAC to stop deleting connections
Ip inspect tcp max-incomplete host	50 sessions	Number of existing half-open sessions with the same Destination address before CBAC begins closing sessions

Example:

```
ip inspect name firewall rpc program-number 10001
ip inspect name firewall rpc program-number 12000 timeout 60
```

For Java blocking, a list of permitted IP addresses must be created using a standard IP access list:

```
access list 1-99 [permit|deny] source [source-wildcard]
ip inspect name inspection-name http [java-list access list]
  [timeout seconds]
```

Example:

```
access list 1 permit 175.100.10.0 0.0.0.255
ip inspect name firewall http java-list 1
```

When both specific application and generic TCP or UDP inspection rules are specified, the specific application inspection takes precedence. For example, if both FTP and TCP are configured for inspection, the FTP inspection rule takes precedence.

Apply the Inspection Rules

The final step is to apply the created inspection rules to an interface. Inspection rules are applied in the same manner as an access list. The inspection rules should be applied in the direction of the outbound traffic. If you are configuring inspection on an internal interface, the outbound traffic is entering the interface—so the inspection rules should be applied inbound. If you are configuring inspection on an external interface, the outbound traffic is leaving the interface—so the inspection rules should be applied outbound. Of course, if you are applying CBAC to inbound traffic from the external interface, an inspection rule should be applied inbound on the external interface as well. You would normally only configure an inspection rule on an external interface if you are configuring CBAC in two directions. The syntax to apply an inspection rule is the following:

```
ip inspect inspection-name {in|out}
```

Additional Details

Several additional commands are available that are useful for gathering information about CBAC. A list of these commands is presented in Table 8–3. The reader should consult the Cisco command reference for IOS Version 12.0 for detailed explanations of their usage.

Additionally, CBAC is capable of logging a wide variety of messages to a syslog server or to the router's log buffer. To configure logging to the routers' log buffer, use the following command:

```
logging buffered
```

To configure logging to a syslog server, use the following command:

```
logging server IP address
```

Table 8–3

A List of Useful
Commands
When Configur-
ing CBAC

```
show ip inspect config

show ip inspect interfaces

show ip inspect session [detail]

show ip inspect name inspection-name

show ip inspect all

debug ip inspect function-trace

debug ip inspect object-creation

debug ip inspect object deletion

debug ip inspect events

debug ip inspect details

debug ip inspect timers

debug ip inspect protocol
```

Again, the reader is referred to the Cisco documentation for detailed information on interpreting the information logged by CBAC.

To disable CBAC, use the following command:

```
no ip inspect
```

This command removes all CBAC configuration entries.

Example Configuration

The sample configuration in Figure 8–4 is for the router in the network shown in Figure 8–3. In this example, we have configured CBAC on two interfaces: inbound on interface Ethernet1, and inbound on interface Serial0. The inspection rule on E1 will create necessary openings in the inbound access list on either Ethernet0, the DMZ, or Serial0 (the Internet connection), depending on the traffic destination. The inspection on Serial0 will create necessary openings in the inbound access list on Ethernet0 and the DMZ. If connections from the Serial0 interface were permitted to Ethernet1, openings would be created on the inbound access list on that interface as well. In this design, we are not permitting connections to be initiated from the Internet to the internal network, so no openings will ever be created on the E1 access list by CBAC.

Figure 8–4
A sample
configuration
showing the use of
CBAC

```
Version 12.0
!
!
service password-encryption
!
! Turn off unneeded TCP and UDP services, they are potential DoS
risks
!
no service udp-small-servers
no service tcp-small-servers
!
! Turn off the finger service
!
no service finger
!
hostname 2514
!
! Always use the enable secret password.  There are many utilities
to crack
! the standard enable password
!
enable secret 5 xxxxxxxxxxxxxxxxx
!
ip subnet-zero
!
! Disable forwarding of IP packets with the source route option
!
no ip source-route
ip domain-name simple.com
ip name-server 160.10.1.1
!
!configure inspection rules
!
ip inspect name from_internal ftp
ip inspect name from_internal http java-list 1
ip inspect name from_internal smtp
ip inspect name from_internal udp
ip inspect name from_internal tcp
!
ip inspect name from_external ftp
ip inspect name from_external smtp
ip inspect name from_external udp
ip inspect name from_external tcp
!
! Always disable forwarding of directed broadcasts to prevent ICMP
flood
! attacks with the 'no ip directed-broadcast' command
!
interface ethernet 0
  description DMZ
  ip address 160.10.1.254 255.255.255.0
  no ip directed-broadcast
  no ip proxy-arp
  no cdp enable
  ip access-group 120 in
!
interface ethernet 1
  description internal network
  ip address 160.11.1.254 255.255.255.0
```

Figure 8–4
Continued

```
   no ip directed-broadcast
   no ip proxy-arp
   ip access-group 101 in
   ip inspect from_internal in
  !
interface serial 0
   description external Internet connection
   ip address 175.100.1.1 255.255.255.252
   ip access-group 110 in
   ip inspect from_external in
   no cdp enable
   !
ip classless
ip route 0.0.0.0 0.0.0.0 serial0
!
! The following access list is for java filtering
! We explicitly type the deny any, but it is on by default
!
access-list 1 permit 160.10.0.0 0.0.255.255
access-list 1 permit 148.100.0.0 0.0.255.255
access-list 1 deny any
!
! Define snmp read-only community string
access-list 10 permit host 160.11.10.1
access-list 10 deny any
!
! Define addresses allowed telnet access to the router. This, in
conjuction
! with the anti-spoofing access-list entries, will prevent any hosts
on the
! Internet from accessing the router via a telnet session
access-list 20 permit 160.11.10.0 0.0.0.255
access-list 20 deny any
!
! This is the access list to specify what packets are inspected by
CBAC on
! E1, the inside interface.
! We could have used a standard access list but the use of an
extended
! list allows us to specify the protocols as well.  No other IP
protocols
! should be in use.
!
access-list 101 permit tcp 160.11.0.0 0.0.255.255 any
access-list 101 permit udp 160.11.0.0 0.0.255.255 any
access-list 101 permit icmp 160.11.0.0 0.0.255.255 any
access-list 101 deny ip any any
!
! This is the inbound access list on S0 where CBAC will create
dynamic
! openings. Openings created by CBAC will be inserted at the
beginning of the
! ACL. The first set of entries are for anti-spoofing.  No packets
coming
! into our network should have these source IP addresses.
!
! loopback addresses
access-list 110 deny ip 127.0.0.0 0.255.255.255 any
! multicast addresses
access-list 110 deny ip 224.0.0.0 31.255.255.255 any
```

Figure 8–4
Continued

```
! unregistered addresses
access-list 110 deny ip 10.0.0.0 0.255.255.255 any
access-list 110 deny ip 172.16.0.0 0.15.255.255 any
access-list 110 deny ip 192.168.0.0 0.0.255.255 any
! our internal and dmz addresses
access-list 110 deny ip 160.11.0.0 0.0.255.255 any
access-list 110 deny ip 160.10.0.0 0.0.255.255 any
! The next entries are to permit access to the services on our DMZ
access-list 110 permit udp any host 160.10.1.1 eq 53
access-list 110 permit tcp any host 160.10.1.1 eq 53
access-list 110 permit tcp any host 160.10.1.1 eq www
access-list 110 permit tcp any host 160.10.1.1 eq ftp
access-list 110 permit tcp any host 160.10.1.1 eq smtp
! The next entries allow all ICMP to the DMZ server and select ICMP
! packets to our internal network
access-list 110 permit icmp any host 160.10.1.1
access-list 110 permit icmp any 160.11.0.0 0.0.255.255 echo-reply
access-list 110 permit icmp any 160.11.0.0 0.0.255.255 time-exceeded
access-list 110 permit icmp any 160.11.0.0 0.0.255.255
administratively-prohibited
access-list 110 permit icmp any 160.11.0.0 0.0.255.255 packet-too-big
access-list 110 deny ip any any
!
! The access list below is applied inbound on ethernet 0, the dmz.
! CBAC will create dynamic entries for sessions initiated from the
internal
! and external network due to the ip inspect rules on the e1 and s0
interface.
access-list 120 deny ip any 160.11.0.0 0.0.255.255
access-list 120 permit tcp host 160.10.1.1 any eq 25
access-list 120 permit tcp host 160.10.1.1 any eq 53
access-list 120 permit udp host 160.10.1.1 any eq 53
access-list 120 deny ip any any
!
snmp-server community nms RO 10
!
line con 0
  exec-timeout 0 0
  password xxxxxxx
line vty 0 4
  exec-timeout 0 0
  access-class 20 in
  password xxxxxx
  transport output none
!
end
```

Traffic from either the Internet or the internal network will have access to the DMZ. The inbound access list on the Serial0, however, will prevent external hosts from initiating connections to the internal network. Similarly, the inbound access list on the Ethernet0 interface will prevent DMZ hosts from initiating connections to the internal network or to the Internet.

The only applications that can be initiated from the DMZ will be SMTP and DNS. No initiated connections of any kind will be enabled from the DMZ to the internal network. This feature will ensure that if the DMZ host is compromised, the DMZ host cannot be used to further compromise internal hosts. Additionally, only limited connections will be permitted to initiate from the DMZ to external networks. If our DMZ host is compromised, the host cannot be used to attack either our site or other Internet sites.

Preventing your hosts from being used to compromise other networks on the Internet is called being a "good Internet citizen" and is strongly encouraged. In the near future, companies that do not take "reasonable measures" to prevent their hosts from being used to compromise other companies' networks will most likely be legally liable for damages. Attempting to prevent your hosts from being used by attackers to compromise other networks, therefore, is in your best interests.

Note that if an internal host were to access the DMZ host, and the DMZ host had been compromised, an attacker could tamper with the connection. Depending on the application used, however, the attacker might be able to cause substantial problems on the internal host. An attacker would not be able to initiate a sustained attack from the DMZ, however, due to the inbound access list on Ethernet0. No method exists to prevent this type of vulnerability. Your internal hosts take the same risk when they access any device on an external network. A DMZ, by definition, enables access by unknown outside parties and should therefore be treated with the same caution as any other external network.

Closely examine the relevant portions of the configuration in Figure 8–4. The use of CBAC on two interfaces makes this example as complex as you are likely to find in a real-world network. This example could have been configured differently so that CBAC was applied on only one interface. We could have simply used a traditional, extended access list on the inbound DMZ interface. CBAC gives greater protection, however, in the event that a host on the DMZ becomes compromised. Despite your best efforts, it is possible that the DMZ host might be compromised—so it is prudent to plan for the worst-case scenario.

Notice that the inspection could have been configured on the outbound side on the interface of SERIAL0 and outbound on interface E0. If this process were done, the inspection rules on each interface would create openings on that interface. If an internal or external host were connecting to the DMZ, a dynamic opening would be created on the inbound access list on interface E0 by the inspection rule on that interface. If an internal or DMZ host connected to the Internet, a dynamic opening would be created on the inbound access list of interface SERIAL0 by the inspection rule on that interface. While there is nothing wrong with configuring CBAC in such a manner, we find it conceptually easier to apply inspection rules closest to the originating traffic and use inbound access lists on all interfaces. This process takes advantage of the intelligence built into CBAC and lets CBAC take care of creating the necessary openings.

If desired, the configuration in Figure 8–4 can be easily modified so that CBAC is configured in only one direction—and a traditional IP access list is configured on the inbound E0 interface.

On an additional note, although the network in Figure 8–3 shows only a single router, the design could be easily modified to use multiple routers all configured with CBAC. You could, for example, configure multiple routers inline to increase your security. One router could have only a Serial connection to the Internet and a single Ethernet connection to the second router. The second router could have an Ethernet connection to the first router, an Ethernet connection to a DMZ segment, and a third Ethernet interface to the inside network. Such a configuration would be useful so that if problems were encountered on the outside router due to a failure or a DoS attack, inside users would still be able to access hosts on the DMZ. This configuration also provides an additional layer of security if a misconfiguration or software bug on the outside router leads to a security breach.

Other IP Security Features

In this section, we discuss several additional router features which can be useful in securing IP networks.

Hardening the Router

The process of "hardening" a network device is a method of systematically examining all of the services that the device provides and determining whether each service is required. Any service that is not absolutely needed to support applications in the network is disabled. Additionally, strict access control is applied so that passwords are required for access of any kind. Although this approach is typically used with general purpose operating systems such as Unix and NT, the same approach can be applied to the Cisco router IOS. A device that is used to control access between an untrusted and a trusted network is often the most likely target of an attack. Properly configured access lists should prevent most attacks against internal hosts. If the router itself is compromised, however, so is the entire network. The steps to harden a Cisco router are listed next.

1. Secure router access
2. Disable unnecessary services

Each of these steps is discussed in the following section.

Secure Router Access

Access to a Cisco router can be obtained in several ways. Each of the following methods listed could lead to a compromise of the routers' configuration.

■ Console and Auxiliary port access

The console and auxiliary ports should *always* have a password set. Additionally, the router should be physically secured in an access-monitored location, such as a data center. Modems that require password access are also available to add an additional layer of security.

■ Remote Telnet access

A password must be set on the vty port configurations to enable remote access. Additionally, access lists can be used to control which IP addresses are permitted Telnet access to the router. We used an access list on our vty port configuration in the CBAC example in Figure 8–4. The use of the command `transport output none` prevents Telnet access from the router to prevent further use of the router as a "jumping off" point, should the router become compromised.

■ SNMP access

SNMP access on a high-security router should be limited to read-only. Additionally, an access list should be used to control which IP addresses are permitted SNMP access. We used an access list with SNMP in the CBAC example in Figure 8–4.

■ Network configuration files

If the router loads its configuration from a TFTP server, the server should be on the internal network. The router should never load its configuration file from a server on an untrusted network.

Disable Unnecessary Services

Several services should be disabled and are listed here:

■ TCP and UDP small services and Finger

Small services are TCP and UDP ports used for diagnostic services. These services include echo, chargen, and discard. Use of these ports is not critical. Conversely, there are known DoS attacks using these ports. Although there are no known attacks using the Finger protocol, its use is also not critical and should be disabled.

Commands

```
no service udp-small-servers
no service tcp-small-server
no service finger
```

■ IP Directed Broadcasts

Directed broadcasts have been used in one of the most popular DoS attacks ever created. The "smurf" attack, named after the original attacking program, sends thousands of ICMP echo-request packets to the directed broadcast address of an attacked hosts network. The source address of the ping is not the attacker's real network but a secondary victim's network. The thousands of requests are multiplied by the number of hosts on the initial target network, and both the original destination and the spoofed source network are denied service. Always disable this service on each router interface.

```
no ip directed-broadcast
```

■ IP Source-Routed Packets

Enabling packets with the source routing option through a router might permit an attacker to gain access to a protected network. This option is rarely used for legitimate purposes and should be disabled, unless there is a specific reason to enable the option.

```
no ip source-route
```

■ ICMP Unreachables

By default, the router will send an ICMP "destination unreachable" message in response to an access list violation. Each ICMP packet sent consumes a small portion of the router's CPU. An attacker could use this feature to overload the routers' CPU and consume valuable network bandwidth—either of which could result in a DoS attack. Disable ICMP Unreachables on the untrusted network interface.

```
no ip unreachables
```

When a Cisco router is properly configured with access control and unnecessary services removed, it is nearly impossible for an attacker to gain privileged access. Only a severe bug in the router IOS would enable the router to be compromised to the extent that an attacker had control of the router. DoS attacks are still possible, but these are far less threatening than an outside attacker gaining complete control of your router.

TCP Intercept—Preventing SYN Flooding

TCP intercept was introduced in IOS Version 11.3 and is available on all router platforms. This feature is designed to prevent known SYN attacks against internal hosts. The attack is simple. The first packet in the TCP three-way handshake sets the SYN bit. When a device receives an initial packet requesting a provided service, the device responds with a packet, setting the SYN and ACK bits, and waits for an ACK from the originator of the conversation. If the originator of the request never responds to the host, the host times out the connection. While the host is waiting for the transaction to complete, however, the half-open connection consumes resources on the host. This action is the essence of the attack.

Thousands of packets with the SYN bit set are sent to a host. The source IP address in these packets, however, is forged. The source address of the forged packets is an unreachable address. In most cases, the source address will either be an unregistered address or the address of a host the attacker knows does not exist. Therefore, the attacked host will never receive a response to its request to complete the initial three-way handshake and must wait to time out thousands of connections. Eventually, the hosts' resources are consumed, and the host becomes unusable.

The TCP intercept feature works by intercepting and validating TCP connection requests. The feature can operate in two modes: intercept and watch. In *intercept* mode, the router intercepts incoming TCP synchronization requests and establishes a connection with the client on the servers' behalf—and with the server on the clients' behalf. If both connections are successful, the router transparently merges the two connections. The router has aggressive timeouts to prevent its own resources from being consumed by a SYN attack. In *watch* mode, the router passively watches half-open connections and will actively close connections on the server after a configurable length of time. Access lists are defined to specify which source and destination packets are subject to TCP intercept.

Enabling TCP Intercept

Only two steps are necessary to enable TCP intercept:

1. Configuring the access list permitting the hosts IP addresses you want to protect

```
access list [1-199] [deny|permit] tcp any destination destination-
    wildcard
```

2. Enabling TCP intercept

```
ip tcp intercept list access list-number
```

Setting the Mode

TCP intercept works in either intercept or watch mode. The default is intercept. In this mode, the router responds to the incoming SYN request on the servers' behalf with a SYN-ACK and waits for an ACK from the client. If an ACK is received, the original SYN packet is sent to the server, and the router completes the three-way handshake with the server on behalf of the originating client.

In watch mode, the router enables SYN requests through to the server. If the session fails to establish itself in 30 seconds (the default), the router sends a RST to the server to clear the connection. The amount of time the router waits is configurable. The mode can be set with the following command:

```
ip tcp intercept mode {intercept|watch}
```

Aggressive Thresholds

When the router believes a server is under attack as defined by its thresholds, the router will begin actively deleting connections until the number of half-open connections falls below this threshold. Oldest connections are dropped first, unless the command `ip tcp intercept drop-mode random` is used. When an aggressive threshold is exceeded, the router performs the following actions:

1. Each new connection causes the oldest (or random) connection to be deleted.
2. The initial retransmission timeout is reduced by half to 0.5 seconds.
3. If in watch mode, the timeout is reduced by half to 15 seconds.

Two factors determine aggressive behavior. If either of the thresholds is exceeded, aggressive behavior begins until both values fall below their threshold mark. The parameters and their default values are shown in the following list. The meaning of the parameters is self-explanatory.

```
ip tcp intercept max-incomplete low number    900
ip tcp intercept max-incomplete high number   1100
ip tcp intercept one-minute low number        900
ip tcp intercept one-minute high number       1100
```

Other useful commands include the following:

```
show tcp intercept connections
show tcp intercept statistics
```

Sample Configuration

```
ip tcp intercept list 101
!
access list 101 permit tcp any host 160.10.1.1
```

Network Address Translation

Network Address Translation (NAT) is a feature that dynamically modifies the contents of IP packets flowing through the router so that the source and/or IP addresses are altered. Packets leaving the router will have the source or destination address translated to a different IP address. This function enables an administrator to hide the IP addresses in use on an internal network behind a router performing NAT. This technique is a requirement for organizations using addresses from the unregistered address space—or for organizations that are using IP addresses registered to other organizations.

NAT can be used to alter both the source and destination IP addresses in IP headers. The IP checksum is updated automatically by the NAT process. Cisco's version of NAT also enables load-sharing TCP traffic by enabling TCP requests to a single IP address to be services by multiple hosts.

Use of NAT is most prevalent at administrative domain boundaries, such as the Internet, or in connections between different organizations. NAT is useful for organizations that have a registered IP address range but have more hosts than can be accommodated by the number of addresses. Unregistered addresses might be used internally, and registered addresses might be used only when packets communicate with external networks. The NAT process is transparent to both source and destination hosts.

Caveats

Although NAT is a useful tool, NAT does have some drawbacks. The central difficulty with NAT is that some applications embed the original source IP address in the data portion of the IP packet. Therefore, the source IP address of the packet, after undergoing NAT, does not match the IP address embedded in the data portion of the packet. This characteristic causes many applications to function improperly. The Cisco implementation of NAT is capable of handling most applications that include the IP address in the data portion of the packet. One notable exception is NetBIOS session services. NetBIOS services are used by Windows NT, so NetBIOS is prevalent in many data networks. Cisco is actively working to enhance its NAT offering to include full support for all NetBIOS services. More information on the services supported and a wide variety of NAT topics can by found at the Cisco Web site NAT page, http://www.cisco.com/warp/public/732/nat/.

NAT Terms

When discussing NAT, several terms are used.

- Inside local address—IP addresses that are assigned to hosts on the internal network, normally only known by internal hosts
- Inside global address—IP addresses assigned to internal hosts by the NAT process (the addresses of internal hosts as seen by external hosts)

■ Outside local addresses—IP addresses assigned to external hosts by the NAT process (the addresses of external hosts as seen by internal hosts)

■ Outside global addresses—IP addresses assigned to hosts on the external network (known by external hosts but might not be known by internal hosts)

Inside addresses are used by the internal network. These addresses might be translated. Outside addresses are used by external networks and might be translated as well. The term *local* refers to addresses as seen by internal hosts. The term *global* refers to addresses as seen by external hosts. Note that outside local and outside global addresses might be the same if outside addresses are not being translated by NAT.

Sample Configurations

We will show several sample NAT configurations:

1. Translating source addresses
2. Translating source and destination addresses
3. TCP load distribution

Translating Source Addresses

In the Figure 8–5 diagram, we will begin by translating inside local addresses from the 10.0.0.0 address range to the inside global address range 160.10.1.0. The 160.10.1.0 address range is what will be seen by external hosts.

The commands to configure this translation to occur are listed in the following display. Only relevant portions of the configuration are shown:

```
ip nat pool 1600net 160.10.1.1 160.10.1.254 prefix-length 24
ip nat inside source list 1 pool 160net
!
interface ethernet 0
  ip address 10.1.1.254 255.255.255.0
  ip nat inside
!
interface serial 0
  ip address 160.10.2.1 255.255.255.0
  ip nat outside
!
access-list 1 permit 10.1.1.0 0.0.0.255
```

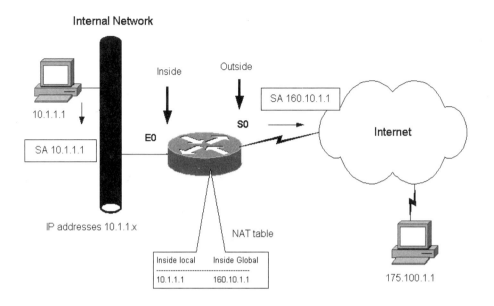

Figure 8–5
The use of NAT to translate internal addresses

Here we have specified a pool of addresses between 160.10.1.1 and 160.10.1.254. Any source address matching access list 1 will cause the NAT service to pick an address from the global pool and assign that source address to outgoing packets. A mapping between the inside local addresses and the inside global addresses is created in a NAT table for future use by the router.

The access list can be an extended IP access list, so that you might specify packets to be translated by both source and destination IP address and protocol. Note that once a packet has triggered a NAT mapping between its inside local address and an inside global address, all future packets from that source IP address will be translated. An extended access list can be used with NAT, so that only packets matching source and destination IP addresses and port numbers create address translation entries. Once a packet triggers an address translation entry for a particular host, however, all future packets from the host will be translated—whether or not they match the extended access list. This condition would occur until the translation entry timeout was reached.

Regarding the commands in the code above, we used a pool of addresses from the 160.10.1.0 range and a separate address range on the Serial0 interface. This event means we would be using two class C networks, which many environments do not have. We can also define the pool of addresses from the same address range as that used on the serial interface. Here's an example of this situation:

```
ip nat pool 1600net 160.10.2.3 160.10.2.254 prefix-length 24
ip nat inside source list 1 pool 160net
!
interface serial 0
  ip address 160.10.2.1 255.255.255.0
  ip nat outside
```

The NAT process on the router will automatically take care of translating incoming packets on the serial link and correctly forwarding them. The same process will work if the outside NAT interface is Ethernet. In this case, the router will answer ARP requests for the inside global pool addresses with its own MAC address.

If we wanted an internal host to be directly accessible from external hosts, we need to provide a static NAT translation so that the internal host is always reachable via the same internal global address. We can assign host 10.1.1.1 a static NAT translation to the global IP address 160.10.2.3. Notice in the following statements that we have removed the .3 inside global host address from the pool.

```
ip nat pool 1600net 160.10.2.4 160.10.2.254 prefix-length 24
ip nat inside source list 1 pool 160net
ip nat inside source static 10.1.1.1 160.20.2.3
```

If we do not want to waste address space or only have a limited number of addresses, we can translate many inside local addresses to one inside global address. In this situation, the router will use source port numbers to differentiate the different inside global addresses, as shown in the diagram in Figure 8–6.

As shown earlier, multiple inside local addresses are translated to a single inside global address. The configuration changes necessary to make this process happen are shown here.

```
ip nat pool 1600net 160.10.2.1 160.10.2.1 prefix-length 304
ip nat inside source list 1 pool 160net overload
!
interface serial 0
  ip address 160.10.2.1 255.255.255.0
  ip nat outside
```

Note that we have defined a single IP address in our address pool, and that the address is the same as the one used on our serial link. This information is useful in situations where the serial link uses a 30-bit mask, and

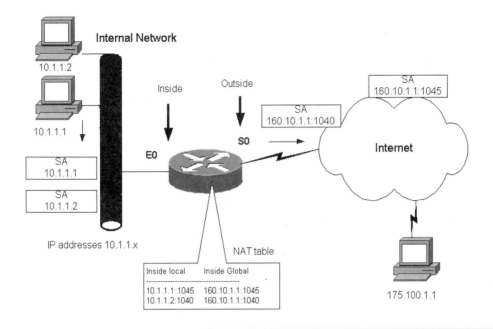

Figure 8–6
The use of a single global IP address to translate all the different inside local IP addresses

there are only two available addresses. The overload parameter on the "ip nat inside source list" command enables the translating of multiple inside local addresses to a single local global address.

Translating Source and Destination Addresses

We will continue to expand our NAT configuration. We have modified our example so that now both internal and external addresses will be translated. This action is useful when the internal and external addresses overlap, as shown in Figure 8–7.

In Figure 8–7, both the internal and external hosts are using IP address 10.1.1.1. NAT can create mappings so that both internal and external IP addresses are modified, as shown here:

```
ip nat pool inside 160.10.1.1 160.10.1.254 prefix-length 24
ip nat pool outside 192.168.1.1 192.168.1.254 prefix-length 24
ip nat inside source list 1 pool inside
ip nat outside source list 1 pool outside
!
interface ethernet 0
  ip address 10.1.1.254 255.255.255.0
  ip nat inside
!
interface serial 0
```

```
    ip address 160.10.2.1 255.255.255.0
    ip nat outside
!
access-list 1 permit 10.0.0.0 0.255.255.255
```

The configuration above relies on internal hosts requesting access to the external host via a DNS lookup. The DNS server must reside on the other side of the router performing address translation. The NAT process will take care of translating the IP address returned in the DNS reply to an outside local address. Normally, a static translation would be used for the external hosts. A static NAT mapping can be configured for outside hosts, just as we saw earlier for inside hosts.

```
    ip nat outside source static 10.1.1.1 192.168.1.1
```

TCP Load Distribution

An additional feature of NAT is the capacity to distribute TCP packets with a single destination IP address among various servers performing the same function. For example, if there were three Web servers providing the same function, an administrator could distribute the load among all of

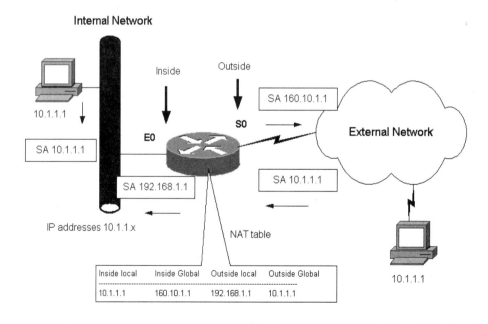

Figure 8–7
The use of address translation to translate both inside and outside IP addresses

them. In the code below, the pool defines the actual addresses of the Web server hosts. The access list defines the virtual IP address that will be the destination IP address for inbound packets. In other words, outside hosts will send IP packets with a destination IP address of 10.1.1.5. The router will take care of sending these packets in a round-robin fashion to the hosts defined by the NAT pool "web-farm."

```
ip nat pool web-farm 10.1.1.1 10.1.1.3 prefix-length 28 type rotary
ip nat inside destination list 1 pool web-farm
!
interface serial 0
  ip address 160.10.2.1 255.255.255.0
  ip nat outside
!
interface ethernet 0
  ip address 10.1.1.254 255.255.255.0
  ip nat inside
!
access-list 1 permit 10.1.1.5
```

Note that the router makes no attempt to determine whether the hosts in the pool are actually functioning. If one of the three servers were to be disabled, the router would continue to try sending packets to the IP address of the failed machine.

Useful Commands

The following commands are useful when configuring NAT. Refer to the Cisco Web site for detailed documentation on the use of each command.

```
clear ip nat translation *
show ip nat translation [verbose]
show ip nat statistics
ip nat translation udp-timeout
ip nat translation tcp-timeout
ip nat translation dns-timeout
ip nat translation finrst-timeout
```

Many more configurations are possible with NAT. Indeed, sample NAT configurations alone could fill an entire book. Refer to the Cisco Web site for additional information on the use of Cisco NAT.

CHAPTER 9

Non-IP Access Lists

In this chapter, we will take a brief look at access lists that can be created for protocols other than IP. All of the previous issues that were discussed with regard to IP access lists apply to non-IP access lists as well. Non-IP access lists are still processed in a top-down fashion; new entries are always added to the bottom of the access list; and the wild card masking principle is the same.

We will initially look at the different kinds of access lists that can be created for the IPX protocol. We will see that there are filters that can be created for IPX that have no direct correlation to those filters used with the IP protocol. We will conclude this chapter by examining the various kinds of filtering that can be done, based on layer 2 information.

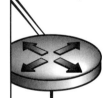

IPX Access Lists

Recall from Chapter 5, "NetWare," that the format of an IPX network number is network.node, where *network* is a four-octet number that identifies the logical network, and *node* is the six-octet MAC layer address. The network number is shared by all devices on a particular physical segment but is unique throughout the Internetwork. No two physical segments can have the same logical network number. The MAC layer address is unique to a particular device and is normally burned into the ROM on an NIC. Another name for the MAC address is *Burned-In Address* (BIA). Both the network and node address are represented in hexadecimal format. Several examples of IPX network.node addresses are shown in Table 9–1.

Notice that the addresses in Table 9–1 are represented in hexadecimal format. As we will see, when specifying a wild card mask to match particular access list entries, the same IP access list rules apply that we saw in Chapter 7, "Cisco Router Access Lists." A binary zero is a match condition, and a binary one is a "don't care" condition. The representation of the address and wild card mask will be in hexadecimal, however, rather than in decimal. For example, if the mask were all binary ones, the representation in decimal for an IP wild card mask would be 255. For an IPX wild card mask, the representation would be FFFFFFFF—indicating the hexadecimal equivalent of all binary ones. A hexadecimal *F* is the equivalent of four binary bits, so eight hexadecimal digits are needed to represent a 4-octet value. In other words, a single octet can be represented by two hexadecimal digits between zero and F (F is 15).

Several different kinds of IPX access lists exist. They generally fall into one of the following categories:

1. IPX data packet filters
2. IPX SAP filters
3. IPX RIP filters

Table 9–1

Examples of
IPX Network
Numbers

IPX Network Number	Network Portion	Node Portion
abcd.0080.1e56.1234	abcd	0080.1356.1234
cddeff.0600.4783.4512	cddeff	0600.4783.4512
f2.0080.0034.7832	f2	0080.0034.7832

We will discuss each of these types of IPX filters in this section.

You can also create IPX access lists to filter NetBIOS packets encapsulated in IPX and to aggregate NLSP routes. These types of access lists are not covered in this book.

Filtering IPX Data Packets

IPX data packet filtering is similar to IP data packet filtering. Both standard and extended IPX data packet filters exist, and each has nearly identical characteristics as those held by their IP counterparts. Standard IPX data filters are capable of filtering only by source and destination IPX network address. Extended IPX data filters are capable of filtering by source and destination IPX address, as well as by protocol and source and destination sockets. Sockets are the IPX equivalent of TCP and UDP port numbers.

The following display shows the syntax of a standard IPX access list:

```
access-list access-list-number {deny | permit} source-
    network[.source-node[source-node-mask]] [destination-
    network[.destination-node [destination-node-mask]]]
```

The access-list-number field must be between 800 and 899. The source-network field is the four-octet source network represented by eight hexadecimal digits. The source-node field is the 6-octet node number represented by 12 hexadecimal digits. The source-node-mask field is an optional network mask, similar to the wild card mask used with IP access lists. A binary zero is a match condition, and a binary one is a "don't care" condition. The principle is the same, except that hexadecimal numbers—instead of decimal numbers—represent the binary values (as with IP).

The use of standard IPX access lists is best illustrated with an example. Figure 9–1 shows a sample IPX network that we will refer to throughout this section.

If we wanted to prevent devices on segment AA from accessing the devices on segment BA, we could implement a standard IPX access list on the router as shown here:

```
interface ethernet 1
  ipx network BA
  ipx access-group 800 out
!
access-list 800 deny AA FFFFFFFF
access-list 800 permit FFFFFFFF
```

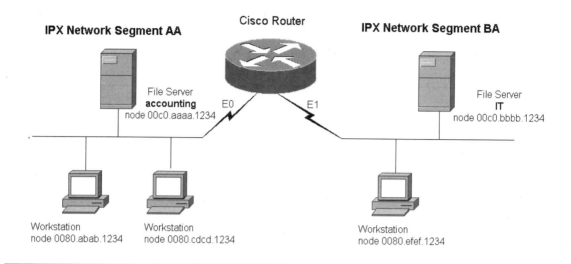

Figure 9–1
A sample IPX network configuration using two IPX servers separated by a router

There are several points of interest in this example. First, notice that the IPX access list is applied to an interface in the same manner as an IP access list, including the specification of a filtering direction. Also notice that the permit entry for access list 800 specifies only the source IPX network number. We could have specified both a source and a destination IPX network number for this entry. We also did not specify a network mask —so, as with IP access lists—an exact match is assumed. Notice that the permit statement specifies all Fs, instead of the keyword *any*.

Instead of using a standard IPX access list, we could use an extended IPX access list to create the same results. The syntax of an extended IPX access list is shown here:

```
access-list access-list-number {deny | permit} protocol [source-
    network[.source-node [source-network-mask.source-node-mask]]
    source-socket [destination-network [.destination-node
    [destination-network-mask.destination-node-mask] destination-
    socket] [log]
```

The *protocol* field is new and enables filtering by a particular IPX protocol type. Table 9–2 shows a list of IPX protocol types.

The *source-socket* and *destination-socket* fields are similar to the TCP and UDP port numbers. They specify particular higher-layer processes within an IPX protocol. A list of IPX socket numbers are shown in Table 9–3.

Table 9–2

IPX Protocol.
Types

Number	Protocol
–1	Wildcard, matches any protocol
0	Undefined protocol, refers to socket numbers.
1	RIP
2	Cisco-specific echo packet (Ping)
3	Error Packet
4	IPX
5	SPX
17	NCP
20	IPX NetBIOS

Table 9–3

IPX Socket
Numbers

Number	Socket
0	All sockets
451	NCP process
452	SAP process
453	RIP process
455	Novell NetBIOS packet
456	Novell diagnostic packet
457	Novell serialization packet
4000-7FFF	Dynamic sockets used by workstations
8000-FFFF	Novell assigned sockets
85BE	IPX EIGRP
9001	NLSP
9004	IPXWAN
9086	IPX official Ping

Returning to our sample network in Figure 9–1, suppose we wanted to block packets from the workstations on segment AA to the devices on segment BA—and enable packets from the accounting server as well. Many methods are available to do this task, but we choose to block based on source network.node numbers. The following display shows an example.

```
interface ethernet 0
  ipx network AA
  ipx access-group 900 in
!
access-list 900 deny 0 AA.0080.0000.0000 FFFFFFFF.000f.ffff.ffff
  BA FFFFFFFF
access-list 900 permit 0 FFFFFFFF
```

This access list will block any protocol from any device on IPX network AA whose node number starts with 008. Notice that the node portion of the wild card mask uses zero in the first three positions and F for everything else, which means that we are matching the first three hexadecimal values (which, in this case, are 008). All of the workstation node numbers start with 008, while the server node address starts with 00C. Therefore, only packets from the workstations to network BA will be blocked. Notice also that the access list has been moved to Ethernet 0 and is applied inbound.

Filtering IPX SAP Updates

Novell uses SAP to enable servers to dynamically advertise which services they are providing. You will sometimes find it desirable to filter out unwanted SAP updates. IPX SAP filters have their own syntax as follows:

```
access-list access-list-number {deny | permit} network[.node]
  [network-mask node-mask] [service-type [scrver-name]]
```

The access-list-number must be between 1,000 and 1,099. The service-type is the SAP type used. Table 9–4 shows a few common SAP types.

Table 9–4

IPX SAP Types

Number	Type
0	Any
1	File Server
2	Print Server
3	SNA Gateway
24	Remote bridge-server

Hundreds of different SAP types exist. A complete list can be found at ftp://ftp.isi.edu/in-notes/iana/assignments/novell-sap-numbers.

The server-name field is the name of a particular server. An asterisk (*) can be used as a wild-card character. Returning to Figure 9–1, suppose we wish to prevent the router from advertising the existence of the accounting server to the devices on segment BA. We can do this task with the following configuration:

```
interface ethernet 1
   ipx network BA
   ipx output-sap-filter 1000
!
access-list 1000 deny -1 0 account*
access-list 1000 permit -1
```

These commands will filter all services that begin with the string "account." We could have specified the entire string, but if the name of the server changed to accounting_1, we would have to alter our access list if we specified the entire string. Because we only specified the first seven letters, in this case we would not have to change the access list. The -1 is equivalent to "any" or all Fs. The zero specifies that any service should be filtered. If we wanted to enable SAP type 4, we could alter the access list as such:

```
interface ethernet 1
   ipx network BA
   ipx output-sap-filter 1000
!
access-list 1000 permit -1 4 account*
access-list 1000 deny -1 0 account*
access-list 1000 permit -1
```

Notice that instead of the command *access-group*, we have used the command *output-sap-filter* on the Ethernet 1 interface. An input-sap-filter command can also be used to filter SAP updates coming into the router. If an input filter is used, the SAP entries will not show up in the SAP table on the router. If an output filter is used, they will show up on the router but will be blocked from being advertised by the router.

Filtering IPX RIP Updates

Novell uses the IPX RIP to advertise information about the IPX networks being used in an Internetwork. Blocking the advertisement of IPX RIP routes by a Cisco router can often be useful. As with SAP filters, both an input and output RIP filter may be configured on a router interface. Returning to Figure 9–1, if we wished to block the router from advertising network AA on segment BA, we could use the following filter:

```
interface ethernet 1
  ipx network BA
  ipx output-network-filter 800
!
access-list 800 deny AA FFFFFFFF
access-list 800 permit -1
```

Notice that a standard IPX access list was used to match the network number we wished to filter. We could also have used an extended IPX access list.

Layer 2 Access Lists

In this section, we cover the use of layer 2 access lists. Layer 2 access lists are used when protocols are being bridged. If a protocol is being routed on an interface, a layer 2 filter will not have any effect on the routed traffic. If you need to filter a protocol based on layer 2 information, you must enable bridging of that protocol on the interface where the layer 2 filter is applied.

Filtering on layer 2 information generally takes one of several forms:

1. Filtering by layer 2 address
2. Filtering by LSAP or Type
3. Filtering by byte offset

We will examine each of these types of layer 2 filters.

Filtering by Layer 2 Address

The first type of layer 2 access list we will examine are the filters that block layer 2 packets based on the layer 2 address. The layer 2 address is also called the MAC layer address and is the simplest type of layer 2 filter. The syntax of a MAC address filter is shown in the following line:

```
access-list access-list-number {permit | deny} mask
```

The access-list-number is a number between 700 and 799. The mask uses the same format as the network mask used on an IP access list: a binary zero represents a match condition, and a binary one represents a "don't care" condition. MAC addresses are a 6-octet number, which is represented by a 12-digit hexadecimal number. A MAC address is applied to an interface through the use of either the *input-address-list* command or the *output-address-list* command. We show an example of these commands:

```
Interface ethernet 0
  bridge-group 1 input-address-list 700
!
access-list 700 deny 0080.0000.0000 000f.ffff.ffff
access-list 700 permit 0000.0000.0000 ffff.ffff.ffff
```

In this example, we are matching the first three hexadecimal values in the deny entry. This action will block all packets that begin with a source MAC address of 008. We could also match based on the exact source MAC address:

```
Interface ethernet 0
  bridge-group 1 input-address-list 700
!
access-list 700 deny 0080.1234.5678 ffff.ffff.ffff
access-list 700 permit 0000.0000.0000 ffff.ffff.ffff
```

This access list will only filter packets that have a source MAC address of 0080.1234.5678.

MAC address filters can also be created for destination addresses. In this case, the output-address-list command is used. When filtering on destination MAC address, an important note is that the filter could deny broadcast packets from the router. When using an output MAC address filter, packets to the broadcast address should be explicitly permitted if the default *deny any* command is used. In the following example, we are permitting packets to a single MAC address and the broadcast address, and we are denying everything else.

```
Interface ethernet 0
  bridge-group 1 output-address-list 700
!
access-list 700 permit 0080.1234.5678 ffff.ffff.ffff
access-list 700 permit ffff.ffff.ffff 0000.0000.0000
access-list 700 deny 0000.0000.0000 ffff.ffff.ffff
```

Notice that the second entry permits packets with the destination MAC address of all ones, which is the broadcast address. The last *deny any* statement is implied and is shown only for clarity.

You can also filter on both source and destination MAC address. This task requires the use of a different access list syntax. We will see an example of this syntax later in this section.

Filtering by LSAP or Type

In addition to filtering by MAC address, layer 2 filters can block packets based on the LSAP or Type fields (depending on the type of packets in use on the Ethernet segment).

If the packets are Ethernet II packets, the twenty-first and twenty-second bytes of the Ethernet packet contain a Type field that identifies the upper-layer protocol in use. For example, 0x0800 identifies the upper-layer protocol as IP.

If the packets are 802.2 packets, the twenty-first and twenty-second bytes of the Ethernet packet contain a *Destination Service Access Point* (DSAP) and *Source Service Access Point* (SSAP) pair. This DSAP/SSAP pair is generically called the LSAP address. For example, the DSAP/SSAP pair 0xF0F0 identifies the packet as NetBIOS.

Both types of filters use the same syntax:

```
access-list access-list-number {permit | deny} type-code mask
```

The access-list-number is a number between 200 and 299. The type-code is the 2-byte Type of LSAP code on which to filter. The format of the *mask* parameter is the same as we have seen with other access lists.

The way the access list is applied to the interface is what determines whether you are filtering by Type of LSAP. If you are filtering by Type, the command *input-type-list* is used. If you are filtering by LSAP, the command *input-lsap-list* is used. We show an example of each in the following display:

```
Interface ethernet 0
  bridge-group 1 input-type-list 200
!
access-list 200 permit 0x0800 0x0000
access-list 200 deny 0x0000 0xffff
```

In this example, we are filtering by Type. This access list permits packets only if the upper-layer protocol is IP (0x0800).

The following example permits packets only if the DSAP/LSAP pair is NetBIOS (0xF0F0):

```
Interface ethernet 0
  bridge-group 1 input-lsap-list 200
```

```
!
access-list 200 permit 0xF0F0 0x0101
access-list 200 deny 0x0000 0xffff
```

When using an LSAP filter, the mask should be specified at least as 0x0101. In both of these examples, the deny entry is unnecessary because it is implied. We show this command only as a reminder.

Filtering by Byte Offset

The most powerful layer 2 filters that can be created are *byte offset filters*. These filters enable you to block layer 2 packets based on arbitrary fields in the layer 2 packet. The syntax of a byte offset filter is shown in the following line:

```
access-list access-list-number {permit | deny} source source-mask
   destination destination-mask offset size operator operand
```

The access-list-number is a number between 1,100 and 1,199. The *source* and *source-mask* identify the source MAC address. The *destination* and *destination-mask* identify the destination MAC address. The *offset* is the number of bytes the fields you are matching are offset from the destination MAC address—not the start of the packet. The destination MAC address field starts eight bytes into the Ethernet packet. To calculate the offset, subtract eight from the number of bytes between the beginning of the packet and the beginning of the field you are filtering. The *size* field is the number of bytes you are matching, between one and four. The *operator* field is a keyword used to compare the arbitrary bytes in the field, such as EQ for equal, NEQ for not equal, LT for less than, and GT for greater than. The *operand* field is the field against which you are comparing the arbitrary bytes.

The use of byte offset filtering is best illustrated with an example. In the following filter, we are comparing two bytes (0x1e) that are 24 bytes (32–8) into the packet to see whether the value is equal to (eq) 0x1F1C:

```
Interface ethernet 0
  bridge-group 1 input-pattern 1100
!
access-list 1100 permit 0000.0000.0000 ffff.ffff.ffff.ffff
   0000.0000.0000 ffff.ffff.ffff.ffff 0x1e 2 eq 0x1f1c
access-list 1100 deny 0000.0000.0000 ffff.ffff.ffff.ffff
```

The format of these types of access lists can be modified to filter only on source and destination MAC address:

```
Interface ethernet 0
  bridge-group 1 input-pattern 1100
!
access-list 1100 permit 0080.0000.0000 000f.ffff.ffff.ffff
  00c0.1234.5678 ffff.ffff.ffff.ffff
access-list 1100 deny 0000.0000.0000 ffff.ffff.ffff.ffff
```

This filter permits layer 2 packets if the source MAC address begins with 008 and the destination MAC address is 00c0.1234.5678. All other layer 2 packets are denied.

Using Access Expressions

The final type of layer 2 filtering we will examine is the use of *access expressions.* An access expression is the joining of a source MAC address filter and a Type of LSAP filter to create a composite expression. For example, suppose we wished to allow packets only if they were from MAC address 0080.1234.5678—and if they were SNA frames (LSAP type 0x0404 0x00010). The following commands create the access expression:

```
Interface ethernet 0
  Access-expression in lsap(200) & smac(700)
!
access-list 200 permit 0x0404 0x0101
!
access-list 700 permit 0080.1234.5678 0000.0000.0000
```

Notice the command *access-expression* is applied to the Ethernet 0 interface. The ampersand (&) symbol designates an AND condition and means that both conditions must be met. The straight-line (|) symbol designates an OR condition, and a tilde (˜) symbol indicates a NOT condition. Parentheses can be used in access expressions to create complex conditions. The following example shows an addition to the access expression that permits packets not only if they are from source MAC address 0080.1234.5678 and SNA—but also if they are NetBIOS packets.

```
Interface ethernet 0
  Access-expression in lsap(201) | (lsap(200) & smac(700))
!
access-list 200 permit 0x0404 0x0101
!
access-list 201 permit 0xF0F0 0x0101
!
access-list 700 permit 0080.1234.5678 0000.0000.0000
```

Notice that the access expression is configured so that NetBIOS packets (0xF0F0 0x0101), OR packets that are both from MAC address 0080.1234.5678 and SNA, are permitted.

10

The Cisco PIX

In this chapter, we focus on a completely different product from Cisco Systems, the *Private Internet Exchange* (PIX). The PIX, unlike a router, is a dedicated firewall platform. As we have seen in Chapter 8, "Advanced Cisco Router Security," a Cisco router can be configured to function as a firewall. However, a router is not designed from the ground up to perform this function. It takes fairly extensive configuration and planning to configure a Cisco router to perform the functions of a firewall. The Cisco router IOS contains many features that enhance its functionality far beyond merely routing packets, yet it is for this reason that it takes extensive configuration to ensure that the router is secure.

The Cisco PIX is very different than the Router IOS. Out of the box the Cisco PIX is secure. Unless specifically configured, no packets from outside administrative domains are allowed to enter your network. No sessions from external domains can be established to the PIX and the PIX itself is generally not vulnerable to attacks due to the very limited number of services it supports. Additionally, it takes very minimal configuration to get the PIX up and

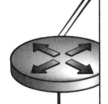

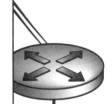

running. Only six commands are necessary to initially configure the PIX and have it protect your network. Assuming the PIX is already cabled and you have a console connection, it can literally be configured and running in about five minutes.

The PIX supports many additional features that require configuration beyond the basic six commands. In release 4.2(3) of the PIX IOS, Cisco has provided many significant enhancements. We will examine both the basic configuration commands and the new enhancements in this chapter. It should also be noted that the configuration commands that will be detailed here are for version 4.2(3). Although many of the commands are similar to later revisions, there have been significant enhancements and changes to commands used in earlier versions. If you are running earlier versions of the PIX IOS, you should contact your local Cisco representative for details on obtaining the latest IOS version.

NOTE: As this book was going to press, Cisco released version 4.3 of the PIX IOS. The authors have examined the release notes for this version and did not find any significant architectural changes to the functions and commands discussed in this chapter, but there may be changes to the default settings for a few commands. If you upgrade to version 4.3, you should review the release notes on the Cisco Web site (www. cisco.com).

Cisco PIX Basics

We will begin our discussion of the PIX by initially answering the question, "just what is the PIX?" The PIX is a complete hardware and software solution, similar in this regard to a router. The PIX IOS runs only on the special PIX hardware and cannot be ported to other hardware platforms. Similarly, the PIX hardware does not support any other operating systems such as Unix or NT. Figure 10–1 shows a view of the PIX from the front.

Figure 10–2 shows a view of the PIX from the back.

The PIX hardware is essentially a hybrid system. In most respects, it resembles a rack mountable personal computer without a hard drive. Instead of a hard drive, the PIX stores both its configuration and its IOS image on a two-MB flash card. Note that this is unlike a Cisco router that stores its configuration in a completely separate NVRAM area. In addition to flash memory, the PIX also has a floppy drive that can be used to

Figure 10–1
Front view of the PIX

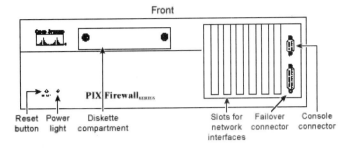

Figure 10–2
Back view of the PIX

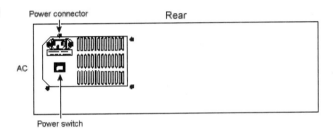

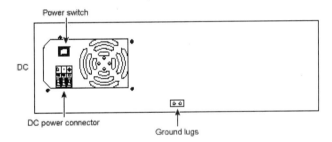

save and restore the configuration. The floppy drive is used to upgrade the IOS image on the two-MB flash memory card using a specially created PIX boot floppy. The utility and instructions for performing this operation are available on the Cisco Web site (www.cisco.com).

The PIX is specifically designed to perform a very limited number of tasks. The PIX has two central purposes:

1. Provide *Network Address Translation* (NAT) functionality

2. Provide network security

All of the functions of the PIX are designed with these two goals in mind.

Although the most current PIX hardware and software can support up to four LAN interfaces, the original PIX supported only two interfaces, a trusted and an untrusted link. In PIX terminology, the trusted link is called the "inside" interface and the untrusted link is called the "outside" interface. These two interfaces are required for the PIX to function.

NOTE: In the context of this chapter, unless specifically stated otherwise, the term "outbound" means connections from a more trusted side of the PIX to a less trusted side of the PIX. The term "inbound" means connections from a less trusted side of the PIX to a more trusted side of the PIX. The trust level of each interface can be set and is called the security level. The inside interface is always the most trusted or highest security interface and the outside interface is always the least trusted or lowest security interface.

The PIX default policy is very simple: allow everything outbound from the inside interface to the outside interface and allow only return connections from the outside interface to the inside interface. The use of more than two LAN interfaces complicates this rule, but this concept is essentially unchanged in all versions of the PIX and grasping this principle is central to understanding the security of the PIX. We will return to this topic throughout this chapter. Figure 10–3 shows a graphical representation of this concept.

The PIX handles connections from an inside interface to an outside interface much differently than connections from the outside to the inside.

Figure 10–3
The default configuration of the PIX allows all connections from the inside interface to the outside but only return connections from the outside interface to the inside.

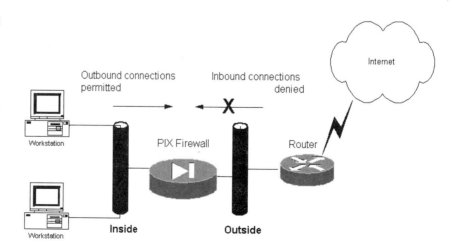

All outbound connections from the inside interface to the outside one are permitted unless specifically denied. In contrast, only established connections are permitted from the outside interface to the inside one. Special commands must be used to permit connections from an outside interface to one inside. We will cover the commands to allow connections from an outside interface to an inside interface later in this chapter.

The PIX maintains information about the state of existing connections in order to know whether packets inbound from an outside interface are part of an existing conversation. If the PIX does not recognize that the incoming packets are part of an existing conversation, the packets are dropped and information about the packet is logged. As mentioned, special commands can be used to allow inbound connections that are not part of an existing conversation.

The PIX IOS is aware of the behavior of many applications, so it can securely handle many multi-channel protocols. In these respects, it has capabilities similar to that of *Context Based Access Control* (CBAC). Recall our discussion of stateful inspection and CBAC earlier in Chapters 8 and 9.

Both 10/100 Ethernet and Token Ring LAN cards can be installed in the PIX. These cards are essentially the same network cards that can be installed in other host devices that support ISA or PCI bus interfaces. However, because the PIX IOS is very specialized, only certain vendor cards are guaranteed to work with the PIX IOS. A list of compatible cards can be obtained from your local Cisco representative. Using non-approved cards in the PIX voids the warranty and is highly discouraged. The PIX does not support *wide area network* (WAN) interfaces, so a router is required for wide area connectivity.

The PIX is initially configured in the same manner as a Cisco router via a direct console cable. The console connection on the PIX allows configuration through a terminal emulation program, such as Windows HyperTerminal. The PIX also supports remote administration via the telnet protocol, but access via telnet must be explicitly enabled. As we will see later, Cisco has introduced a management console called the PIX Manger that provides a GUI interface for managing single or multiple PIX boxes.

Models and Specifications

There are two current versions of the PIX, the 510 and the 520. The specifications of these models are listed in Table 10–1.

Table 10–1

The Specifications
for the PIX510
and PIX520

Model	CPU	Memory
PIX510	Pentium II 166 Mhz	16 MB
PIX520	Pentium II 233 Mhz	32 MB

Currently the maximum memory that can be installed in the PIX is 32 MB.

Several versions of the PIX hardware have been introduced previously by Cisco, such as the PIX 10000. These models are not covered, but the PIX IOS principles discussed in this chapter are the same regardless of the model used.

The PIX is currently capable of supporting up to 4 10/100 Ethernet cards or three Token Ring cards. Both Ethernet and Token Ring cards can be combined in the same chassis as long as the total number of cards does not exceed four. The PIX also provides for an additional encryption card to create secure private network connections to other PIX units. The use of a private link card reduces the number of available network interface cards by one.

A concept that is introduced with the PIX that we did not see when covering Cisco routers is licensing. A Cisco router does not keep track of the number of connections used through its interfaces. This is not true for the PIX. It counts each TCP conversation as a connection and limits the number of connections that can be used, depending on the licensing agreement. The current licensing options for the PIX are 128, 1024, and unlimited. The maximum number of connections is also limited by the amount of RAM installed in the PIX. The current maximum RAM that can be installed in the PIX is 32 MB, which allows 65,536 simultaneous connections.

Note that a connection is not the same as the number of IP addresses. A single host station can use multiple connections, depending on the application used. Telnet, for example, uses only one connection, while FTP uses two and Web Browsing can use as many as 20 for a single session. The recommended rule of thumb is to plan for four to eight connections per active user and order your licensing based on that number. If you have 100 users, it would be wise to order at least the 1024 license version because it's likely that the 128 connection limit may be reached with only 30 to 40 active users. We will see later that there are ways to limit the number of connections used by particular IP address ranges.

Two additional caveats apply when talking about the number of connections allowed. First, UDP connections are not counted against the license. If the license is for 128 connections, that many TCP connections and an unlimited number of UDP connections are allowed. Second, only connections from a higher security interface to a lower security interface are counted against the license. On a PIX with only two interfaces, this means that no connections from an outside interface to an inside interface are counted against the license. When more than two interfaces are in use, the security values of the source and destination interfaces are used to determine whether or not a TCP connection counts against the license. Interface security levels will be covered later in this chapter.

Special Features of the PIX

As we stated earlier, the PIX is secure out of the box. It provides a limited number of services, which makes it far more secure in its default configuration than a router. In its default configuration, only six commands are needed to enable basic functionality.

The PIX must be configured with at least two active interfaces. One interface must be configured as the *inside* interface and one as the *outside* interface. The PIX does not support WAN interfaces.

By default, once the interfaces of the PIX have been assigned IP addresses and made active, all traffic from the inside interface is allowed outbound through the outside interface, while only return traffic is allowed inbound from the outside interface. Any traffic initiated from hosts on the untrusted network side of the PIX is dropped at the outside interface. The PIX monitors the state of existing connections so that packets arriving at the outside interface are only allowed access if they are part of a legitimate network conversation. This feature is called the Adaptive Security Algorithm and is the heart and soul of PIX security.

There is one caveat to the algorithm described above. As described, the definition is correct only for TCP- or UDP-based network connections; ICMP is handled differently. In pre-4.2 releases, the default behavior of the PIX was to allow the following types of ICMP packets inbound: echo-reply, source-quench, unreachable, and time-exceeded. These ICMP packets were used for ping, traceroute, and flow control by inside stations. In version 4.2, this behavior was altered so that no ICMP packets were allowed inbound by default. This means that even if a ping or traceroute is initiated from the inside interface, the procedure fails because the PIX blocks the inbound ICMP packets at the outside interface. Each type of ICMP packet that is needed must be explicitly allowed through the outside interface. We will cover this topic later in this chapter when we discuss ways to allow traffic inbound from the outside interface to the inside interface.

The other main function of the PIX is to perform *Network Address Translation* (NAT). Recall our discussion of NAT from Chapter 8. The PIX was designed to support NAT, but this functionality can be disabled if needed. The PIX can also be configured to support *Port Address Translation* (PAT) so that only one IP address is used to translate many addresses. In the latest version of the PIX IOS, the use of NAT in both directions is supported. This is commonly referred to as *dual NAT* and is useful if there are overlapping addresses on an inside and outside network.

The PIX is capable of securely handling many applications. In general, the only applications that do not work through the PIX are those that use changing and/or random port numbers during a TCP or UDP conversation. Many multimedia applications exhibit this behavior and the PIX is specifically aware of many of the popular multimedia applications' behaviors. What this means is that if an application requires that the server end of a multimedia connection opens a return connection to a multimedia client in a range of ports, the PIX will allow packets back from the server but only on the range necessary. No unnecessary holes will be opened up that could be exploited by an attacker. A list of the multimedia applications that the PIX is capable of handling securely is given in Table 10–2.

Table 10–2

The Multimedia Applications the PIX Is Capable of Handling Securely

Intel Internet Video Phone
Microsoft NetMeeting
Microsoft Netshow
RealNetworks RealAudio and RealVideo
VDOnet VDOlive
Vxtreme WebTheater
VocalTec Internet Phone
White Pine CU-SeeMe
White Pine Meeting Point
Xing Streamworks

As you can see, the list is quite extensive. Cisco has worked very hard to ensure that the PIX will work correctly and securely with most of popular multimedia applications on the market. For those multi-channel applications of which the PIX is not specifically aware, the PIX provides an option to modify the standard adaptive security policy through the use of the *established* command, which will be covered later in this chapter.

The PIX provides many additional features above and beyond merely maintaining information about the state of connections and the address translation. A list of additional features and a brief description is shown in Table 10–3.

Table 10–3

Additional Features Provided by the PIX

Feature	Description
DNS Guard	All outgoing DNS requests are allowed by default, but only the first reply is allowed to return through the PIX. This feature cannot be disabled.
Mail Guard	Only the SMTP commands specified in RFC 821 are allowed to a SMTP server on an inside interface, which include HELO, MAIL, RCPT, DATA, RSET, NOOP, and QUIT. All other SMTP commands are dropped and the PIX responds with OK to confuse attackers. This feature is configured through the fixup protocol command.
IP Fragguard	This feature requires that all non-initial IP fragments be associated with an already-seen initial fragment. It also limits the number of IP fragments to 100 full-fragmented packets per second per internal host. This prevents many IP fragment attacks such as teardrop, land.c, and so on. It is on by default but can be disabled by using the sysopt security fragguard command. It cannot be selectively enabled on a per-interface basis.
Flood Defender	This feature allows you to limit the total number of connections and the number of embryonic connections in use with a nat or static command. An embryonic connection is either a connection that has not completed the TCP three-way handshake or, if UDP is the transport, that has not received a response to an initial connection request. The nat and static commands will be covered further in this chapter.
Flood Guard	This feature is used with the Authentication services of the PIX, which is able to authenticate inbound and outbound user connections. To do so, the PIX uses a user authentication subsystem. It is possible for this subsystem to run out of resources if a large number of user requests are pending. If this occurs, the PIX dynamically begins reclaiming system resources from the user authentication subsystem. This prevents a denial of service (DoS) attack by someone sending many failed user authentication attempts to the PIX.

continues

Table 10–3

Continued.

Feature	Description
Default ICMP Deny	By default, the PIX denies any inbound ICMP packets, even if they are in response to an ICMP query initiated from the inside interface. This is a new feature of the 4.2 IOS. All inbound ICMP packets must be explicitly permitted by using the conduit command, which will be discussed in this chapter.
Sequence Number Randomization	By default, the PIX automatically randomizes the TCP sequence numbers used by outgoing connections. This makes it nearly impossible for an attacker to successfully hijack a TCP session because they cannot predict what the sequence numbers will be during the initial TCP three-way handshake (refer to Chapter 8, "Advanced Cisco Router Security," for more on this topic). This feature can be disabled on individual nat and static command entries, which are discussed later in this chapter.

Some of these features are always on and cannot be disabled. For others, the only modification option is to disable or enable them. The features that are configurable are noted in the table above and are covered later in this chapter.

On a final note, one of the central features of the PIX is its packet throughput rate. In the industry, the PIX has shown its capability to forward and receive packets at rates of 170 Mbps on a full-duplex Fast Ethernet link. This is about two to three times faster than the rates attainable by most competing firewall solutions based on either Unix or NT platforms. This packet throughput rate is one of the biggest advantages of using an integrated hardware and software solution. The PIX is inherently scalable for large transaction environments.

Limitations of the PIX

The benefits of the PIX notwithstanding, every firewall solution has some limitations and the PIX is no exception. In this section, we detail the most significant limitations of the PIX.

Closed Implementation

With the benefits of an integrated firewall solution come some drawbacks. Because the PIX is a complete hardware and software solution, you are locked into a particular hardware platform. If you outgrow your hardware implementation, your only option may be to purchase an additional

PIX. Since the PIX is capable of handling large volumes of traffic, this issue may not be as problematic as it sounds.

Additionally, the PIX IOS is a completely closed operating system, so no details on its underlying security structure are publicly available. This is in contrast to general-purpose operating systems such as NT or Unix. Note, however, that the underlying security of the firewall software on those operating systems is normally closed as well unless an open-source solution is implemented. Most vendors do not like to disclose the source code for the products they sell.

Limited Routing Support

The PIX is not a router. Although it supports some functions of RIP, it is not designed to fully participate in the routing process. This limitation is usually only an issue in designs that involve multiple, active PIX units. We cover the use of static routing and RIP on the PIX later in this chapter.

Limited VPN Support

The current PIX implementation only provides PIX to PIX *Virtual Private Network* (VPN) support. As of this writing, there is no capability to establish an encrypted connection to the PIX using an end-station such as Windows or Unix. Cisco has announced plans to have a client VPN solution available for the PIX sometime in 1999 and has also discontinued its partnership with a third-party vendor to develop a VPN client solution for the PIX and is developing its own solution internally.

Limited Client Authentication

Client authentication is the requirement that end-users are authenticated and authorized by the PIX before they can establish connections from an inside or outside interface. Authentication answers the question "who are you?," while authorization answers the question "what are you allowed to do?" The PIX supports client authentication and authorization, but it requires a TACACS+ sever. A RADIUS server can be used if only authentication is required, but the PIX does not support authorization when using a RADIUS server. The users are prompted for authentication only when they attempt to use FTP, Telnet, or HTTP. If the application is not one of these three, special procedures must be used.

PIX authentication will be covered further later in this chapter. In the next section, we begin our discussion of the specific commands used to configure the PIX.

Configuring the Cisco PIX

As we mentioned earlier, the basic PIX configuration is very simple. The PIX comes prebuilt to allow all connections from the inside interface access to the outside interface and to block all connections from the outside interface to the inside interface. All that is necessary to enable this functionality is to configure and enable the interfaces, add a static route and the NAT commands, and your system is ready to go. It should be noted here that a NAT command is necessary even if NAT is not used, because NAT functionality is imbedded in the core of the PIX IOS.

Before covering the default configuration of the PIX, it is worth mentioning that the maximum size of the PIX configuration is one MB minus the size of the IOS image loaded. This is because both the configuration file and the IOS image are stored on the same two-MB flash memory card. Currently, a bug prevents the upper one MB of the flash memory card from being used, which is why the size of the IOS image is subtracted from one MB and not two.

The number of megabytes free is the number of characters that can occur in the configuration. If the IOS image is 600 KB, the number of characters that can appear in the configuration is 400 KB or 409,600. This translates roughly to about 7,500 to 10,000 lines of configuration, depending on the commands used, and should be sufficient for almost all environments.

Default Configuration

In this section, we display the default configuration of the PIX when it is initially booted using PIX IOS 4.2.3. Figure 10–4 shows the default configuration and each of the default commands will be covered in detail later.

Each section is displayed with a corresponding line number to facilitate discussion. In the actual configuration, no line numbers are shown.

Naming Interfaces

The first command in the configuration is on lines 2 and 3. The `nameif` command provides a mechanism to assign a name to each interface on the PIX and to specify its security level. The syntax of this command is shown below:

```
nameif hardware_id if_name security_level
```

```
1     PIX version 4.2.3
2     nameif ethernet0  outside security0
3     nameif ethernet1 inside security100
4     enable password 3Ey27xUiv19Tl80 encrypted
5     passwd KQn.2YVVoU58Bzp8 encrypted
6     hostname pixfirewall
7     fixup protocol ftp 21
8     fixup protocol http 80
9     fixup protocol smtp 25
10    fixup protocol h323 1720
11    fixup protocol rsh 514
12    fixup protocol sqlnet 1521
13    names
14    no failover
15    failover timeout 0:00:00
16    failover ip address outside 0.0.0.0
17    failover ip address inside 0.0.0.0
18    pager lines 24
19    no logging console
20    no logging monitor
21    no logging buffered
22    no logging trap
23    logging facility 20
24    interface ethernet0 auto
25    interface ethernet1 auto
26    interface ethernet2 auto
27    interface ethernet3 auto
28    ip address outside 0.0.0.0 0.0.0.0
29    ip address inside 0.0.0.0 0.0.0.0
30    ip address 0.0.0.0 0.0.0.0
31    arp timeout 14400
32    no rip outside passive
33    no rip outside default
34    no rip inside passive
35    no rip inside default
36    timeout xlate 3:00:00 conn 1:00:00 udp 0:02:00
37    timeout rpc 0:10:00 h323 0:05:00
38    timeout uauth 0:05:00 absolute
39    no snmp-server location
40    no snmp-server contact
41    snmp-server community public
42    no snmp-server enable traps
43    mtu outside 1500
44    mtu inside 1500
45    mtu 1500
46    floodguard 1
```

The if_name is a name assigned from the administrator for the interface that is used in all configuration references to the interface. It consists of up to 255 characters and can be upper- or lowercase. The name of the inside interface cannot be changed.

The hardware_id is the hardware name assigned by the PIX IOS to each network card. The network cards are numbered from the leftmost slot nearest the power supply and begin at 0. The inside interface must be in slot 1, the lowest security level interface is in slot 0, the next lowest in slot 2, and so on.

The security_level is a number between 0 and 100. The lowest security interface is typically named outside and has a default security level of 0, as seen in Figure 10–4. The highest security level interface is named inside and has a security level of 100. Neither the name nor the security level can be changed for the highest security interface (the inside interface).

The security level is purely a relative value. It designates whether an interface is inside or outside relative to another interface. An interface is considered inside in relation to another interface if its security level is higher than the other interface's security level. As stated earlier, the highest security level is 100, while the lowest is 0. Security levels should be unique so that no two interfaces have the same one. Because the inside interface has the highest possible security value, it is obvious that all other interfaces are considered outside in relation to the outside interface. It is also obvious that all other interfaces are considered inside in relation to it because the outside interface has the lowest possible security value.

Whether or not an interface is considered inside or outside another interface is relevant due to the default behavior of the PIX. Remember we stated earlier that the default behavior of the PIX is to allow all connections from the inside interface to the outside interface and to block all connections from the outside to the inside. Although this concept is very simple to understand when there are only two interfaces, it becomes a bit more difficult to apply when there are three or more. This is where the security level comes into play.

The security level is used by the PIX to determine the default behavior for connections initiated from an interface. If the connection is initiated from a higher security interface to a lower one, the connection is allowed by default. If the connection is initiated from a lower security interface to a higher one, the connection is denied by default. An example will serve to illustrate this purpose.

Figure 10–5
A PIX firewall with
four interfaces of
varying security levels

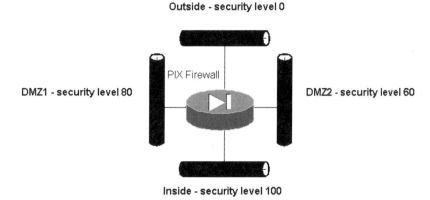

In Figure 10–5, we show a PIX with four interfaces. Each interface is labeled with a name and a security level.

Because the interface labeled "inside" always has a security level of 100, we know that all connections from that interface to all other interfaces are allowed by default. Similarly, because the interface labeled "outside" has a default value of 0, we know that connections from that interface to all other interfaces are denied by default. The question arises when we consider the other interfaces, dmz1 and dmz2. What is the default behavior of the PIX when connections are initiated from these interfaces?

To answer this question, we examine the security levels that have been configured on each interface. We see that dmz1 has a security level of 80 and that dmz2 has a security level of 60. This means that dmz1 is considered *more* secure than dmz2. Thus, connections from dmz1 to dmz2 are allowed by default and connections from dmz2 to dmz1 are denied by default. As already mentioned, all connections to the inside interface are denied by default and all connections to the outside interface are allowed by default. Our selection of the security level 80 for dmz1 and 60 for dmz2 was somewhat arbitrary. We could have chosen any values between 1 and 99 as long as the values are unique for each interface.

At this point in our configuration, we do not have any reason to believe that one DMZ interface will be more secure than another interface. We will discuss methods for determining which interface should be configured with a higher security level when we discuss NAT later in this chapter. We will also see ways in which the default behavior can be overridden so that connections from a lower security interface to a higher one can be allowed and connections from a higher security interface to a lower one can be blocked.

Interface Settings

The interface commands are shown on lines 24 through 27 in Figure 10–4.

NOTE: We have skipped some of the configuration to facilitate discussion. We will return to the commands we have skipped after discussing the interface settings.

An interface command automatically appears for any recognized Ethernet board that is installed in the PIX. Token Ring boards may not initially appear in the configuration but should appear once they are referenced with the interface command. The syntax of the command is shown below:

```
Interface hardware_id hardware_speed
```

The `hardware_id` value is the same value referenced with the nameif command. It is automatically chosen by the PIX, based on the interface board's location in relation to the power supply. The `hardware_speed` can take on one of multiple values, depending on the type of interface card installed. For Ethernet cards, the value can be one of the following:

10baset	Sets 10 Mbps half duplex
100basetx	Sets 100 Mbps half duplex
100basefull	Sets 100 Mbps full duplex
aui	Sets 10 Mbps half duplex for an AUI interface
auto	Automatically detects speed and duplex
bnc	Sets 10 Mbps half duplex for a BNC interface

For Token Ring cards, the value can be either four or 16, indicating either a four or 16 Mbps connection.

Passwords

Line 4 is the enable password and line 5 is the telnet password in Figure 10–4. These passwords serve the same purpose as those used on a Cisco router. The telnet password is equivalent to the VTY password on a router, and the enable password is equivalent to the enable secret password on a router. Both passwords are always encrypted. Each password is case-sensitive and can be up to 16 alphanumeric characters. The default telnet password is *cisco,* and there is no default enable password.

Both passwords should be changed immediately after initially booting your PIX. Although a telnet session cannot be established to the PIX until telnet has been specifically enabled, it is always good practice to change any default password settings immediately. Believe it or not, many documented security breaches have occurred because an administrator neglected to change the default passwords that shipped with various hardware and software platforms.

Hostname

The hostname command is shown on line 6 in Figure 10–4. The default setting is *pixfirewall.* This command is used to set the name of the PIX and can be up to 16 alphanumeric characters.

Fixup Commands

Lines 7 through 12 show the default values for the fixup command in Figure 10-4. The fixup command is used to modify how the PIX handles connections for particular applications. Some applications, such as FTP, require that the PIX understand special properties of the application so that connections that are legitimately part of the application are permitted access. During an FTP transfer, for example, the PIX needs to be aware of the second data channel that is opened from the server to the initiating workstation. Similarly, the PIX implements a feature called Mail Guard, which allows only the SMTP commands HELO, MAIL, RCPT, DATA, RSET, NOOP, and QUIT access to a protected SMTP server.

The PIX identifies applications by the TCP or UDP port number contained in the IP packets. It identifies FTP by port number 21 and SMTP by port number 25, for example. In most cases, there is no reason to change these port numbers, but in rare cases you may have a service listening on a non-standard port number. For instance, you might have an FTP server listening on port 5140. In this case, the PIX would not recognize that port 5140 is being used for an FTP transfer and might incorrectly believe that the return FTP data connection from the server should be blocked. This problem could be resolved by adding port 5140 to the fixup protocol command as shown below:

```
fixup protocol ftp 5140
```

This command allows the PIX to recognize that connections to port 5140 should be treated in the same manner as connections to port 21.

Another use of the fixup command is to disable the normal handling of certain applications by the PIX. If for some reason you wished to allow more SMTP commands than those allowed in the default configuration, you could disable the fixup command for SMTP as shown below:

```
no fixup protocol smtp 25
```

This disables the Mail Guard feature. The default processing of other applications can be disabled similarly. The RSH application is somewhat special in that the default value of 514 cannot be changed, but additional RSH values can be added.

Names

The names command is shown on line 13 in Figure 10–4. The use of this command enables you to configure a list of name-to-IP address mappings on the PIX. This allows the use of names in the configuration instead of the IP addresses. You can specify a name by using the following syntax:

```
name ip_address name
```

The name is case-sensitive and must consist of alphanumeric characters. Use of an underscore is also supported, but the name cannot exceed 16 characters. Once a name is defined, it can be used in any PIX command that references an IP address. An example is shown below:

```
names
name 10.1.1.1 pix_inside
ip address inside pix_inside
show ip address
inside ip address pix_inside mask 255.255.255.255
```

The names in the PIX configuration can be cleared by issuing the command:

```
no names
```

Although the use of names instead of IP addresses can be useful, we have found that the names feature does not scale very well and can be an additional administrative burden if many IP addresses are in use on the PIX. Use of this command is strictly optional and is at the administrator's discretion.

Failover

Lines 14 through 17 of the configuration in Figure 10–4 show the failover commands. These commands are used when there are two PIX units configured in a primary and secondary configuration. If the PIX is not configured in a failover configuration, these commands can be ignored and they do not affect normal PIX behavior. This topic is covered in detail later in this chapter.

Pager Lines

This command is shown on line 18 in Figure 10–4. It is used to set the number of lines that will appear on your screen before the "More" prompt is displayed. The syntax of this command is shown below:

```
pager lines lines
```

You can set the *lines* value to 0 to disable paging. Entering the command `pager` with no options restores the default setting of 24.

Logging

The logging commands appear on lines 19 through 23 in Figure 10–4. This command is used to enable or disable the logging of SNMP and syslog messages. Messages from these services can be sent to the console, telnet sessions, the system buffer, or an external server. Additionally, the syslog facility can also be set. It is recommended that you enable logging to a syslog server and perform regular audits of the messages that are logged to determine which type of activity is normal for your site. Large deviations in the logs from traditional traffic patterns may be a sign of an attacker at work.

IP Addressing

Lines 28 through 30 show the use of the IP address command in Figure 10–4. Each interface in use on the PIX must be configured with an IP address and must be configured in a different subnet. The syntax of the IP address command is shown below:

```
ip address if_name ip_address [mask]
```

The `if_name` parameter is the same as that used in previous commands discussed in this section. If a mask is not specified, the default network mask is assumed. Do not specify that an all-ones subnet mask (255.255.255.255) or processing on the interface will be disabled.

ARP

Line 31 of the default configuration shows the value of the ARP timeout in seconds in Figure 10–4. This value determines how long an ARP entry remains in the ARP table of the PIX. The default value is four hours or 14,400 seconds. You can optionally manually install ARP entries in the routers ARP cache. The line breaks down like this:

```
arp if_name ip_address mac_address [alias]
```

Here's an example with the values included:

```
arp outside 171.10.1.1 00e0.568a.1258 alias
```

The value for if_name is the same as that discussed with other commands and should match an entry defined with the nameif command. The optional alias keyword means that the router retains the ARP entry permanently. ARP entries entered with the alias keyword do not timeout and survive reboots of the PIX.

Routing Commands

The commands influencing the use of the IP RIP routing protocol on the PIX are on lines 32 through 35 of the default configuration in Figure 10–4. As we stated previously, the PIX is not a router. It has two basic functions that relate to RIP:

1. Listen for RIP updates
2. Broadcast a default route via RIP

To enable the capability of the PIX to listen to RIP updates on an interface, use the command rip *if_name* passive. The PIX then installs routes received via RIP on the interface specified in the routing table. To enable the PIX to broadcast a default route via RIP, use the command rip *if_name* default. This allows any devices on the specified interface to receive a default route from the PIX. Both of these functions are disabled by default on all interfaces.

No static routes are shown in the configuration because no static routes are in the default configuration. Static routes can be added to the PIX using the route command:

```
route if_name ip_address netmask gateway_ip [metric]
```

Here's an example with its values included:

```
route outside 150.10.0.0 255.255.0.0 171.10.1.1 1
```

The use of the if_name parameter is the same as we have seen in previous commands. The ip_address is the IP address of the network we are installing a static route for, and the netmask is the associated network mask for the network specified in the ip_address command. The gateway_ip is the next-hop IP address that the PIX should send packets to for the ip_address. The metric value specifies the RIP routing metric, which is the hop count. This parameter is optional and defaults to one.

Two default routes can be specified *if only two interfaces are physically installed.* If only the inside and outside boards are installed, a default route can be specified for both the outside and inside interfaces. If a third interface is physically installed in the PIX, even if it is not configured, only a single default route can be defined. The default route is specified by using either 0.0.0.0 for both the ip_address and netmask or by simply specifying 0 for these parameters.

```
route outside 0 0 171.10.1.1
route inside 0 0 10.1.1.1
```

If more than two interfaces are installed in the PIX, only one default route can be specified. In this case, the default route would be normally configured to point to a router on the outside interface and specific routes for all internal subnets would be configured to point to a router on the inside interface.

Translation Timeouts

The commands to configure translation table timeouts are shown on lines 36 through 38 in Figure 10–4. These timeout commands control how long inactive NAT translations and connections are allowed to remain in the translation tables of the PIX. These timeout values apply to connections that are in use and only connections that the PIX has not seen activity on during the specified time interval will be closed. All values are in seconds. The default values are listed below:

xlate	NAT translations, default three hours
conn	TCP connections, default one hour
udp	UDP connections, default two minutes
rpc	RPC connections, default 10 minutes

h323	H.323 connections, default five minutes
uauth	User authentication and authorization. The use of the absolute keyword requires even active connections to re-authenticate once the timeout value is reached. This behavior can be overridden by using the keyword "inactivity" instead of absolute.

SNMP Commands

The commands to enable SNMP on the PIX are found on lines 39 through 42 in Figure 10-4. Basic SNMP functionality can be enabled on the PIX using these commands, and only read functions are supported. You cannot set any values on the PIX using the SNMP protocol. The command to specify the SNMP server that SNMP traps are sent to does not appear in the default configuration and is shown below:

```
snmp-server host if_name local_ip
```

The syntax is straightforward. The if_name is the name of the interface where the SNMP server resides and the local_ip is the IP address of the SNMP server. Up to five SNMP servers can be specified.

Maximum Transmission Unit (MTU) Commands

The commands to specify the *Maximum Transmission Unit* (MTU) or maximum packet size are found on lines 43 through 45. The default values are 1,500 bytes for Ethernet and 8,192 bytes for Token Ring. These values can be modified if necessary. The minimum value is 64 bytes and the maximum value is 65,536 bytes. The PIX supports Path MTU Discover and will send ICMP "packet too big" messages if a large packet is sent with the Don't Fragment bit set. In most environments, the default MTU values should work fine.

Floodguard

The floodguard command is used to prevent a DoS attack on the PIX's authentication processes. Each request for user authentication consumes resources on the PIX. If the number of resources used by the user authentication subsystem becomes too great, it is possible that the PIX will stop functioning. To remedy this possibility, if the user authentication subsystem runs out of resources, the PIX will actively begin reclaiming TCP user resources. This feature is enabled by default. We recommend that you leave this feature enabled. It can be disabled with the command:

```
floodguard 0
```

Getting the PIX Up and Running

Now that we have covered each of the default commands, we return to our earlier statement that the basic PIX configuration requires only six commands. These commands are covered in the following three steps:

1. You must configure an IP address on the inside and outside interfaces. Once this is done, you should verify that the interfaces are up and running by pinging a device on the inside and outside interfaces from the PIX using the ping command.

```
ping inside 10.1.1.1
ping outside 171.10.1.1
```

Both the interface and the IP address are required. You should be able to ping active devices on both the inside and outside interfaces before continuing. Configuring IP addresses consists of two commands, one for the inside interface and one for the outside interface.

2. You must configure a default route for the outside and inside interfaces. Strictly speaking, if you have only one physical network on the inside interface of the PIX, you don't need to specify a default route for the inside network because the PIX will simply ARP for the host MAC addresses. This type of configuration is rare, so we will assume that a default route on the inside network is needed. Once the default routes are configured, you should verify that IP addresses on non-directly connected subnets are reachable. In other words, you should ping IP addresses that are on the other side of a router on both the inside and outside interfaces.

A word of caution: You will not be able to ping the PIX inside interface from the outside network or the outside interface from the inside network. Do not let this confuse you. If you can ping inside networks from the inside interface and outside networks from the outside interface, the PIX is functioning normally and your routes are correct. The configuration of the inside and outside default routes comprises two commands, bringing the total number used so far to four. Two more commands to go!

3. The final step requires the use of two commands we have not seen yet, global and nat. We cover these two commands in the next section.

Defining NAT and Global Pools

As we stated earlier, the use of the nat command is required by the PIX, even if network address translation is not actually being used. If address translation is used, a companion command, global, must also be configured to define the pool of translation IP addresses.

The basic procedure is to first identify which IP address or addresses will be used as the global pool. The global pool defines the IP addresses that will be seen by devices on the outside of the PIX. If the PIX is being used to connect to the Internet, these addresses must be registered addresses obtained from your ISP or the Internet. The syntax of the global command is shown below. This command is required if you are using address translation.

```
global [(if_name)] nat_id global_ip[-global_ip] [netmask
    global_mask]
```

The if_name command is the external network interface name where you will use the global addresses. In most cases, this is the outside interface, although it could be either the third or fourth interface on the PIX. As we will explain later, the inside interface is never referenced by the global command. The nat_id is a positive number between 1 and 2,147,483,647. This number is used to identify the global pool and match it with its respective nat command. This number is how a particular global command is matched to a particular nat command. Remember, if address translation is used, every nat command must have at least one corresponding global command.

The global_ip is either a single IP address or a range of IP addresses. If a single IP address is used, *Port Address Translation* (PAT) will be performed. If PAT is used, the single IP address cannot be the outside interface of the PIX. This is a change from the behavior of PAT when used with a Cisco router, as we saw in Chapter 8. This means that at a minimum three legal IP addresses are required if you are using the PIX to connect to the Internet: one for the PIX outside interface, one for the PAT address, and one for the outside routers' LAN interface.

When defining the global_ip, both an IP address range and a single IP address can be specified, but only one global statement specifying a PAT address is permitted in the entire configuration. In other words, the following is invalid:

```
global (outside) 1 171.10.1.5 netmask 255.255.255.0
global (outside) 2 171.10.1.6 netmask 255.255.255.0
```

Only one PAT address can be defined on the PIX. The following configuration is legal:

```
global (outside) 1 171.10.1.6-171.10.1.20 netmask 255.255.255.0
global (outside) 1 171.10.1.5 netmask 255.255.255.0
```

Addresses are used from the global pool first, starting at the highest IP address and working down to the lowest. Once all the IP addresses from the global pool have been used, PAT is performed on the single IP address defined. When using a single IP address in conjunction with a pool of addresses, the single IP address should be a lower IP address than the lowest IP address in the pool. Note in our example that the IP address used for PAT is .5 and the lowest pool address used is .6.

The nat command can be used either alone or in conjunction with the global command. In most cases, the two commands are used together. When used with the global command, the nat command specifies which IP address ranges are allowed to use the global IP addresses defined with the corresponding global command. The syntax of the nat command is shown below:

```
nat [(if_name)] nat_id local_ip [netmask[max_conns[em_limit]]]
    [norandomseq]
```

The if_name parameter we have seen before. Its value is typically the inside interface but could be the third or fourth interface on the PIX. The nat and global commands are used when a connection is initiated from a higher security interface to a lower security interface. They are not used when connections are required from a lower security interface to a higher one. For example, you would not use the nat and global commands to allow connections from the outside interface to the inside interface.

Returning to Figure 10–5, we would use nat and global commands to connect from dmz1 to either the dmz2 or the outside interface because the security level of dmz1 is higher than the security level on either of those two interfaces. However, we would not use nat and global commands to connect from dmz1 to the inside because the security level of the inside interface is higher than that of the dmz1 interface. It is important to remember this concept. The nat and global commands are used only when connecting from a higher security interface to a lower one. Connecting from a lower security interface to a higher one requires a different set of commands, as we will see later in this chapter.

A word should be said about selecting the security level of the third and fourth interface (note that these interfaces are referred to as "perimeter" interfaces). When selecting the security level of perimeter interfaces, such as dmz1 and dmz2 in Figure 10–5, it is recommended that the interface with the most hosts be configured with the higher security level. This is so that when hosts on one perimeter interface access another perimeter interface, fewer exceptions need to be made to the PIX adaptive security algorithm. Be aware that perimeter interfaces always have a higher security level than the outside interface and a lower security level than the inside interface. Since this is the case, no matter what the security level is on a perimeter interface, access from the outside interface is always denied by default and access from the inside interface is always permitted by default. Therefore, you only need to consider the number of hosts on a perimeter interface in relation to other perimeter interfaces in order to determine which interface the highest security level should be given.

Returning to the nat command, the nat_id parameter must either match the number defined in a global pool or be zero. If it is zero, this indicates that address translation is not being used and therefore no global pool is associated with nat_id 0. The local_ip parameter, in conjunction with the netmask parameter, specifies the range of IP addresses that are allowed to obtain translation IP addresses from the global pool defined by the nat_id. If the nat_id is zero, this field determines which IP addresses are allowed to initiate outbound connections from the inside interface.

The commands in Figure 10–6 define a global pool of IP addresses between 171.10.1.5 and 171.10.1.100. The nat command allows IP addresses from the 10.0.0.0 255.0.0.0 network to obtain IP addresses from the global pool. If an internal host has an IP address that is not in the 10.0.0.0 255.0.0.0 network, it will not be able to obtain an IP address from the global pool and will not be able to communicate through the PIX. Figure 10–6 shows a graphical representation of this concept.

As shown in Figure 10–6, IP packets arriving at the inside PIX interface from host 10.1.1.1 are allowed by the nat command to obtain an IP address from the pool defined by the global command. IP packets arriving at the inside PIX interface from host 192.168.1.1 are not allowed by the nat command, are not translated, and are not allowed through the PIX.

Figure 10–7 illustrates the use of the nat 0 command. No global command is defined because we are not using address translation. In this case, the internal IP addresses appear unchanged on networks on the outside interface.

Notice in Figure 10–7 the absence of the global command that we saw in Figure 10–6. Also notice that IP packets from host 192.168.1.1 are still not allowed. The nat command only allows hosts from the 10.0.0.0 255.0.0.0 network. You can specify that any host can use the nat command by using 0.0.0.0 or simply 0 for the local_ip and netmask parameters, instead of specifying an actual IP network as shown below.

These commands are equivalent:

```
nat 1 0.0.0.0 0.0.0.0
nat 1 0 0
```

NOTE: In general, you can specify 0 or 0.0.0.0 in most PIX commands that use an IP address if you want any IP address to match a particular parameter. You can also specify 0 for the TCP or UDP port with commands that use source and or destination ports to match any port. The use of the 0 value with a PIX command is equivalent to using the any keyword in a Cisco router access-list.

Figure 10–6

Only hosts that have IP addresses in the range defined by the nat 1 command can obtain an IP address from the pool of addresses defined by the global 1 command.

PIX Commands
nat (inside) 1 10.0.0.0 255.0.0.0
global (inside) 1 171.10.1.5-171.10.1.100

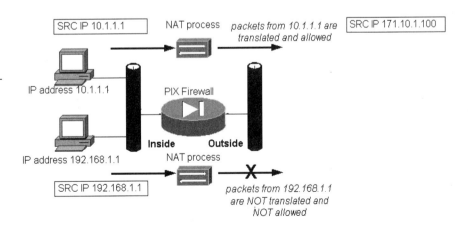

Figure 10–7
The use of nat 0
indicates that we are
not using address
translation. No global
pools are necessary.

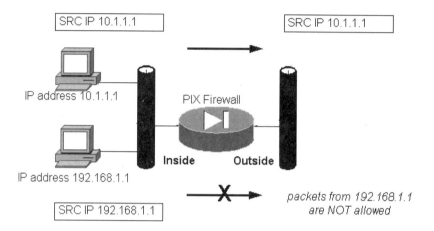

PIX Commands
nat (inside) 0 10.0.0.0 255.0.0.0

SRC IP 10.1.1.1

SRC IP 10.1.1.1

IP address 10.1.1.1

PIX Firewall

IP address 192.168.1.1

Inside   Outside

SRC IP 192.168.1.1

packets from 192.168.1.1
are NOT allowed

Although specifying 0 for the local_ip is fine as long as nat 0 is not used, special problems occur if local_ip is defined as 0 when using nat 0. The problem occurs because when nat 0 is used the PIX will proxy-arp for all IP addresses defined by the local_ip address range. If a host on the outside interface issues an arp request for a host defined in the local_ip address range, the PIX will answer.

This is not a problem as long as the local_ip is not 0. If it is 0, the PIX will proxy-arp for *any* IP addresses. If a host on the outside interface issues an ARP request for a host on the outside subnet, the PIX will answer the ARP request with its own MAC address—even if the ARP request should legitimately be answered by another host on the outside segment!

This issue is exacerbated by the fact that most hosts issue an ARP request for their own IP address during the initialization of their IP stack to check for the existence of a duplicate IP address on the LAN. This process is called a *gratuitous ARP*. In such a case, the PIX replies to the ARP request and the originating host believes there is an IP address conflict. The host would therefore never be able to initialize its IP stack and would not be able to communicate with other devices. Cisco recommends that you *never* set the local_ip to 0 in conjunction with nat 0. If you always use nat 0, explicitly specify what inside networks are allowed to use the nat command.

If you research the PIX information on the Cisco Web site, you will see examples where the local_ip is set to 0 when using nat 0. Cisco has acknowledged that these examples are in error and should not be used.

The max_conns parameter of the nat command specifies how many connections are allowed by hosts using this address translation instance. Since multiple nat commands are allowed, this gives you the ability to limit the number of connections taken up by certain IP address ranges. For example, assume you have only a 128 connection license and your IT staff uses the Internet for business purposes, while your marketing staff uses it for casual Web browsing. You've also decided to limit the number of connections that can be used by the marketing staff to 40 and reserve the rest for the IT staff. In Figure 10–8, we show the commands that would allow 40 connections for the marketing staff and reserve the rest to the IT staff.

As shown in Figure 10–8, IP addresses from the 192.168.1.0 255.255.255.0 address range are limited to 40 connections. The remaining IP addresses are limited only by the license maximum. Notice that we used 0.0.0.0 for the local_ip because we are not using nat 0. If we were using nat 0, we would have explicitly defined the IP address ranges in use on our inside networks.

The em_limit value sets the number of embryonic connections that the IP addresses matching the nat command are allowed to have. An *embryonic connection* is a connection that has not completed the TCP three-way

Figure 10–8
The marketing group on subnet 192.168.1.0 is allowed only 40 connections. The remaining subnets are used by IT and are allowed unlimited connections up to the license maximum.

PIX Commands
nat (inside) 1 192.168.1.0 255.255.255.0 40
nat (inside) 1 0.0.0.0 0.0.0.0
global (inside) 1 171.10.1.5-171.10.1.100

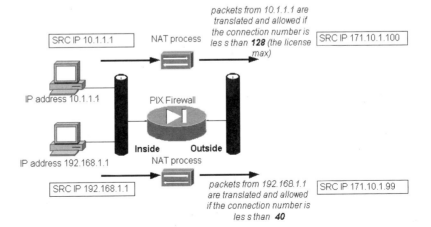

handshake or, if the transport is UDP, a return packet has not been received. Cisco recommends setting the embryonic connection limit to your license limit minus 30%. If your connection limit is 128, you would set the embryonic limit to 90 embryonic connections ($128 \times .7$). You may want to set this number higher if you have slow network links that cause large delays in setting up initial connections. The maximum value is the license limit and the minimum value is one.

The norandomseq parameter is used to disable the randomizing of TCP sequence numbers by the PIX. This option should only be used if another firewall is also randomizing the TCP sequence numbers. As described in Table 10–2, the PIX randomizes the TCP sequence numbers so that TCP sequence number prediction is much more difficult, if not impossible. This prevents TCP session hijacking, which we discussed in Chapter 8.

As we have seen in this section, the use of the nat and global commands enable connections to be initiated from a higher security interface to a lower one. As promised, we have now completed coverage of the six commands necessary to initially configure the PIX. Configuring the inside and outside interface IP addresses made up two commands, configuring a default route for the inside and outside interfaces was an additional two commands, and the global and nat commands bring the total to six. Of course, if nat 0 is used, there is no global command, in which case the total number of commands needed would be five.

We still haven't covered some administrative tasks such as setting passwords, setting up an address to allow telnet connections, renaming our PIX, and so on. But with only these six commands, the PIX is ready to accept user connections from the inside interface to the outside interface and protect your internal network.

Up to this point, we have only covered connections from a higher security interface to a lower security interface. In the next section, we discuss ways to allow connections from a lower security interface to a higher one.

Using Static NAT and Conduits

Although the majority of network activity will most likely be from a higher security interface to a lower one, it is often desirable to allow direct connections from a lower to a higher. We have seen how to allow connections from a higher security interface to a lower one by using the nat and global commands. We will now show how to allow connections from a lower security interface to a higher security interface by using the static and conduit commands.

The static command is used to create a permanent mapping between an inside IP address and a global IP address. Under normal conditions, when a connection is initiated from a higher security interface to a lower security interface and address translation is used, whatever address is available is just picked from the IP address range defined by the global command. There is also no way to know beforehand which IP address will be made available from the global IP address pool. By using the static command, you can dedicate a particular global IP address to a particular inside IP address. This is a necessary first step to allow communication from a lower security interface to a higher one. The syntax of the static command is shown here:

```
static [(internal_if_name, external_if_name)] global_ip local_ip
    [netmask network_mask] [max_conns[em_limit]] [norandomseq]
```

The internal_if_name is the higher security interface you are allowing access to, while the external_if_name is the lower security interface from which you are allowing access. The global_ip is the IP address as it is seen on the lower security interface, while the local_ip is the IP address used on the higher security interface. The netmask parameter is optional and defaults to 255.255.255.255.

NOTE: If nat 0 is used, the global_ip and the local_ip will be the same address. This is because when using nat 0 there is no global pool of IP addresses to map to the internal IP addresses.

The max_conns, em_limit, and norandomseq parameters are all optional and are used in the same manner as they are with the nat command that was discussed earlier in this chapter.

Notice that the format of the static command is a bit confusing when defining the internal_if_name, external_if_name, global_ip, and local_ip parameters. The order of the internal_if_name and the external_if_name is high, low. The order of the global_ip and the local_ip is low, high. That is, the global_ip parameter is the IP address that appears on the interface named by the external_if_name parameter. The local_ip parameter is the IP address that appears on the interface named by the internal_if_name parameter. We show an example of the static command in Figure 10–9.

Notice that even though we have created the static mapping, connections from the outside interface to the inside interface are still blocked by the adaptive security algorithm of the PIX. Outbound connections

Figure 10–9

A static translation creates a permanent mapping between an outside address and an inside address, but it does not allow connections from devices on the outside to the statically translated IP address by itself.

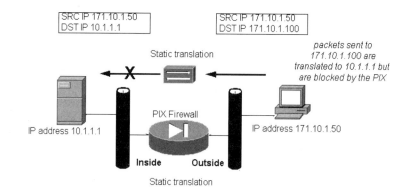

PIX Commands
static (inside, outside) 171.10.1.100 10.1.1.1 netmask 255.255.255.255

from the inside host would be allowed and the return connections would be allowed just as they would normally if the inside host had obtained an IP address from a global pool.

If both a global pool and static mappings are used on the same inside interface, the IP addresses defined in the static mappings should not be in the range of IP addresses defined by the global pool. Also, the global_ip parameter for your static mappings cannot use the IP address assigned to the outside interface of the PIX.

In order to allow connections inbound from a lower security interface to a higher security interface, a conduit command must be used. The conduit command is what actually creates exceptions to the standard PIX adaptive security algorithm. The static command is only used to define a global IP address that is always mapped to a particular inside IP address. The syntax of the conduit is shown below:

Version #1

```
conduit permit|deny protocol global_ip global_mask [operator
    port[port]] foreign_ip foreign_mask [operator port[port]]
```

Version #2

```
conduit permit|deny icmp global_ip global_mask foreign_ip
    foreign_mask [icmp-type]
```

Notice that there are two versions of the conduit command. The first version is used to allow TCP or UDP protocols and the second is used for the ICMP protocol. The global_ip and global_mask define the IP address or addresses where connections are being permitted. This is the same global_ip that is referenced in a static command. The operator is a comparison value, such as GT for greater than, LT for less than, EQ for equal, NEQ for not equal, and RANGE to specify a range of ports. The operator is applied to the port parameter.

The port parameter immediately following the global_mask parameter is the destination port you are allowing access to on the host using the IP address defined by the global_ip parameter. The foreign_ip and foreign_mask define the IP address or addresses you are allowing access from on an outside network.

The port parameter immediately following the foreign_mask parameter is the source port from which the hosts defined by the foreign_ip and foreign_mask are allowed to initiate connections. Notice that in the ICMP version, the destination ICMP type is used instead of a source and destination port number. As we have seen previously, a port number of 0 indicates any port can be used. In the ICMP version, you could just leave off the ICMP type to signify that any ICMP type can be used. To specify that any IP address can be used, either 0.0.0.0 or the keyword any should be used with the global_ip and foreign_ip parameters.

In Figure 10–10, we show conduits that will allow access to the server on the inside interface from devices on the outside interface.

Figure 10–10

Several conduit statements allowing access for a variety of protocols to the server on the inside network

PIX Commands
static (inside, outside) 171.10.1.100 10.1.1.1 netmask 255.255.255.255
conduit permit tcp host 171.10.1.100 eq 23 host 171.10.1.50
conduit permit udp host 171.10.1.100 eq 53 any
conduit deny icmp 171.10.1.0 255.255.255.0 any echo-request
conduit permit icmp 171.10.1.0 255.255.255.0 any

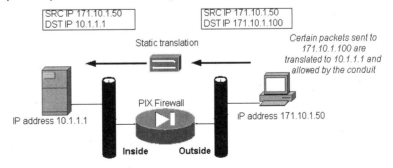

In Figure 10–10, we are allowing host 171.10.1.50 to access the static translation 171.10.1.100 on port 23 (telnet) from any port. We are also allowing UDP on port 53 (DNS) from any host on any port. ICMP packets of type echo-request are denied, but all other ICMP packet types are allowed to any host on the inside network.

Many different configuration options are available with the conduit command, which has roughly the same functionality as an inbound Cisco router access list. Note that conduits are processed from the top down, like a Cisco router access list. The ICMP deny statement would deny ICMP packets of type echo-request before the final ICMP `permit any` would be reached.

One final word on the use of the static and conduit commands. Although our example shows that we are permitting access from the outside interface to the inside interface, the principles discussed are the same for access from any lower security interface to any higher security interface. If the lower security interface had been dmz2 and the higher security interface had been dmz1 from Figure 10–5, the format of the static and conduit commands would have been the same and the same principles apply. The same can be said regarding the use of the nat and global commands. Although our previous examples showed access from the inside interface to the outside interface, the same principles apply to access from any higher security interface to a lower security interface.

Dual NAT—Using the Alias Command

In some situations, it may be necessary to perform address translation on both the inside IP addresses *and* the outside IP addresses. This can occur if the IP addresses used on the inside network overlap with IP addresses on the outside network, which could happen if an organization is using IP addresses on their internal network that were registered to another organization. The two organizations would consequently not be able to communicate without using dual address translation. The format of the alias command is shown below:

```
alias [(if_name)] dnat_ip foreign_ip [netmask]
```

The if_name is the inside interface that is using IP addresses that overlap with IP addresses on an outside network. The dnat_ip is the IP address that will be used on the internal network by the hosts on the outside interface. The foreign_ip is the IP address on the outside network that overlaps with IP addresses on the inside network. If you were using the 10.1.1.0 255.255.255.0 subnet internally, for example, and another organization was also using IP addresses from the 10.1.1.0 255.255.255.0 network, we could choose another IP address range to translate the host IP addresses on the external network. We chose IP network 192.168.1.0 255.255.255.0, but any IP network number not currently being used in our internal network would work. IP addresses from the chosen network range will only appear on our internal network. The alias command is shown below:

```
alias (inside) 192.168.1.0 10.1.1.0 255.255.255.0
```

Notice that we have specified the inside interface because that is the interface where we want the IP addresses from the outside network to be translated. Also notice that we have specified the entire 10.1.1.0 subnet by using the netmask 255.255.255.0. We could also have specified each individual host.

The use of the alias command requires that the hosts on the inside network access the hosts on the outside network by IP address or that they use a DNS on the outside of the PIX. If a DNS request is returned through the PIX with the outside host's IP address, the PIX will dynamically translate the DNS reply to an aliased IP address. If the DNS resides on the inside network, however, the PIX will not be able to translate the DNS reply and unpredictable results will occur.

Suppose a host on the inside network using IP address 10.1.1.1 requested the IP address for host fubar from an external DNS. The host fubar has an IP address of 10.1.1.100. The DNS reply would contain IP address 10.1.1.100. When the PIX sees the inbound DNS reply, it will dynamically translate the contents of the DNS reply from 10.1.1.100 to 192.168.1.100 before sending the packet to the internal host.

When the internal host gets the reply, it sends packets for host fubar to IP address 192.168.1.100. When these packets reach the PIX, it dynamically translates the destination IP address to 10.1.1.100 and translates the source IP address to an IP address from the global pool 171.10.1.5 through 171.10.1.100. The PIX then sends the packet to the outside host fubar. Note that the DNS must reside on the outside interface of the PIX for this operation to work correctly. Also, if connections are going to be initiated to the host 10.1.1.1 from the outside, appropriate static and conduit commands would have to be used so that inside host 10.1.1.1 is reachable from outside networks (both of these commands have been covered previously).

Figure 10–11 illustrates the use of the alias command to enable an inside host at IP address 10.1.1.1 to communicate with an outside host at IP address 10.1.1.100.

Figure 10-11

The PIX dynamically translates the DNS reply from the outside DNS server so that the inside host 10.1.1.1 accepts that the IP address of host fubar is 192.168.1.100. Packets from host 10.1.1.1 will be sent to IP address 192.168.1.100 and both the source and destination IP address will be translated by the PIX.

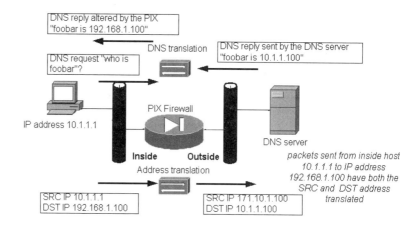

PIX Commands
nat (inside) 1 10.0.0.0 255.0.0.0
global (inside) 1 171.10.1.5-171.10.1.100
alias (inside) 192.168.1.0 10.1.1.0 255.255.255.0

PIX Access Lists

PIX access lists are used to restrict connections going outbound from a higher security interface to a lower one. Remember that the adaptive security algorithm allows all connections from a higher security interface to a lower one by default. If you want to limit the type of connections that users on an inside interface can initiate to an outside interface, you must use an access list. A PIX access list can also be used to block the downloading of HTTP-imbedded Java applets from a lower security interface to higher security interface.

We should initially note a few things about PIX access lists. First, with the exception that there is both a creation and application step, PIX access lists are *nothing* like Cisco router access lists. PIX access lists are "best-fit;" the entire access list is examined to find the best matching entry. This is unlike Cisco router access lists that are "first-fit;" once a matching entry is found in the Cisco router access list, the matching process ends. When using PIX access lists, it does not matter what the order of the permit or deny entries are; each of the entries will be examined individually to determine which entry is the best match.

The second thing that should be noted about PIX access lists is that they are used to filter connections from a higher security interface to a lower security interface only. There is no reason to attempt to filter connections from a lower security interface to a higher one because the adaptive security algorithm drops all inbound connections except those that are specifically permitted. The PIX access list can filter on either the outbound source IP address or the outbound destination IP address. Filtering on outbound destination port is also permitted, but not on the outbound source port.

The only similarity that PIX access lists have to Cisco router access lists is there are two steps to enable a PIX access list. The list must first be defined and then the list must be applied. The outbound command is used to create the access list and then the apply command is used to actually enable the access list. The syntax of a PIX access list is shown below:

```
outbound list_id permit|deny ip_address [netmask[java[port[-port]]]
   [protocol]
outbound list_id except ip_address [netmask[java[port[-port]]]
   [protocol]
apply [(if_name)] list_id outgoing_src|outgoing_dst
```

Notice that there are two versions of the outbound command. The first version uses the permit or the deny keyword. This version lets you specify whether a particular source or destination IP address will be permitted or denied. The second version of the outbound command uses the except keyword. This version lets you permit specific exceptions to a previously defined permit or deny access list entry.

The list_id is a number used to identify the access list. The list_id parameter used with the outbound command must be the same list_id referenced in the apply command.

The ip_address can specify either 0.0.0.0 or 0 if any IP address is to be matched by the entry. Similarly, the port parameter can use a 0 to specify any port. The value of the protocol parameter can be TCP, UDP, or ICMP. If a value is specified for the port but the protocol is not specified, TCP is assumed to be the protocol.

The use of a PIX access list is best illustrated with an example. We'll permit outbound access from the inside interface to the destination IP address 171.10.0.0 255.255.0.0 and block all other destination IP addresses:

```
outbound 1 deny 0.0.0.0
outbound 1 permit 171.10.0.0 255.255.0.0
apply (inside) 1 outgoing_dst
```

Notice that the permit entry appears after the deny entry. This is fine because the PIX access list is best-fit, not first-fit. Also notice that the apply command specifies the interface where the packets being blocked are originating from and that the filter is on the destination IP address.

We could use an except entry to specify an exception to a deny entry that would permit a specific host complete access.

```
outbound 1 deny 0.0.0.0
outbound 1 except 10.1.1.1 255.255.255.255
apply (inside) 1 outgoing_dst
```

In this example, the except entry specifies an exception to the previous deny entry. The deny entry denies access to all destination IP addresses because the matching apply statement is set to filter on the outgoing destination. The except statement specifies an exception to the source IP address and allows connections from 10.1.1.1 access to any destination IP address. The except entry specifies exceptions to the source IP address because the access list is applied to the outgoing destination.

This may seem a little confusing and even backward at first glance, but remember that PIX access lists are best-fit. If we wanted to permit access to the destination IP address 10.1.1.1, we would just have added a permit entry and would not need an except entry:

```
outbound 1 deny 0.0.0.0
outbound 1 permit 10.1.1.1 255.255.255.255
apply (inside) 1 outgoing_dst
```

This access list says that access is permitted to destination IP address 10.1.1.1 and all other destination IP addresses are blocked. This is very different than saying that access to all destinations is blocked unless the packets have a source IP address of 10.1.1.1.

The rule is that an except entry permits exceptions for source IP addresses if the access list is applied to the outgoing destination IP address. An except entry also permits exceptions for destination IP addresses if the access list is applied to the outgoing source IP address. We'll present another example to drive this point home. In the following example, the access list denies access from any source IP address unless the destination IP address is 171.10.1.100. The destination port must be either 23 or 80 for TCP or 53 for UDP.

```
outbound 1 deny 0 0 0
outbound 1 except 171.10.1.100 255.255.255.255 tcp 23
outbound 1 except 171.10.1.100 255.255.255.255 tcp 80
outbound 1 except 171.10.1.100 255.255.255.255 udp 53
apply (inside) 1 outgoing_src
```

Notice that the apply command is applying the access list to the out-going source IP address, so the except entries permit exceptions to certain destination IP addresses.

We'll also illustrate a final access list example. We'll prevent inside users from downloading Java applets from all sites unless the destination IP address is on the 171.10.0.0 255.255.0.0 network.

```
outbound 1 deny 0 0 0 java
outbound 1 except 171.10.0.0 255.255.0.0
apply (inside) 1 outgoing_src
```

Notice again that the except entry permits exceptions to the destination IP address because the access list is applied on the outgoing source IP address. Note that the use of the Java keyword implies that the destination protocol is TCP and the port is 80. In other words, it only filters out Java applets imbedded in the HTTP protocol.

One final note about PIX access lists. If multiple access lists are in use, an outgoing source filter and an outgoing destination filter are filtered independently. If a packet matches a deny entry, the packet is denied. If there are conflicting entries in multiple access lists, the most specific match wins, based on the IP address and port numbers. If there is a tie, a permit overrides a deny.

Handling Multi-Channel Protocols

Earlier in this chapter, we discussed the multimedia applications that the PIX is capable of handling securely. The problem in dealing with these types of applications is that many of them select random port numbers to be used during the course of the conversation. Since the port numbers aren't known beforehand, it is difficult to know whether a connection is part of a legitimate conversation or not. Even though the PIX is capable of handling many of these types of applications, it's a moving target to attempt to handle all the current multimedia applications. It is for this reason that Cisco developed the established command. The syntax of the established command is shown below:

```
established protocol dst_port_1 [permitto protocol [dst_port_2[-
    dst_port_2]]] [permitfrom protocol [src_port[-src_port]]]
```

The established command lets you specify a condition so that if a connection already exists between an inside client to a certain destination port, the server that the client has an established connection with is allowed to open certain connections back to the client. In the command syntax, the protocol and dst_port_1 parameters specify the original destination protocol and port used on the connection between the client on a higher security interface to a server on a lower security interface.

The permitto parameter allows you to specify the destination protocol and port on the connection initiated from the server on the lower security interface to the client on the higher security interface. The permitfrom parameter allows you to specify the source destination and port on the connection initiated from the server on the lower security interface to the client on the higher security interface.

You can specify the original outbound destination protocol and port, the return inbound source protocol and port, the return inbound destination protocol and port, or none of the above. Only TCP and UDP can be specified for the protocol parameter. As we have seen previously, 0 is used to match any address or port. In this case, it would match any port because IP addresses are not used with the established command.

The use of the established command is best illustrated with an example. Refer to Figure 10–12.

Figure 10–12
The use of the established command. If a connection exists from a host on the inside network to a host on the outside network and the outside TCP port number is 4178, we will permit the outside host to initiate connections to the inside host if the destination UDP port is between 3000 and 4000 and the source UDP port is between 6000 and 65536.

PIX Commands

established tcp 4178 permitto udp 3000-4000 permitfrom udp 6000-65536

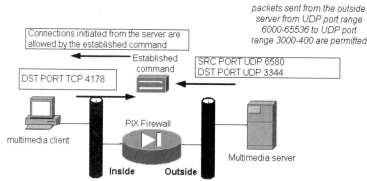

packets sent from the outside server from UDP port range 6000-65536 to UDP port range 3000-400 are permitted

Connections initiated from the server are allowed by the established command

Established command

SRC PORT UDP 6580
DST PORT UDP 3344

DST PORT TCP 4178

PIX Firewall

multimedia client

Inside   Outside

Multimedia server

In Figure 10–12, an inside client has opened a multimedia connection to an outside server on TCP port 4178. We know from either talking with the application developer or from the return packets sent by the outside server that the server will open a return connection to a UDP port between 3000 and 4000 on the client. We also know that the server will choose a random UDP port above 6000 as its source port for this return connection.

Notice that although the initial connection uses TCP, the return connection uses UDP. The established command is used so that if a connection already exists from any inside workstation to an outside server on destination port 4178, the outside server is allowed to open a return connection to the client on destination UDP port range 3000–4000 with source UDP port range 6000–65536. Notice that no IP addresses are specified with the established command.

It may not always be possible to limit the source and destination port numbers used with a multimedia application. In such a case, it is *strongly* urged that you at least specify the initial destination port:

```
established tcp 4178
```

This allows any outside host to initiate connections to any inside host if there is already an existing connection from the inside host to the outside host on TCP port 4178.

You should *not* allow the initial destination port to be just any port as shown below. The following command is *not* recommended:

```
established tcp 0
```

If you do not specify at least the destination port, the result will be that *any* outside device can initiate connections to *any* clients that have active connections on *any* port. Worse still, if static and conduit commands are used, connections can be opened to those devices as well.

It does not matter whether the initial connection is from an inside interface or an outside interface. The established command considers all connections equally, regardless of the direction in which the connection was initially opened. If used improperly, the established command can open large holes in your PIX configuration. If you have any doubts about how to use this command, you should contact either the Cisco TAC or your local Cisco representative. If you don't absolutely need the features of this command, it is best to avoid it completely.

Setting Passwords

As discussed in the section on the default configuration of the PIX, there are two passwords. The first password is to allow either console or telnet access to the PIX. This password is equivalent to the VTY password on a Cisco router and the default value is cisco. There is also an enable password that is exactly equivalent to the enable password on a Cisco router, but there is no default enable password. Both of these passwords should be changed as soon as possible after the PIX is brought online. The commands to do so are shown below:

```
passwd password
enable password password
```

Both passwords can be up to 16 characters and can be composed of both alphanumeric and special characters. The passwords on the PIX are case-sensitive and are always encrypted.

Managing the PIX

A few final administrative tasks should be completed before the PIX can be deemed production-ready. First, many administrators like to manage the PIX from a remote device without having to physically visit the PIX. Traditionally, this has been done via the telnet protocol. In order to access the PIX via a remote telnet session, the IP address of the machine from which you will be administering the PIX must be entered in the PIX configuration. The command to do this is

```
telnet local_ip [netmask]
```

The local_ip is the IP address that is allowed to open a telnet session to the PIX. The netmask parameter is used to determine the mask of the local_ip. The netmask parameter can be used to allow an entire subnet to access the PIX via a telnet session, although we discourage this practice. The default value is 255.255.255.255. Up to 16 host addresses can be specified, and five hosts can access the PIX simultaneously, although we encourage limiting access to one administrator at a time. An idle timeout on telnet session can also be set:

```
telnet timeout minutes
```

The default value is five minutes, while the lowest value is one minute. Cisco recommends values between one and 60. We would not recommend increasing the default timeout, although decreasing it is OK.

There are several issues regarding the use of the telnet protocol to manage the PIX. The central problem is that the session is not encrypted on the network, so anyone with a sniffer could see the password used to access the PIX as the packets pass between the administrator's workstation and the PIX. Although telnet sessions cannot be initiated from the outside interface, it is still a security risk. Not all or even most threats come from outside entities. Internal users often pose threats equal to or greater than those posed by outside parties.

Cisco addressed this issue beginning with PIX IOS version 4.1 by introducing a new PIX management tool called the PIX manager. The PIX manager is a software package that runs on an NT server or NT workstation. It uses encrypted telnet sessions to configure the PIX and you attach to the PIX manager through a standard Web browser. Sessions between the client Web browser and the PIX manager use encrypted Java calls. Using the PIX manager is also much more secure than using standard telnet. All that is necessary to use the PIX manager is the PIX manager software running on an NT device and a client station with a Web browser. The PIX manager must be setup as a telnet client in the PIX configuration; it cannot reside on the outside interface. We cover the PIX manager in greater detail later in this chapter.

Proper management of the PIX also involves saving your configurations. The PIX configuration can saved by using the write command, which can be used to save the PIX configuration to NVRAM, to a floppy disk, or to a *trivial file transfer protocol* (TFTP) server. We recommend all of the above. Your configuration should always be saved to NVRAM by issuing a write mem command after making any configuration changes. The configuration should then further be saved to a floppy with the command write floppy. And finally, in case you have problems with your floppy or the floppy drive, you should always save your configuration to a TFTP server. As one of us was reminded of very recently, floppy disks fail fairly often. Use the following command to save your configuration to a TFTP server:

```
write net [[server_ip]:[filename]]
```

If you previously used the tftp-server command, you do not need to specify the server_ip parameter with the write net command. The TFTP server used should reside on the internal network or should at least not reside on the outside network. Unless the hard drive of the TFTP server is encrypted, anyone with access to the files on the TFTP server could read the configuration of the PIX. Although this may not be catastrophic, it is better not to reveal any more information than absolutely necessary about your network security configuration. It is also always a good idea to save a hard copy of your configuration in a secure location. In a worst case scenario, you can rebuild your configuration by hand from a physical printout.

Advanced Configuration Topics

In this section, we look briefly at some of the more advanced configuration features that are available on the Cisco PIX.

User Authentication

We mentioned earlier that the PIX provides the capability to authenticate users on both inbound and outbound connections. This capability is typically referred to as AAA: Authentication, Authorization, and Accounting. Authentication and authorization have been covered earlier, and accounting answers the question "what did you do?" Each of these services is enabled separately and can be used independently of the others. The use of any of these services requires that either a TACACS+ server or a RADIUS server has been previously defined. Authorization only works with a TACACS+ server, while RADIUS authorization is not supported. The syntax of the commands needed to establish AAA services is shown below:

```
tacacs-server [(if_name)] host ip_address [key] [timeout seconds]
radius-server [(if_name)] host ip_address [key] [timeout seconds]
```

Up to 16 TACACS+ and RADIUS servers can be specified. Servers are used in the order entered until a server is found that responds. The key parameter is used to encrypt communications between the PIX and the authentication server. The value of the key must be the same on the PIX and the authentication server. If no key is used, communication is not encrypted. The timeout value specifies how long the PIX will attempt to contact a particular authentication server. Authorization is not supported for RADIUS servers.

```
aaa accounting authen_service|except inbound|outbound|if_name
   local_ip local_mask foreign_ip foreign_mask tacacs+|radius
aaa authentication authen_service|except inbound|outbound|if_name
   local_ip local_mask foreign_ip foreign_mask tacacs+|radius
aaa authorization $/#|except inbound|outbound|if_name local_ip
   local_mask foreign_ip foreign_mask
```

The *authen_service* can be either FTP, HTTP, telnet, or the keyword any. The inbound parameter specifies that connections originate from the outside interface, while the outbound parameter specifies that connections originate from the inside interface. Alternatively, the if_name command can be used to specify the originating interface. The local_ip and foreign_ip specify the source and destination IP addresses that are checked for a particular AAA entry. For authorization services, the $ indicates the protocol used and the # parameter indicates the port used, such as UDP/53.

If AAA services are enabled for any service, the PIX only prompts for user credentials if FTP, HTTP, or telnet is the service. Therefore, if a user wishes to use a service other than FTP, HTTP, or telnet, they must first authenticate using one of these protocols. This is done by setting up a virtual IP address on the PIX for users to connect to via the telnet protocol.

```
virtual telnet ip_address
```

The user would then open a telnet session to the IP address identified in the virtual telnet ip_address parameter. Once the user has been authenticated and authorized, the telnet session to the virtual IP address will be closed and the user can use whatever protocols for which he is authorized. If users on outside interfaces need to connect to the virtual IP address, appropriate static and conduit commands must be entered on the PIX. The virtual IP address is treated as if it were a physical host on the inside network.

A virtual HTTP server can be designated as well, which allows HTTP sessions to be authenticated by the authentication server and then redirected to the real HTTP server. This prevents problems with HTTP servers that interpret the authentication requests in HTTP GET commands as additional requests for authentication on the HTTP server itself. Microsoft IIS server exhibits this behavior. The user of the virtual HTTP command prevents problems with the Microsoft IIS server or other HTTP servers that interpret authentication commands imbedded in the HTTP GET request. The syntax for this command is the same as it is for the virtual telnet command.

```
virtual http ip_address
```

As with the virtual telnet command, the ip_address specified by this command is considered to reside on the inside network, so appropriate static and conduit commands must be used to allow connections from outside networks.

Once the user has been authenticated and authorized by the AAA server, the user is not prompted again until the authorization timer expires. The timeout value, discussed earlier, is set with the timeout uauth command.

Problems can arise when using AAA if the specifications of the AAA commands on the PIX differ from the commands used on the AAA server. It is usually easier to set the AAA commands on the PIX to specify any service or IP address and let the authentication server decide whether the connection will be permitted or denied. The commands below specify that any outbound connections from the inside interface will be authenticated and authorized by the TACACS+ server at IP address 10.1.1.100. We have also specified a virtual telnet IP address so that users can authenticate via a telnet session before using applications other than FTP, HTTP, or telnet.

```
tacacs-server (inside) 10.1.1.100
aaa authentication any outbound 0 0 0 0 tacacs+
aaa authorization any outbound 0 0 0 0 tacacs+
virtual telnet 10.1.1.99
```

The TACACS+ server at IP address 10.1.1.100 takes care of ensuring proper authentication and authorization for outbound connections. If you are a registered Cisco user, you can download the source Unix code for TACACS+ at

```
http://www.cisco.com/cgi-bin/tablebuild.pl/tacacs_plus
```

Commercial versions of TACACS+ are available for the Windows NT platform from several vendors including Cisco.

Virtual Private Networks

We noted earlier that the PIX supports *Virtual Private Network* (VPN) connections between PIX units. A VPN is an encrypted connection between two devices that allows secure communication across an unsecure network, such as the Internet. The VPN feature of the PIX is called a private link and requires an additional private link card to be installed in the PIX. The use of a private link requires two commands. The first command, link, specifies the IP address of the PIX box you are creating a VPN connection to and the encryption key used:

```
link [(if_name)] foreign_external_ip key_id key|md5
```

Here's an example:

```
link (inside) 171.10.1.100 1 abbdccddeeffaf
```

The if_name parameter indicates the interface where the private link connection originates. If an interface other than the inside is used, packets are processed using normal nat and global commands before being transmitted across the private link. The key_id specifies a unique key number, and a maximum of seven keys can be defined for each remote VPN peer. The key is a value of up to 14 hexadecimal digits and is used to establish a VPN connection. The key value must match on both sides of the VPN link. The md5 parameter puts an md5 digital signature on each packet before it is sent across the VPN link.

The second command, linkpath, specifies the networks that are reachable through a particular PIX specified by the link command.

```
linkpath foreign_internal_ip netmask foreign_external_ip
```

Here's an example:

```
linkpath 150.10.0.0 255.255.0.0 171.10.1.100
```

The foreign_internal_ip and netmask specify the network that can be reached by the VPN connection to the PIX defined by the foreign_external_ ip parameter. The foreign_external_ip parameter must be the same as that specified on a previously defined link command, while the linkpath command is essentially a route statement.

Redundant PIX Design

The PIX supports a redundant design using two PIX boxes through the use of a special cable connected to each PIX box. This cable is called a *failover cable* and is specially designed by Cisco. The cable has a limited distance, so the PIX boxes must be in close physical proximity, and the distance between them cannot be extended. The specifications for this cable can be found on the Cisco Web site.

In a failover configuration, one PIX is the active unit and one is the standby unit. The interfaces on the standby unit are not active until a failure of the active unit is detected. The standby PIX must have a physical interface on the same networks as the active PIX. A failover IP address must also be assigned to each interface on the standby PIX that will be used.

```
failover ip address if_name ip_address
```

Here's an example:

```
failover ip address inside 10.1.1.10
failover ip address outside 171.1.10.10
```

For obvious reasons, the configuration on the standby PIX must be identical to the configuration on the active PIX. During normal operation, the active PIX will automatically update the configuration of the standby PIX as new commands are entered on the active PIX. Also, if the active PIX is rebooted, it will replicate its entire configuration to the standby PIX. You can force the active PIX to replicate its configuration to the standby PIX by using the command write standby. All configuration changes should be made on the active PIX because any changes made on the standby PIX will not be propagated to the active unit.

You can observe the state of the failover connection with the command show failover. The command determines whether failover is enabled and which device is the active unit. No sharing of information about existing connections is shared between the active and the standby PIX units. When the active PIX fails, it takes approximately 30 to 45 seconds for the standby PIX to take over. When the standby PIX becomes active, it has no information about the state of existing connections and therefore all active sessions would most likely be dropped. You can use the failover timeout command to specify a time interval during which the standby PIX allows all traffic in and out so it can build a connection table:

```
failover timeout hh:mm:ss
```

During this period of time, adaptive security is totally disabled. Once the period of time expires, normal adaptive security resumes. By default, this command is disabled. If used, Cisco recommends it be set to two minutes or less:

```
failover timeout 0:02:00
```

Filtering Web Traffic

The PIX is capable of using a product from WebSENSE to allow URL filtering that allows you to filter Web pages that contain content that is deemed objectionable by your security policy, such as pornography. You must first designate the IP address of the WebSENSE server and then designate which source and destination IP addresses will be sent to the server for content filtering. The url-server command is then used to define the IP address of the WebSENSE server.

```
url-server [(if_name)] host ip_address [timeout seconds]
```

An example follows:

```
url-server (inside) host 10.1.1.99
```

The timeout parameter specifies the maximum idle time permitted before the PIX attempts to contact another WebSENSE server. The default timeout is five seconds and up to 15 WebSENSE servers can be defined. The filter command defines which source and destination IP addresses are to be sent to the WebSENSE server.

```
filter url http|except local_ip local_mask foreign_ip foreign_mask
   [allow]
```

Here's an example:

```
Filter url http 10.0.0.0 255.0.0.0 0 0 allow
Filter url except 10.1.1.1 255.255.255.255 0 0
```

In this example, all HTTP connections with a source IP address on the 10.0.0.0 255.0.0.0 network to any destination IP addresses will have their incoming URLs sent to the WebSENSE server for filtering. HTTP connections from host 10.1.1.1, however, are exempt from having its URLs filtered. The allow command states that connections will be allowed if the PIX is unable to contact the WebSENSE server.

The PIX is also capable of caching the responses from the WebSENSE server to speed up HTTP connections. The command to do this is url-cache.

```
url-cache dst|src_dst size
```

An example follows:

```
url-cache src_dst 128
```

Use the dst parameter if all the internal hosts use the same WebSENSE policy. Use the src_dst if the policy differs among internal hosts. The size parameter indicates the size in KB between 1 and 128 of the url-cache. Statistics on the url-cache can be obtained by using the command show url-cache stats. Further information on WebSENSE products is available at the company Web site `http://www.websense.com`.

The PIX Manager

We discussed the use of the PIX manager earlier in this chapter. The PIX manager is a program that runs on an NT server or NT workstation that allows you to configure the PIX through any Web browser that supports Java.

You must first set the IP address of the NT server running the PIX manager as a permitted telnet client on the PIX. Once this is done, you can establish a HTTP browser session to the PIX manager on the port specified during the installation of the PIX manager program (8080 by default). All sessions between the client HTTP browser and the PIX manager use encrypted Java calls, while sessions between the PIX manager and the PIX use encrypted telnet calls. This provides a significantly higher security level than managing the PIX through clear-text telnet. The PIX manager cannot reside on the outside interface.

We have included six screenshots of the PIX manager, Figure 10-13 to Figure 10-18, to give you an idea of this tool's capabilities.

Figure 10–13
The initial PIX
manager screen

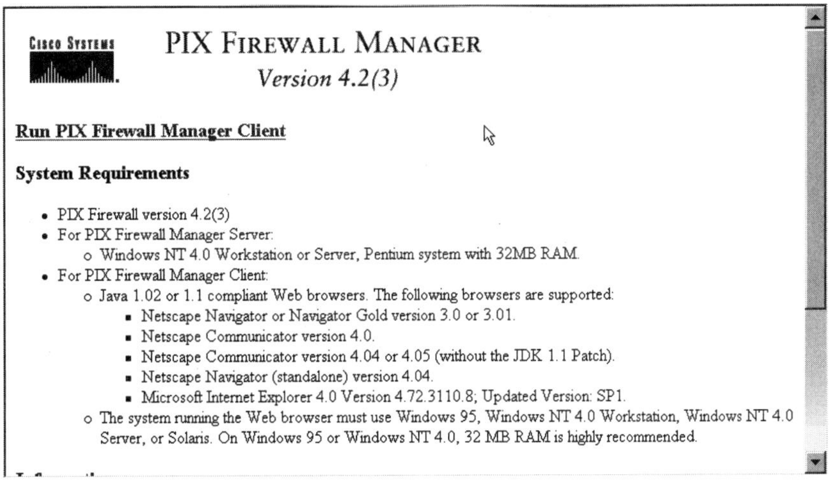

CISCO SYSTEMS

PIX FIREWALL MANAGER
Version 4.2(3)

Run PIX Firewall Manager Client

System Requirements

- PIX Firewall version 4.2(3)
- For PIX Firewall Manager Server:
  - o Windows NT 4.0 Workstation or Server, Pentium system with 32MB RAM.
- For PIX Firewall Manager Client:
  - o Java 1.02 or 1.1 compliant Web browsers. The following browsers are supported:
    - Netscape Navigator or Navigator Gold version 3.0 or 3.01.
    - Netscape Communicator version 4.0.
    - Netscape Communicator version 4.04 or 4.05 (without the JDK 1.1 Patch).
    - Netscape Navigator (standalone) version 4.04.
    - Microsoft Internet Explorer 4.0 Version 4.72.3110.8; Updated Version: SP1.
  - o The system running the Web browser must use Windows 95, Windows NT 4.0 Workstation, Windows NT 4.0 Server, or Solaris. On Windows 95 or Windows NT 4.0, 32 MB RAM is highly recommended.

Figure 10–14
The login prompt to
enable managing of
a particular PIX box

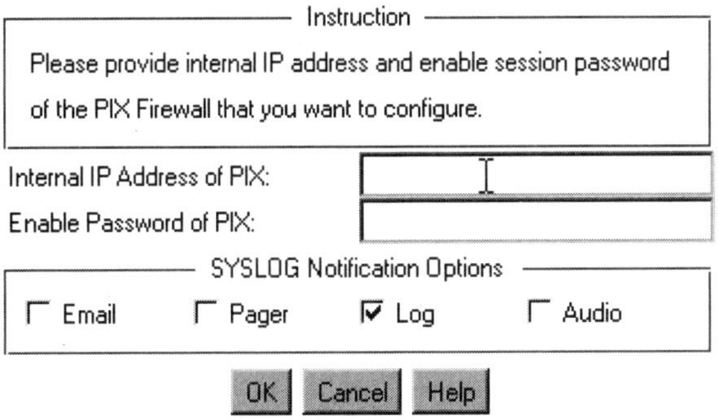

Instruction

Please provide internal IP address and enable session password
of the PIX Firewall that you want to configure.

Internal IP Address of PIX:

Enable Password of PIX:

SYSLOG Notification Options

☐ Email   ☐ Pager   ☑ Log   ☐ Audio

OK   Cancel   Help

Figure 10-15
The different categories available on the PIX manager

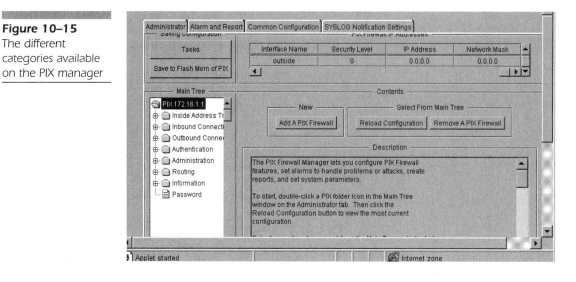

Figure 10-16
Adding a static route

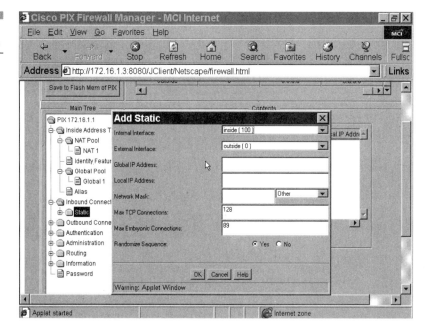

Figure 10–17
Adding a global pool

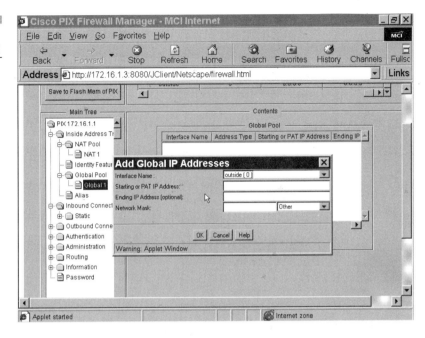

Figure 10–18
Adding a nat
translation

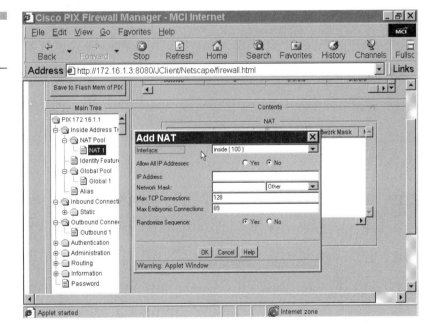

APPENDIX A

Determining Wildcard Mask Ranges

In this section, we present an algorithm that can be used to determine the correct wildcard mask ranges when attempting to summarize an arbitrary range of IP addresses. We will first present the algorithm and then show a detailed example of how it can be used.

The algorithm is presented below. Key sections of the algorithm are referenced by an index number.

```
       Convert the octet you are summarizing from decimal to binary
       Set the beginning IP address to BEGIN
       Set the ending IP address to END
 1 While BEGIN < END do
       2 Find the lowest order bit in BEGIN that is 1, this is the
         FOUND bit
       3 If there is a binary 1 in END that is a higher order bit
         than the HIGHEST order bit in BEGIN then
             All bits to the right of the FOUND bit are included
             in the range.
       4 Else
             5 Find the highest order bit in END less than the
               FOUND bit.
               This is the NEW-FOUND bit.
             6 If none found then
                   All bits to the right of the FOUND bit are
                   included
             7 Else
                   8 If all bits lower than NEW-FOUND in END are 1
                     then All bits lower than NEW-FOUND including
                     NEW-FOUND are included in the range
                   9 Else IF there is at least 1 bit in END that
                     is a higher order bit than FOUND that is a 1
                     while the corresponding bit in BEGIN is 0
                     then
                          All bits lower than NEW-FOUND including
                          NEW-FOUND are included in the range
                  10 Else
                          All bits to the right of NEW-FOUND are
                          included in the range
      11 Set MASK equal to the value of the range found
      12 BEGIN and MASK represent a contiguous range
      13 Set BEGIN equal to BEGIN + MASK + 1
      14 Return to While
```

The use of this algorithm is best illustrated with an example. In chapter 7 we summarized the range of IP addresses between 175.100.38.0/24 and 175.100.92.0/24. We will show how the wildcard masks for each access-list entry was created.

We begin by concentrating on the third octet of the beginning and ending IP address networks. The first two octets match, so we are not concerned with them. The last octet is the host octet, so we are not concerned with it either.

The first step is to represent the value of the beginning and ending numbers in binary.

```
38 = 00100110
92 = 01011100
```

Phase 1

```
Begin = 00100110 (38)
End   = 01011100 (92)
(1) While begin is less than end do
```

Begin is less than end, so we continue.

```
(2) Find the lowest order bit in BEGIN that is 1, this is the
FOUND bit
```

The lowest order bit in BEGIN that is 1 is in bit position 2 going from right to left, `00100110`. Bit position 2 is the FOUND bit position.

```
(3) If there is a binary 1 in END that is a higher order bit than
the HIGHEST order bit in BEGIN
```

We see that bit position 7 in END is a binary 1:

```
01011100
```

The highest bit position in BEGIN that is a binary 1 is in position 6:

```
00100110
```

Therefore this condition is met.

```
Then All bits to the right of the FOUND bit are included in the
range.
```

The FOUND bit is in position 2, so bits in position 1 are included in the range.

```
(11) Set MASK equal to the value of the range found.
```

Only the bits in position 1 are included in the range, so the value of MASK is 2 raised to the 0th power or 1. In binary, the value of each bit is 2 raised to the n−1 power where n is the bit position.

```
(12) BEGIN and MASK represent a contiguous range
```

BEGIN is `00100110` or `38`, MASK is `1`. Using these numbers we can create an access-list entry:

```
access-list 100 permit ip 175.100.38.0 0.0.1.255
```

Notice that we used the BEGIN and MASK values in the 3rd octet of the IP address and wildcard mask for this access-list entry.

> (13) Set BEGIN equal to BEGIN + MASK + 1

BEGIN = 38 + 1 + 1 = 40

> (14) Return to While

Repeat the process

Phase 2

```
Begin = 00101000 (40)
End   = 01011100 (92)
(1) While begin is less than end do
```

Begin is less than end, so we continue.

> (2) Find the lowest order bit in BEGIN that is 1, this is the FOUND bit

The lowest order bit in BEGIN that is 1 is in bit position 4 going from right to left, `00101000`. Bit position 4 is the FOUND bit position.

> (3) If there is a binary 1 in END that is a higher order bit than the HIGHEST order bit in BEGIN

We see that bit position 7 in END is a binary 1:

```
01011100
```

The highest bit position in BEGIN that is a binary 1 is in position 6:

```
00101000
```

Therefore this condition is met.

> Then All bits to the right of the FOUND bit are included in the range.

The FOUND bit is in position 4, so bits in positions 1–3 are included in the range.

```
(11) Set MASK equal to the value of the range found.
```

The bits in positions 1–3 are included in the range, so the value of MASK is 2 to the 2nd power, 2 to the 1st power and 2 to the 0th power. This is $4 + 2 + 1 = 7$.

```
(12) BEGIN and MASK represent a contiguous range
```

BEGIN is 00101000 or 40, MASK is 7. Using these numbers we can create an access-list entry:

```
access-list 100 permit ip 175.100.40.0 0.0.7.255
```

```
(13) Set BEGIN equal to BEGIN + MASK + 1
```

BEGIN = $40 + 7 + 1 = 48$

```
(14) Return to While
```

Repeat the process

Phase 3

```
Begin = 00110000 (48)
End   = 01011100 (92)
```

```
(1) While begin is less than end do
```

Begin is less than end, so we continue.

```
(2) Find the lowest order bit in BEGIN that is 1, this is the
FOUND bit
```

The lowest order bit in BEGIN that is 1 is in bit position 5 going from right to left, 00110000. Bit position 5 is the FOUND bit position.

```
(3) If there is a binary 1 in END that is a higher order bit than
the HIGHEST order bit in BEGIN
```

We see that bit position 7 in END is a binary 1:

```
01011100
```

The highest bit position in BEGIN that is a binary 1 is in position 6:

```
00110000
```

Therefore this condition is met.

```
Then All bits to the right of the FOUND bit are included in the
range.
```

The FOUND bit is in position 5, so bits in positions 1–4 are included in the range.

```
(11) Set MASK equal to the value of the range found
```

The bits in positions 1–4 are included in the range, so the value of MASK is 2 to the 3rd power, 2 to the 2nd power, 2 to the 1st power and 2 to the 0th power. This is $8 + 4 + 2 + 1 = 15$.

```
(12) BEGIN and MASK represent a contiguous range
```

BEGIN is `00110000` or `48`, MASK is `15`. Using these numbers we can create an access-list entry:

```
access-list 100 permit ip 175.100.48.0 0.0.15.255
```

```
(13) Set BEGIN equal to BEGIN + MASK + 1
```

$BEGIN = 48 + 15 + 1 = 64$

```
(14) Return to While
```

Repeat the process

Phase 4

```
Begin = 01000000 (64)
End   = 01011100 (92)
(1) While begin is less than end do
```

Begin is less than end, so we continue.

```
(2) Find the lowest order bit in BEGIN that is 1, this is the
FOUND bit
```

The lowest order bit in BEGIN that is 1 is in bit position 7 going from right to left, `01000000`. Bit position 7 is the FOUND bit position.

```
(3) If there is a binary 1 in END that is a higher order bit than
the HIGHEST order bit in BEGIN
```

We see that bit position 7 in END is a binary 1:

```
01011100
```

The highest bit position in BEGIN that is a binary 1 is in position 7:

```
01000000
```

Therefore this condition is **NOT** met. We now operate on the **4** ELSE condition.

```
(5) Find the highest order bit in END less than the FOUND bit.
This is the NEW-FOUND bit.
```

The FOUND bit is in position 7 of BEGIN: `01000000`. The highest order bit in END less than the FOUND bit is in position 5: `01011100`. Bit position 5 is the NEW-FOUND bit.

```
(6) If none found
```

A bit was found, so we execute the **7** ELSE portion

```
(8) If all bits lower than NEW-FOUND bit in END are 1
```

The NEW-FOUND bit position is 5, so we examine the bits in END to the right of the 5th bit: `01011100`. We can see that not all of the bits are 1, so we execute the **9** Else IF.

```
(9) Else IF there is at least 1 bit in END that is a higher
order bit than FOUND that is a 1 while the corresponding bit in
BEGIN is 0
```

The FOUND bit is position 6, so we are looking for bits in END that are in bit positions higher than 6 that are 1 where the corresponding bit in BEGIN is 0. By examining the bits higher than the 6th position is END, we see that there is no bit position that meets the criteria. There is a binary 1 in bit position 7 in END: `01011100` but there is a corresponding binary 1 in bit position 7 in BEGIN: `01000000`. This condition is not met, so we execute the **10** Else.

```
(10) Else all bits to the right of NEW-FOUND are included in the
range
```

The NEW-FOUND bit is in position 5, so bits 1–4 are included in the range

```
(11) Set MASK equal to the value of the range found
```

The bits in positions 1-4 are included in the range, so the value of MASK is 2 to the 3rd power, 2 to the 2nd power, 2 to the 1st power and 2 to the 0th power. This is $8 + 4 + 2 + 1 = 15$.

```
(12) BEGIN and MASK represent a contiguous range
```

BEGIN is 01000000 or 64, MASK is 15. Using these numbers we can create an access-list entry:

```
access-list 100 permit ip 175.100.64.0 0.0.15.255
```

```
(13) Set BEGIN equal to BEGIN + MASK + 1
```

$BEGIN = 64 + 15 + 1 = 80$

```
(14) Return to While
```

Repeat the process

Phase 5

```
Begin = 01010000 (80)
End   = 01011100 (92)
(1) While begin is less than end do
```

Begin is less than end, so we continue.

```
(2) Find the lowest order bit in BEGIN that is 1, this is the
FOUND bit
```

The lowest order bit in BEGIN that is 1 is in bit position 5 going from right to left, 01010000. Bit position 5 is the FOUND bit position.

```
(3) If there is a binary 1 in END that is a higher order bit than
the HIGHEST order bit in BEGIN
```

We see that bit position 7 in END is a binary 1:

```
01011100
```

The highest bit position in BEGIN that is a binary 1 is in position 7:

```
01010000
```

Therefore this condition is **NOT** met. We now operate on the 4 ELSE condition.

```
(5) Find the highest order bit in END less than the FOUND bit.
This is the NEW-FOUND bit.
```

The FOUND bit is in position 5 of BEGIN: 01010000. The highest order bit in END less than the FOUND bit is in position 4: 01011100. Bit position 4 is the NEW-FOUND bit.

```
(6) If none found
```

A bit was found, so we execute the **7** ELSE portion

```
(8) If all bits lower than NEW-FOUND bit in END are 1
```

The NEW-FOUND bit position is 4, so we examine the bits in END to the right of the 4th bit: 01011100. We can see that not all of the bits are 1, so we execute the **9** Else IF.

```
(9) Else IF there is at least 1 bit in END that is a higher
order bit than FOUND that is a 1 while the corresponding bit in
BEGIN is 0
```

The FOUND bit is position 5, so we are looking for bits in END that are in bit positions higher than 5 that are 1 where the corresponding bit in BEGIN is 0. By examining the bits higher than the 5th position is END, we see that there is no bit position that meets the criteria. There is a binary 1 in bit position 7 in END: 01011100, but there is a corresponding binary 1 in bit position 7 in BEGIN: 01000000. This condition is not met, so we execute the **10** Else.

```
(10) Else all bits to the right of NEW-FOUND are included in the
range
```

The NEW-FOUND bit is in position 4, so bits 1–3 are included in the range

```
(11) Set MASK equal to the value of the range found
```

The bits in positions 1–3 are included in the range, so the value of MASK is 2 to the 2nd power, 2 to the 1st power and 2 to the 0th power. This is $4 + 2 + 1 = 7$.

```
(12) BEGIN and MASK represent a contiguous range
```

BEGIN is 01010000 or 80, MASK is 7. Using these numbers we can create an access-list entry:

```
access-list 100 permit ip 175.100.80.0 0.0.7.255
```

```
(13) Set BEGIN equal to BEGIN + MASK + 1
```

BEGIN = 80 + 7 + 1 = 88

```
(14) Return to While
```

Repeat the process

Phase 6

```
Begin = 01011000 (88)
End   = 01011100 (92)
(1) While begin is less than end do
```

Begin is less than end, so we continue.

```
(2) Find the lowest order bit in BEGIN that is 1, this is the
FOUND bit
```

The lowest order bit in BEGIN that is 1 is in bit position 4 going from right to left, 01011000. Bit position 4 is the FOUND bit position.

```
(3) If there is a binary 1 in END that is a higher order bit than
the HIGHEST order bit in BEGIN
```

We see that bit position 7 in END is a binary 1:

```
01011100
```

The highest bit position in BEGIN that is a binary 1 is in position 7:

```
01011000
```

Therefore this condition is **NOT** met. We now operate on the **4** ELSE condition.

```
(5) Find the highest order bit in END less than the FOUND bit.
This is the NEW-FOUND bit.
```

The FOUND bit is in position 4 of BEGIN: 01011000. The highest order bit in END less than the FOUND bit is in position 3: 01011100. Bit position 3 is the NEW-FOUND bit.

```
(6) If none found
```

A bit was found, so we execute the **7** ELSE portion

```
(8) If all bits lower than NEW-FOUND bit in END are 1
```

The NEW-FOUND bit position is 3, so we examine the bits in END to the right of the 3rd bit: 01011100. We can see that not all of the bits are 1, so we execute the **9** Else IF.

```
(9) Else IF there is at least 1 bit in END that is a higher
order bit than FOUND that is a 1 while the corresponding bit
in BEGIN is 0
```

The FOUND bit is position 4, so we are looking for bits in END that are in bit positions higher than 4 that are 1 where the corresponding bit in BEGIN is 0. By examining the bits higher than the 4th position in END, we see that there is no bit position that meets the criteria. There is a binary 1 in bit position 7 and 5 in END: 01011100, but there is a corresponding binary 1 in bit positions 7 and 5 in BEGIN: 01011000. This condition is not met, so we execute the **10** Else.

```
(10) Else all bits to the right of NEW-FOUND are included in the
range
```

The NEW-FOUND bit is in position 3, so bits 1–2 are included in the range

```
(11) Set MASK equal to the value of the range found
```

The bits in positions 1-2 are included in the range, so the value of MASK is 2 to the 1st power and 2 to the 0th power. This is $2 + 1 = 3$.

```
(12) BEGIN and MASK represent a contiguous range
```

BEGIN is 01011000 or 88, MASK is 3. Using these numbers we can create an access-list entry:

```
access-list 100 permit ip 175.100.88.0 0.0.3.255
```

```
(13) Set BEGIN equal to BEGIN + MASK + 1
```

BEGIN $= 88 + 3 + 1 = 92$

```
(14) Return to While
```

Repeat the process

Phase 7

```
Begin = 01011100 (92)
End   = 01011100 (92)
(1) While begin is less than end do
```

Begin is less NOT than end, so we exit the loop.
Since BEGIN is now equal to END, we are done but we still have to add the last entry to cover the 175.100.92.0/24 network:

```
access-list 100 permit ip 175.100.92.0 0.0.0.255
```

We have now completed the summarization process. Collecting all of the access-list entries we have created, we now have the complete access-list:

```
access-list 101 permit ip 175.100.38.0 0.0.1.255 any
access-list 101 permit ip 175.100.40.0 0.0.7.255 any
access-list 101 permit ip 175.100.48.0 0.0.15.255 any
access-list 101 permit ip 175.100.64.0 0.0.15.255 any
access-list 101 permit ip 175.100.80.0 0.0.7.255 any
access-list 101 permit ip 175.100.88.0 0.0.3.255 any
access-list 101 permit ip 175.100.92.0 0.0.0.255 any
```

This is the same access-list presented in chapter 7.

APPENDIX B

Creating Access Lists

We now turn our attention to the creation and operation of access lists. The basic syntax of an access list is:

```
Access-list [1-1199] [permit|deny] [protocol|protocol-keyword]
    [source source-wildcard|any] [source port] [destination destina-
    tion-wildcard|any] [destination port] [precedence precedence#]
    [options]
```

We will discuss each of these fields in detail next. Actual commands are in bold, and the other statements are English equivalents of the command syntax. Each section of the command is separated on its own line with a number to facilitate discussion. In practice, each access list entry normally appears on a single line in the router configuration.

```
Access-list
[access list number 1-1199]
[permit or deny]
[some protocol]
[source address and mask]
[source port number or range]
[destination address and mask]
[destination port number or range]
[options]
```

A few words need to be said about the above command structure. First, not all the fields are required. Only fields 1, 2, and 4 are required in every type of access list. Most access lists also include fields 3 and 6. Each field is discussed below:

```
[access list number 1-1199]
```

The actual number that is used varies, depending on the type of access list used. Different types of access lists use different numbers. An IP access list, for example, uses a different number than an IPX access list. There are many different types of access lists.

```
[permit or deny]
```

A permit or deny statement is always required. This is how you specify whether the packets that match an access list entry are to be allowed or denied access.

```
[some protocol]
```

Quite a few different protocols can be filtered using an access list. A short list includes IP, IPX, AppleTalk, DECnet, VINES, and XNS. It is also possible to filter on MAC layer addresses. Within most protocol stacks, there are usually additional protocols that can be filtered. For example, filters can also be created for TCP, UDP, and ICMP, all of which use IP at the network layer.

```
[source address and mask]
```

The source address and mask of the packets is always required. The source address is normally the layer 3 address of the packet, unless the access list is a MAC layer filter. The mask portion tells the router how much of the address to match when filtering packets. The concept is similar to a subnet mask. For instance, you may want to match all packets originating from the 10.10.0.0 255.255.0.0 subnet. The mask allows you to tell the router to match only the first two octets of the address. If no mask is specified, an exact match is assumed. If 10.10.0.0 is typed, the access list entry would only match packets with a source address of 10.10.0.0 (a very unlikely source address). Although the principle is the same, the syntax of this mask is different than a network mask. We cover this topic in greater detail later. In addition to the use of an actual address, many protocols also support the use of the "any" keyword.

```
[source port number or range]
```

This field is used when filtering on layer 4 information. It allows you to specify a particular higher-layer port. If the access list protocol is TCP, for example, you could specify a source TCP port of 25 (SMTP). You can also use symbols like GT for "greater than," LT for "less than," and RANGE to create specific ranges of port numbers.

```
[destination address and mask]
```

This field has the same parameter structure as the source address and mask.

```
[destination port number or range]
```

This field has the same parameter structure as the source port number or range.

```
[options]
```

This field allows a variety of additional fields to be matched in the access list entry. The contents of the field vary depending on the type of access list. A typical option for a TCP access list would be "established," indicating the access list entry would examine the packet to see if the ACK or RST bit is set. The "log" option is also common, indicating that matches of the access list entry should be logged to the router's buffer or a syslog server. Other options include filtering on TOS and IP precedence.

APPENDIX C

Standard Access Lists

The basic format of a standard IP access list is:

```
Access-list [1-99] [permit|deny] [ip address] [mask] [log]
```

NOTE: The log keyword is available only in IOS 11.3 and later versions.

Each access list is given a unique number that is used to inform the IOS of the type of access list you are defining. This number is also used in all subsequent references to the access list. Standard IP access lists are defined within the range 1–99. In IOS version 11.2, named access lists were introduced, allowing you to define names for your access lists. These lists were created so you can delete specific entries in the access list without recreating the entire list. Additional entries, however, are still added to the end of the access list.

APPENDIX D

Extended IP Access Lists

Extended IP access lists provide much greater functionality and flexibility than standard IP access lists. Extended access lists provide the capability to filter by source address as in standard access lists, but they can also filter by destination address and upper layer protocol information. Very complex packet filters can be built with extended access lists. Extended access lists are numbered from 100–199 and their format is

```
Access-list [100-199] [permit|deny] [protocol|protocol-keyword]
    [source source-wildcard|any] [destination destination-
    wildcard|any] [precedence precedence#] [tos tos] [log]
```

A list of possible protocols includes

- IP
- TCP
- UDP
- ICMP
- IGMP
- GRE
- IGRP
- EIGRP
- IPINIP
- OSPF
- NOS
- Integer in the range 0 through 255

To match any Internet protocol, use the keyword IP. Some of the protocols, such as TCP, UDP, and ICMP, have more options that are supported by alternate syntax. We will examine the more common protocols in this section. Extended access lists allow you to filter by IP precedence and type of service fields as well, although few organizations actually use these features. Additionally, you can log access list matches by using the optional LOG keyword at the end of an access list entry. Log entries will be sent to whatever logging facility you have enabled on the router.

APPENDIX E

Glossary

access control list   A list defining the kinds of access granted or denied to users of an object.

address   In data communication, this is a designated identifier.

address class   Traditional method of assigning blocks of addresses to organizations.

address mask   A bit mask used to select bits from an IP address for subnet addressing.

address resolution   Conversion of an IP address into a corresponding physical address, such as ETHERNET or token ring.

address resolution protocol (ARP)   A TCP/IP protocol used to dynamically bind a high-level IP address to low-level physical hardware addresses. ARP works across single physical networks and is limited to networks that support hardware broadcast.

address space   Addresses used to uniquely identify network-accessible units, sessions, adjacent link stations, and links in a node for each network in which the node participates.

addressing   In data communication, the way in which a station selects the station to which it is to send data. An identifiable place.

AppleTalk   A networking protocol developed by Apple Computer for use with its products.

application layer   According to the ISO OSI model, this is layer 7. It provides application services.

ARPANET   The world's first packet-switching network. For many years it functioned as an Internet backbone.

autonomous system (AS)   An internetwork that is part of the Internet and has a single routing policy. Each Autonomous System is assigned an Autonomous System Number.

bandwidth   The quantity of data that can be sent across a link, typically measured in bits per second.

baud   A unit of signaling speed equal to the number of times per second that a signal changes state. If there are exactly two states, the baud rate equals the bit rate.

carrier-sense multiple access with collision detection (CSMA/CD)   A protocol utilizing equipment capable of detecting a carrier which permits multiple access to a common medium. This protocol also has the ability to detect a collision, because this type of technology is broadcast-oriented.

classless inter-domain routing (CIDR)   A method of routing used to enable the network part of IP addresses to consist of a specified number of bits.

collision   An event in which two or more devices simultaneously perform a broadcast on the same medium. This term is used in ETHERNET networks, and also in networks where broadcast technology is implemented.

collision detection   Term used to define a device that can determine when a simultaneous transmission attempt has been made.

congestion   A network state caused by one or more overloaded network devices. Congestion leads to datagram loss.

connected   To have a physical path from one point to another.

connection   A logical communication path between TCP users.

connection-oriented internetworking   A set of subnetworks connected physically and thus rendered capable of connection-oriented network service.

connection-oriented service   A type of service offered in some networks. This service has three phases: connection establishment, data transfer, and connection release.

cracker   Someone who attempts to break into computer systems, often with malicious intent.

data circuit-terminating equipment (DCE)   Equipment required to connect a DTE to a line or to a network.

data-link control (DLC)   A set of rules used by nodes at layer 2 within a network. The data link is governed by data-link protocols such as ETHERNET or token ring for example.

data-link control (DLC) protocol   Rules used by two nodes at a data-link layer to accomplish an orderly exchange of information. Examples are ETHERNET, channel, FDDI, and token ring.

data-link layer   Layer 2 of the OSI reference model. It synchronizes transmission and handles error correction for a data link.

data-link level   The conceptual level of control logic between high-level logic and a data-link protocol that maintains control of the data link.

data terminal equipment (DTE)   A source or destination for data. Often used to denote terminals or computers attached to a wide area network.

DECnet   Digital Equipment Corporation's proprietary network protocol. Versions are identified by their phase number—such as Phase IV and Phase V.

directed broadcast address   In TCP/IP-based environments, an IP address that specifies all hosts on a specific network. A single copy of a directed broadcast is routed to the specified network where it is broadcast to all machines on that network.

DIX Ethernet   Version of Ethernet developed by Digital, Intel, and Xerox.

domain name server   In TCP/IP environments, it is a protocol for matching object names and network addresses. It was designed to replace the need to update/etc/hosts files of participating entities throughout a network.

domain name system (DNS)   The online distributed database system used to map human-readable machine names into IP addresses. DNS servers throughout the connected Internet implement a hierarchical name space that allows sites freedom in assigning machine names and addresses. DNS also supports separate mappings between mail destinations and IP addresses.

dotted-decimal notation   A phrase typically found in TCP/IP network conversations. Specifically, this refers to the addressing scheme of the Internet protocol (IP). It is the representation of a 32-bit address consisting of four 8-bit numbers written in base 10 with periods separating them.

encapsulate   Generally agreed on in the internetworking community to mean surrounding one protocol with another protocol for the purpose of passing the foreign protocol through the native environment.

ETHERNET   A data-link-level protocol. It (Version 2.0) was defined by Digital Equipment Corporation, Intel Corporation, and the Xerox Corporation in 1982. It specified a data rate of 10 Mbits/s, a maximum station distance of 2.8 km, a maximum number of stations of 1024, a shielded coaxial cable using baseband signaling, functionality of CSMA/CD, and a best-effort delivery system.

exterior gateway protocol (EGP)   Routers in neighboring Autonomous Systems use this protocol to identify the set of networks that can be reached within or via each Autonomous System. EGP is being supplanted by BGP.

filter   A device or program that separates data, signals, or material in accordance with specified criteria.

firewall A system that controls what traffic may enter and leave a site.

frame One definition generally agreed on as being a packet as it is transmitted across a serial line. The term originated from character-oriented protocols. According to the meaning in OSI environments, it is a data structure pertaining to a particular area of data. It also consists of slots that can accept values of specific attributes.

hierarchical routing From a TCP/IP perspective, this type of routing is based on a hierarchical addressing scheme. Most TCP/IP routing is based on a two-level hierarchy in which an IP address is divided into a network portion until the datagram reaches a gateway that can deliver it directly. The concept of subnets introduces additional levels of hierarchical routing.

hop count (1) A measure of distance between two points in the Internet. Each hop count corresponds to one router separating a source from a destination (for example, a hop count of 3 indicates that three routers separate a source from a destination). (2) A term generally used in TCP/IP networks. The basic definition is a measure of distance between two points in an internet. A hop count of n means that n routers separate the source and the destination.

interior gateway protocol (IGP) Any routing protocol used within an internetwork.

International Organization for Standardization (ISO) An organization of national standards-making bodies from various countries established to promote development of standards to facilitate international exchange of goods and services, and develop cooperation in intellectual, scientific, technological, and economic activity.

Internet According to different documents describing the Internet, it is a collection of networks, routers, gateways, and other networking devices that use the TCP/IP protocol suite and function as a single, cooperative virtual network. The Internet provides universal connectivity and three levels of network services: unreliable, connectionless packet delivery; reliable, full-duplex stream delivery; and application-level services such as electronic mail that build on the first two. The Internet reaches many universities, government research labs, and military installations and over a dozen countries.

Internet address According to TCP/IP documentation, it refers to the 32-bit address assigned to the host. It is a software address that on local ("little i") internets is locally managed, but on the central ("big I") Internet is dictated to the user (entity desiring access to the Internet).

Internet Assigned Numbers Authority (IANA) The authority responsible for controlling the assignment of a variety of parameters, such as well-known ports, multicast addresses, terminal identifiers, and system identifiers.

Internet control message protocol (ICMP) A protocol that is required for implementation with IP. ICMP specifies error messages to be sent when datagrams are discarded or systems experience congestion. ICMP also provides several useful query services. Specific to the TCP/IP protocol suite. It is an integral part of the Internet protocol. It handles error and control messages. Routers and hosts use ICMP to send reports of problems about datagrams back to the original source that sent the datagram. ICMP also includes an echo request/reply used to test whether a destination is reachable and responding.

Internet gateway routing protocol (IGRP) A proprietary protocol designed for Cisco routers.

Internet group management protocol (IGMP) A protocol that is part of the multicast specification. IGMP is used to carry group membership information.

Internet packet exchange (IPX) A Novell protocol that operates at OSI layer 3. It is used in the NetWare protocols; it is similar to IP in TCP/IP.

Internet protocol (IP) A protocol used to route data from its source to its destination. A part of TCP/IP protocol.

IP Internet protocol. The TCP/IP standard protocol that defines the IP datagram as the unit of information passed across an internet and provides the basis for connectionless, best-effort packet delivery service. IP includes the ICMP control and error message protocol as an integral part. The entire protocol suite is often referred to as TCP/IP because TCP and IP are the two fundamental protocols.

IP address The 32-bit dotted-decimal address assigned to hosts that want to participate in a local TCP/IP internet or the central (connected) Internet. IP addresses are software addresses. Actually, an IP address consists of a network portion and a host portion. The partition makes routing efficient.

IP datagram A term used with TCP/IP networks. It is a basic unit of information passed across a TCP/IP internet. An IP datagram is to an internet as a hardware packet is to a physical network. It contains a source address and a destination address along with data.

link A medium over which nodes can communicate using a link layer protocol.

link state protocol A routing protocol that generates routes using detailed knowledge of the topology of a network.

Logical link control (LLC) According to OSI documentation, a sub-layer in the data-link layer of the OSI model. The LLC provides the basis for an unacknowledged connectionless service or connection-oriented service on the local area network.

loopback address Address 127.0.0.1, used for communications between clients and servers that reside on the same host.

MAC address A physical address assigned to a LAN interface.

MAC protocol A Media Access Control protocol defines the rules that govern a system's ability to transmit and receive data on a medium.

Maximum transfer unit (MTU) The largest amount of data that can be transferred across a given physical network. For local area networks implementing ETHERNET, the MTU is determined by the network hardware. For long-haul networks that use aerial lines to interconnect packet switches, the MTU is determined by software.

multicast A technique that allows copies of a single packet to be passed to a selected subset of all possible destinations. Some hardware supports multicast by allowing a network interface to belong to one or more multicast groups. Broadcast is a special form of multicast in which the subset of machines to receive a copy of a packet consists of the entire set. IP supports an internet multicast facility.

multicast address According to Apple documentation, an ETHERNET address for which the node accepts packets just as it does for its permanently assigned ETHERNET hardware address. The low-order bit of the high-order byte is set to 1. Each node can have any number of multicast addresses, and any number of nodes can have the same multicast address. The purpose of a multicast address is to allow a group of ETHERNET nodes to receive the same transmission simultaneously, in a fashion similar to the AppleTalk broadcast service.

multicasting A directory service agent uses this mode to chain a request to many other directory service agents.

multicast IP address A destination IP address that can be adopted by multiple hosts. Datagrams sent to a multicast IP address will be delivered to all hosts in the group.

NetBEUI Local area network protocol used for Microsoft LANs.

NETBIOS A network programming interface and protocol developed for IBM-compatible personal computers.

network A collection of computers and related devices connected together in such a way that collectively they can be more productive than standalone equipment.

network address In general, each participating entity on a network has an address so that it can be identified when exchanging data. According to IBM documentation, in a subarea network, an address consists of subarea and element fields that identify a link, link station, PU, LU, or SSCP.

network layer According to ISO documentation, it is defined as OSI layer 3. It is responsible for data transfer across the network. It functions independently of the network media and the topology.

octet Eight bits (a byte).

open shortest path first (OSPF) A routing protocol based on the least cost for routing.

packet A term used generically in many instances. It is a small unit of control information and data that is processed by the network protocol.

physical address An address assigned to a network interface.

physical layer A term used in OSI circles. It refers to the lowest layer defined by the OSI model. However, layer 0 would be the lowest layer in such a model. This layer (layer 0) represents the medium, whether hard or soft.

point-to-point protocol (PPP) A protocol for data transfer across serial links. PPP supports authentication, link configuration, and link monitoring capabilities and allows traffic for several protocols to be multiplexed across the link.

presentation layer According to the OSI model for networks, this is layer 6. Data representation occurs here. Syntax of data such as ASCII or EBCDIC is determined at this layer.

protocol An agreed-upon way of doing something.

proxy ARP In TCP/IP networks, this is a technique where one machine answers ARP requests intended for another by supplying its own physical address.

RARP Reverse address resolution protocol. A TCP/IP protocol for mapping ETHERNET addresses to IP addresses. It is used by diskless workstations who do not know their IP addresses. In essence, it asks "Who am I?" Normally, a response occurs and is cached in the host.

Request for comments (RFC)   Proposed and accepted TCP/IP standards.

reverse address resolution protocol (RARP)   A protocol that enables a computer to discover its IP address by broadcasting a request on a network.

routing   The moving of data through paths in a network.

routing information protocol (RIP)   A simple protocol used to exchange information between routers. The original version was part of the XNS protocol suite.

routing policy   Rules for which traffic will be routed and how it should be routed.

routing table   A table containing information used to forward datagrams toward their destinations.

segment   A Protocol Data Unit consisting of a TCP header and optionally, some data. Sometimes used to refer to the data portion of a TCP Protocol Data Unit.

session layer   According to the OSI reference model, this is layer 5. It coordinates the dialog between two communicating application processes.

shortest path first   A routing algorithm that uses knowledge of a network's topology in making routing decisions.

sliding window   A scenario in which a protocol permits the transmitting station to send a stream of bytes before an acknowledgment arrives.

stub network   A network that does not carry transit traffic between other networks.

subnet address   A selected number of bits from the local part of an IP address, used to identify a set of systems connected to a common link.

subnet mask   A configuration parameter that indicates how many bits of an address are used for the host part. It is expressed as a 32-bit quantity, with 1s placed in positions covering the network and subnet part of an IP address and 0s in the host part.

switch   A layer 2 device that enables many pairs of LAN devices to communicate concurrently.

T1   A digital telephony service that operates at 1.544 megabits per second. DS1 framing is used.

T3   A digital telephony service that operates at 44.746 megabits per second. DS3 framing is used.

TELNET   The TCP/IP TCP standard protocol for remote terminal service.

10Base T   An ETHERNET implementation using 10 Mbits/s with baseband signaling over twisted-pair cabling.

Time to live (TTL)   A technique used in best-effort delivery systems to avoid endlessly looping packets. For example, each packet has a "time" associated with its lifetime.

token   The symbol of authority passed successively from one data station to another to indicate which station is temporarily in control of the transmission medium.

token ring   A network with a ring topology that passes tokens from one attaching device to another.

token-ring network   A ring network that allows unidirectional data transmission between data stations by a token-passing procedure.

Transmission control protocol (TCP)   The TCP/IP standard transport-level protocol that provides the reliable, full-duplex, stream service on which many application protocols depend. It is connection-oriented in that before transmitting data, participants must establish a connection.

transport layer   According to the OSI model, it is the layer that provides an end-to-end service to its users.

Trivial file transfer protocol (TFTP)   A TCP/IP UDP standard protocol for file transfer that uses UDP as a transport mechanism. TFTP depends only on UDP, so it can be used on machines such as diskless workstations.

well-known-port   A term used with TCP/IP networks. In TCP/IP, applications and programs that reside on top of TCP and UDP, respectively, have a designated port assigned to them. This agreed-on port is known as a well-known-port.

APPENDIX F

Acronyms and Abbreviations

AAA	Autonomous administrative area
AAI	Administration authority identifier
AARP	AppleTalk address resolution protocol
AC	Access control
ACK	Positive acknowledgment
ACL	Access control list
ADSP	AppleTalk data stream protocol
AEP	AppleTalk echo protocol
ANS	American National Standard
ANSI	American National Standards Institute
ARP	Address resolution protocol
ARPA	Advanced Research Projects Agency
ARQ	Automatic repeat request
ARS	Automatic route selection
ASCII	American Standard Code for Information Interchange
bits/s	bits per second
BOC	Bell Operating Company
BRI	Basic rate interface
BSD	Berkeley standard distribution
BTU	Basic transmission unit
CCITT	Consultative Committee in International Telegraphy and Telephony
CO	Central office
CODEC	Coder/decoder
CPE	Customer premises equipment
CSMA/CD	Carrier-sense multiple access with collision detection

CSU	Channel service unit
DA	Destination address
DAD	Draft addendum
DARPA	Defense Advanced Research Projects Agency
DEC	Digital Equipment Corporation
DES	Data Encryption Standard
DIS	Draft International Standard
DIX	DEC, Intel, and Xerox
DNS	Domain name service (also system)
DoD	U. S. Department of Defense
DSU	Digital services unit
E-mail	Electronic mail
ECC	Enhanced error checking and correction
EIA	Electronic Industries Association
FCC	Federal Communications Commission
FCS	Frame-check sequence
FDX	Full-duplex
FRAD	Frame relay access device
FTP	File transfer protocol in TCP/IP
Gbits	Gigabits
Gbits/s	Gigabits per second
Gbyte	Gigabyte
GUI	Graphical user interface
HDLC	High-level data-link control
HDX	Half-duplex (also HD)
hex	Hexadecimal
IAB	Internet Architecture Board
ICMP	Internet control message protocol

IEEE	Institute of Electrical and Electronic Engineers
I/O	Input/output
IP	Internet protocol
IPX	Internetwork packet exchange
IRSG	Internet Research Steering Group
IRTF	Internet Research Task Force
IS	International Standard
ISO	International Standards Organization
ISP	Internet Service Provider
IT	Information technology
ITC	Independent telephone company
ITU	International Telecommunication Union
kbits	Kilobits
kbits/s	Kilobits per second
kbyte	Kilobyte
kHz	Kilohertz
LAN	Local area network
LE	Local exchange
LEC	Local exchange carrier
LLC	Logical link control
Mbits	Megabits
Mbits/s	Megabits per second
Mbyte	Megabyte
Mbytes/s	Megabytes per second
MS	Management services; message store
MTU	Maximum transfer unit
NCP	Network Core Protocol
ns	Nanosecond

NSF	National Science Foundation
NSFNET	National Science Foundation Network
OS	Operating System
OSE	Open-systems environment
OSF	Open Software Foundation
OSI	Open-systems interconnection
OSPF	Open shortest path first
PCM	Pulse-code modulation
PDN	Public data network
PDU	Protocol data unit
PING	Packet Internet Groper
POP	Point of presence
POTS	Plain old telephone service
PRI	Primary rate interface
PSDN	Packet-switched data network
RBOC	Regional Bell Operating Company
RFC	Request for comment
RFP	Request for proposal
RFQ	Request for price quotation
RIF	Routing information field
RIP	Router information protocol
RISC	Reduced instruction-set computer
s	Second
SA	Source address (field); subarea; sequenced application
SNMP	Simple network management protocol
SPX	Sequenced packet exchange
TA	Terminal adapter
TC	Transport connection or technical committee

TCP	Transmission control protocol
TCP/IP	Transmission control protocol/Internet protocol
TDM	Time-division multiplexing; topology database manager
TELNET	Remote log-on in TCP/IP
TFTP	Trivial file transfer protocol
TTL	Time to live
VAC	Value-added carrier
VAN	Value-added network
VAS	Value-added service
VT	Virtual terminal

INDEX

Note: Boldface numbers indicate illustrations.

U

ABOUT THE AUTHORS

Gil Held is an award-winning lecturer and author. He is the author of over 40 books covering computer and communications technology. A member of the adjunct faculty at Georgia College and State University, Gil teaches courses in LAN Performance and was selected to represent the United States at technical conferences in Moscow and Jerusalem.

Kent Hundley (CCNA) is a Senior Network Consultant for International Network Services, a global provider of network integration and management services. He specializes in Cisco-centric security issues for Fortune 500 companies.